Third Workshop on Natural Language Processing and Computational Social Science 2019

Minneapolis, Minnesota, USA
6 June 2019

ISBN: 978-1-5108-8775-6

NAACL HLT 2019

The Workshop on Natural Language Processing and Computational Social Science

Proceedings of the Third Workshop

June 6, 2019
Minneapolis, USA

Microsoft® Research

Capital One®

facebook

Introduction

Welcome to the Third Workshop on NLP and Computational Social Science!

This workshop series builds on a successful string of iterations, with dozens of interdisciplinary submissions to make NLP techniques and insights standard practice in CSS research. Our focus is on NLP for social sciences - to continue the progress of CSS, and to integrate CSS with current trends and techniques in NLP.

We received 36 submissions, and due to a rigorous review process by our committee, we accepted 12 archival entries, and 2 non-archival abstracts. The program this year includes 6 papers presented as spotlight talks, and 14 posters. We are especially excited to see so many submissions from outside of NLP, and hope to continue the tradition to foster a dialogue between NLP researchers and users of NLP technology in the social sciences. We are also glad to present a fantastic selection of invited speakers from various aspects of computational social science.

We would like to thank all authors of the accepted papers, our invited speakers, and the fantastic organizing committee that made this workshop possible, and, last but not least, all attendees! Special thanks to our sponsors, whose generous contributions have allowed us to support student scholarships and the travel of our inivted speakers.

We hope you enjoy the workshop!

The NLP and CSS workshop organizing team.

Organizers :

Svitlana Volkova (Pacific Northwest National Laboratory)
David Jurgens (University of Michigan)
Dirk Hovy (Bocconi University)
David Bamman (UC Berkeley)
Oren Tsur (Ben Gurion University)

Program Committee :

Abram Handler
A. Seza Doğruöz
Afshin Rahimi
Alexandra Balahur
Alice Oh
Amittai Axelrod
Anja Belz
Ann Clifton
April Foreman
Asad Sayeed
Barbara Plank
Brendan O'Connor
Caroline Brun
Carolyn Rose
Chris Brew
Christopher Potts
Courtney Napoles
Dan Goldwasser
Dan Simonson
Daniel Preoţiuc-Pietro
David Bamman
Diana Maynard
Djamé Seddah
Ekaterina Kochmar
Eric Bell
François Yvon
Gideon Mann
Glen Coppersmith
Guenter Neumann
H. Andrew Schwartz

Ian Stewart
Jacob Eisenstein
John Beieler
Jonathan K. Kummerfeld
Joseph Hoover
Julian Brooke
Juri Ganitkevitch
Kaiping Chen
Kenneth Joseph
Kristen Johnson
Kristen M. Altenburger
Kristy Hollingshead
Loring Ingraham
Ludovic Rheault
Lyle Ungar
Marie-Catherine de Marneffe
Marti A. Hearst
Massimo Poesio
Matko Bošnjak
Michael Bloodgood
Michael Heilman
Molly Ireland
Molly Roberts
Natalie Ahn
Natalie Schluter
Nikola Ljubešić
Oul Han
Pedro Rodriguez
Peter Makarov
Philipp Koehn

Pierre Nugues
Rada Mihalcea
Rahul Bhagat
Raquel Fernández
Rebecca Resnik
Reihane Boghrati
Rob Voigt
Roman Klinger
Sara Rosenthal
Sara Tonelli
Sebastian Padó
Seyed Abolghasem Mirroshandel
Shachar Mirkin
Sravana Reddy
Steve DeNeefe
Steven Bethard
Steven Wilson
Sunghwan Mac Kim
Swede White
Taylor Berg-Kirkpatrick
Teresa Lynn
Thierry Poibeau
Timothy Baldwin
Valery Dzutsati
Vinodkumar Prabhakaran
Yvette Graham
Zeerak Waseem

Table of Contents

Workshop Program

Thursday, June 6, 2019

9:00–10:30   *Session 1*

9:00–9:45   *Invited Talk 1: Using Computational Social Science to Understand the "Social Science of Computing"*
Brent Hecht

9:45–10:30   *Invited Talk 2: From Words To People And Back Again*
Rada Mihalcea

10:30–11:00   ***Coffee Break***

11:00–12:30   ***Session 2: Poster Session***

11:00–12:30   *Not My President: How Names and Titles Frame Political Figures*
Esther van den Berg, Katharina Korfhage, Josef Ruppenhofer, Michael Wiegand and Katja Markert

11:00–12:30   *Identification, Interpretability, and Bayesian Word Embeddings*
Adam Lauretig

11:00–12:30   *Tweet Classification without the Tweet: An Empirical Examination of User versus Document Attributes*
Veronica Lynn, Salvatore Giorgi, Niranjan Balasubramanian and H. Andrew Schwartz

11:00–12:30   *Geolocating Political Events in Text*
Andrew Halterman

11:00–12:30   *Neural Network Prediction of Censorable Language*
Kei Yin Ng, Anna Feldman, JIng Peng and Chris Leberknight

11:00–12:30   *Modeling performance differences on cognitive tests using LSTMs and skip-thought vectors trained on reported media consumption.*
Maury Courtland, Aida Davani, Melissa Reyes, Leigh Yeh, Jun Leung, Brendan Kennedy, Morteza Dehghani and Jason Zevin

12:30–14:00   ***Lunch break***

14:00–15:30   *Session 3: Spotlight Paper Session*

14:00–14:15   *Using time series and natural language processing to identify viral moments in the 2016 U.S. Presidential Debate*
Josephine Lukito, Prathusha K Sarma, Jordan Foley and Aman Abhishek

14:15–14:30   *Stance Classification, Outcome Prediction, and Impact Assessment: NLP Tasks for Studying Group Decision-Making*
Elijah Mayfield and Alan Black

14:30–14:45   *A Sociolinguistic Study of Online Echo Chambers on Twitter*
Nikita Duseja and Harsh Jhamtani

14:45–15:00   *Uphill from here: Sentiment patterns in videos from left- and right-wing YouTube news channels*
Felix Soldner, Justin Chun-ting Ho, Mykola Makhortykh, Isabelle W.J. van der Vegt, Maximilian Mozes and Bennett Kleinberg

15:00–15:15   *Simple dynamic word embeddings for mapping perceptions in the public sphere*
Nabeel Gillani and Roger Levy

15:15–15:30   *Modeling Behavioral Aspects of Social Media Discourse for Moral Classification*
Kristen Johnson and Dan Goldwasser

15:30–16:00   *Afternoon coffee break*

16:00–17:45   *Session 4*

16:00–16:45   *Invited Talk 3: Subtle Differences in Other Varieties of English: Implications for language-related research and technology*
Lisa Green

16:45–17:15   *Invited Talk 4: Treasure Trove or Pandora's Box? Investigating Unstructured User-Generated Data from Online Support Communities*
Lana Yarosh

17:15–17:30   *Closing remarks and wrap-up*
Organizers

Not My President: How Names and Titles Frame Political Figures

Esther van den Berg[*], **Katharina Korfhage**[†], **Josef Ruppenhofer**[*‡],
Michael Wiegand[*] **and Katja Markert**[†]
[*]Leibniz ScienceCampus, Heidelberg/Mannheim, Germany
[†]Institute of Computational Linguistics, Heidelberg University, Germany
[‡]Institute for German Language, Mannheim, Germany
`{vdberg|korfhage|markert}@cl.uni-heidelberg.de`
`{ruppenhofer|wiegand}@ids-mannheim.de`

Abstract

Naming and titling have been discussed in sociolinguistics as markers of status or solidarity. However, these functions have not been studied on a larger scale or for social media data. We collect a corpus of tweets mentioning presidents of six G20 countries by various naming forms. We show that naming variation relates to stance towards the president in a way that is suggestive of a framing effect mediated by respectfulness. This confirms sociolinguistic theory of naming and titling as markers of status.

1 Introduction

Framing is a field of research in communication theory and political science investigating how information is presented to audiences, especially in news media. According to a common definition, to frame is to "to select some aspects of a perceived reality and make them more salient in a communication text, in such a way as to promote a particular problem definition, causal interpretation, moral evaluation, and/or treatment recommendation" (Entman, 1993, p. 52). Most work on framing has focused on issues and events, rather than entities (Card et al., 2015; Fulgoni et al., 2016; Field et al., 2018).

We therefore introduce *entity framing*, which we define as a presentation of an entity which intentionally or unintentionally promotes a particular viewpoint towards that entity. We focus on the framing of political figures on social media, in order to better understand computer-mediated civil political discourse.

Online political discussion has been said to have an increasing influence on the democratic process, including on the tone and civility of political debates (Persily, 2017; Ott, 2017). Tweets on political themes are indeed retweeted more often when their content is emotionally charged, and espe-

cially when they contain negative appraisals of political parties and figures (Dang-Xuan et al., 2013).

We explore one way in which respect or solidarity can be expressed towards political figures: the use of their names and titles. Sociolinguistic studies have suggested that names and titles convey status or solidarity (Allerton, 1996; Dickey, 1997). Of these functions we confirm the status-indicating function on a larger scale than in sociolinguistic studies and on social media data, by demonstrating that formality in naming is positively related to the stance of tweets towards the presidents.

We thus contribute:

- a corpus of stance-annotated tweets mentioning presidents of six G20 countries, which we make publicly available.[1]

- quantitative evidence of the status-indicating function of names and titles on Twitter

2 Related work

According to sociolinguists, names and titles reflect two aspects of relationships: difference in status (based on e.g. age or professional role) and degree of solidarity (also referred to as intimacy or group membership) (Brown and Gilman, 1960; Allerton, 1996; Dickey, 1997).[2] Studies have also observed that naming patterns are context-specific and may be violated to achieve a specific communicative purpose (Ervin-Tripp, 1972; Dickey, 1997). These studies have been qualitative and/or based on real-time observations or

---

[1] `https://www.cl.uni-heidelberg.de/english/research/downloads/resource_pages/TwitterTitlingCorpus/twitles.shtml` To follow Twitter usage guidelines, we provide tweet ids rather than tweet texts.

[2] These observations were made for spoken language, where names are used either as a form of address to refer to the conversation partner or as a form of reference to refer to a third party. For reasons described in Section 5, we do not make this distinction.

Proceedings of the Third Workshop on Natural Language Processing and Computational Social Science, pages 1–6
Minneapolis, Minnesota, June 6, 2019. ©2019 Association for Computational Linguistics

interviews, whereas our work examines naming quantitatively and on social media data.

The concept of framing has been applied to a variety of issues and events (Card et al., 2015; Tsur et al., 2015; Fulgoni et al., 2016; Field et al., 2018), and in one case to the framing of entities (Card et al., 2016), but not previously on social media data. Use of social media to express political opinions has instead been studied to forecast elections (Burnap et al., 2016), political mobilisation (Weeks et al., 2017), and assess political polarization (Bail et al., 2018).

A prominent area of NLP that focuses on expressions of favour is stance detection, the detection of sentiment towards a specified target. Most systems focus on stance towards products, companies and abstract topics rather than persons (Somasundaran and Wiebe, 2010; Meng et al., 2012; Jiang et al., 2011; Mohammad et al., 2016).

The datasets for SemEval 2017 (Task A and B) (Rosenthal et al., 2017) and RepLab (Amigó et al., 2012, 2013, 2014) as well as the dataset created by (Taddy, 2013) do include a variety of person entities, but no stance detection work has investigated the influence of naming on stance.

3 Data

To study how names and titles affect stance towards political figures in social media, we created a corpus of 4002 English-language tweets that mention presidents by different naming forms and which are annotated for stance.

3.1 Collection and cleaning

We focused on leaders of G20 countries with a presidential system whose names followed the order *first-name last-name*. We collected tweets between 18 June 2017 and 30 August 2017 using three query types: last-name, #first-name and first-name + (last-name/country).[3] After removing duplicates, we reduced the number of headlines in the data, as headlines are bound by journalistic style conventions with respect to naming (Siegal and Connolly, 1999). We defined as a *news tweet* any tweet from an account with the string *news* in the username or description. From country subsets with an above average number of news tweets we removed the excess number.

Subcorpus	FE worker agr.	Expert agr.
France	0.77	0.78
Indonesia	0.80	0.91
Russia	0.77	0.72
South Africa	0.77	0.87
Turkey	0.44	0.65
United States	0.65	0.78

Table 1: Inter-annotator agreement for the on-target/off-target task (Krippendorff alpha): agreement among FE workers and agreement between two experts adjudicating tweets where FE worker judgment was not unanimous.

Subcorpus	Adj. tweets	Diff. w/ expert 1	Diff. w/ expert 2
France	281	0.07%	0.05%
Indonesia	290	0.04%	0.03%
Russia	121	0.06%	0.06%
South-Africa	227	0.04%	0.04%
Turkey	128	0.05%	0.04%
United States	192	0.07%	0.06%

Table 2: Adjudication for the on-target/off-target task of tweets where FE worker judgment was not unanimous: number of adjudicated tweets and percentage of tweets given a different label by either expert 1 or 2 than to the FE majority vote.

Manual inspection of 50 tweets per country subset revealed that one subset consisted of very homogenous tweets, and two others contained many tweets that did not refer to the intended target. These subsets were omitted from the data.

The tweets for the remaining six subsets - France, Indonesia, Russia, South Africa, Turkey and the United States - were then automatically labeled for their naming forms. Possible labels were: first name only (FN), last name only (LN), full name (FNLN), title and full name (TFNLN) and title and last name (TLN). Oversampling rarer naming forms, we sampled 1000 tweets per country.

To remove tweets that refer to a namesake rather than the intended target, we crowd-sourced three *on-target/off-target* judgments per tweet via Figure Eight (FE).[4] If workers could not unanimously agree whether a tweet was on-target, we collected two additional judgments from the authors (Table 1). We compared the expert judgments to the majority vote from the FE annotations and found very few differences (Table 2). We thus consider the majority vote reliable. Off-target tweets were removed from the dataset, leaving 4002 tweets.

3.2 Stance annotation

Stance-annotations of the 4002 on-target tweets were collected via Amazon Mechanical Turk

---

Subcorpus	Tweets	Workers	Agreement
France	638	39	0.55
Indonesia	477	27	0.58
Russia	754	66	0.49
South Africa	698	82	0.51
Turkey	692	53	0.62
United States	743	43	0.64
Overall	4002	204	0.58

Table 3: Statistics on stance annotation after removing least reliable annotators: number of tweets, number of workers and agreement among workers (Krippendorff's alpha)

(AMT).[5] Workers were required to pass an English proficiency and instruction comprehension test. They had to have a minimum number of completed HITs (500), a minimum HIT approval rate (97%) and a task-internal 97% accuracy rate based on gold questions making up roughly 4% of the data. Their compensation was $0.02 per HIT for approximately 7 HITs per minute.

Each tweet was labeled by seven annotators. Inspired by the finding in Joseph et al. (2017) that political stance annotation on Twitter suffers when too little context is shown, we provided annotators with the tweet location, user photo, user name and user description. If the tweet was a response to another tweet, that tweet was shown also. The prompt was: *How would a supporter of President X feel about this tweet?* Possible answers were: *positive (+1), neither positive nor negative (0), negative (-1)* and *cannot read / understand*.

Our prompt is based on the reader-perspective elicitation prompt in Buechel and Hahn (2017). We expect it to better capture differences between tweets which are neutral in tone but reflect differently on the president, such as '*Trump trailing in primaries*' vs '*Jobs market improving under Trump*'. Crucially, the prompt also allows annotators to give different ratings to '*President Trump visits France*' and '*Trump visits France*'. As in Card et al. (2015), the perspective is anchored to that of a proponent of the target in order to combat the lower reliability of reader-perspective prompts (Buechel and Hahn, 2017).

After annotation we used Multi-Annotator Competence Estimation (MACE) (Hovy et al., 2013) to identify and remove the least reliable annotators. We collected an additional two judgments per tweet for the country subsets with lowest agreement (Russia and South Africa). Table 3 shows the agreement scores. The data's gold standard was obtained using MACE, which has been shown to retrieve reliable gold labels even under very unfavourable conditions.[6]

4 Framing through naming

We now examine the relation between the use of names and titles for presidents and stance towards them in the collected tweets. Sociolinguistic work suggests that naming expresses status or solidarity. Lower status and high solidarity are both signalled with less formal naming forms such as FN, while higher status and low solidarity are both signalled with more formal naming forms like TLN (Brown and Ford, 1961; Allerton, 1996; Dickey, 1997).

This dual social function gives rise to two possible main relations between naming and stance corresponding to the following hypotheses:

H0 Variation in naming and stance are not related.

H1 Naming primarily downplays or emphasises the president's **status**. Therefore, formality of naming is positively related to stance.

H2 Naming primarily conveys the degree of **solidarity** with the president. Therefore, formality of naming is negatively related to stance.

Table 4 gives examples of tweets which can be interpreted to support either H1 or H2, or to support the existence of alternative, context-specific functions of naming, such as sarcasm.

We group tweets country-independently by naming form and perform a Kruskal-Wallis test of the difference in average stance. This reveals a statistically significant difference between the stance of tweets with different naming forms ($\chi^2(4)$=424.67, p<0.001). A post-hoc Dunn's test with Bonferroni correction shows statistically significant differences between all naming forms (p<0.001) except for LN and FN, possibly due to the small size of the FN group. We reject the null-hypothesis that naming and stance are not related.

To examine which alternative hypothesis is more likely between H1 and H2, we rank the naming forms according to their formality:

---

[5]We chose AMT over FE for this task so we could include a questionnaire asking for country of residence, native language, age, gender, education level, and familiarity with twitter. A study of how annotator demographic impacts annotation is planned but goes beyond this paper.

[6]We conducted experiments with synthetic data to verify that MACE was likely to obtain a reliable gold standard from our data.

Function	Stance	Form	Tweet text
status	pos	TFNLN	*Dear **President Joko Widodo**, Happy Birthday. God bless you @jokowi*
status	neg	FN	*That's the truth!!! Double-standard **#Donald** at it again*
solidarity	pos	LN	*Duterte & **Widodo** are truly public servants. Saving their countries fr the menace of society.*
solidarity	neg	TLN	***President Trump** probably won't like next week's newsstands*
sarcasm	neg	TLN	*Of course, I know, everything is sweetness & light in the wonderful democratic Paradise of **President Erdogan**!*

Table 4: Possible examples of a *status* or *solidarity* function of naming forms in tweets, as well as of an alternative function.

Subcorpus	FN	LN	FNLN	TLN	TFNLN
France	0.00 (10)	-0.29 (377)	-0.08 (117)	-0.04 (80)	0.04 (54)
Indonesia	-0.60 (15)	-0.03 (134)	0.14 (167)	0.08 (50)	0.37 (111)
Russia	-0.56 (54)	-0.71 (442)	-0.31 (122)	-0.26 (74)	0.24 (62)
South Africa	-0.50 (6)	-0.53 (405)	-0.40 (109)	-0.08 (106)	0.18 (72)
Turkey	-0.75 (4)	-0.67 (440)	-0.23 (124)	0.06 (82)	-0.17 (42)
United States	-0.80 (59)	-0.53 (363)	-0.50 (141)	0.15 (94)	0.03 (86)
Overall	-0.63 (148)	-0.52 (2161)	-0.21 (780)	-0.02 (486)	0.14 (427)

Table 5: Average stance and in brackets the absolute number of tweets containing naming forms from least to most formal.

FN<LN<FNLN<TLN<TFNLN.[7] Table 5 shows that the average stance of tweets increases with each increase in formality. A Spearman's rank-order correlation test confirms a statistically significant positive correlation between naming formality and stance ($r_s(4002) = .32$, $p = .001$).

Furthermore, a chi-square test shows that the difference between the stance of tweets with and without a title in them (Table 6) is significant for each of the six subcorpora ($p<0.05$).

These findings support the *status* hypothesis: due to naming mainly indicating status, status-indicating function of names, formality in naming is positively related to stance.

5 Discussion

Although we show a clear framing effect of naming and titling, our study has several limitations. First, we do not distinguish between address and reference. Our data contains both names used as forms of address (e.g. *'Making things "Great Again" huh #Donald?'*) and as forms of reference (e.g. *'#Donald just cant handle competing for the title.'*). Studying these types separately would require additional manual annotation. In addition, this distinction is not as clear for Twitter data as for face-to-face conversations, as many tweets mix both functions.

Second, some of the naming forms occur only rarely, particularly FN. This hinders the finding of significant differences between each of the naming forms for each individual country subset. Nevertheless, a significant difference in stance could be observed between tweets with and without titles in each subcorpus.

Third, we consider tweets from a limited time span. This means the content of the tweets and therefore the naming used in them may be influenced by the occurrence of specific events (e.g. Joko Widodo's birthday).

Fourth, we only consider English tweets. Tweets about presidents which are not well-known to native English speakers may be unrepresentative of local ways of referring to the president. They may also be more neutral in tone and may use (T)FNLN to be informative rather than respectful.

These limitations as well as certain social media/Twitter-specific properties (the character limit, the often unspecified audience) increased the chance that any primary function of naming would be lost among noise. It is therefore interesting to still see the clear trend across country subsets that informal naming of presidents co-occurs with perceived hostility, while formal naming co-occurs with perceived supportiveness of a tweet. This suggests that in tweets on politicians naming primarily emphasises status and conveys respect.

6 Conclusions and future work

We present an analysis of the way political figures are named in social media and how this naming relates to stance in a corpus of stance-annotated tweets mentioning presidents of six G20 countries.

---

[7]Based on the following criteria:
1) Naming with title is more formal than without title.
2) Longer names are more formal than shorter names.
3) Last names are more formal than first names.

Subcorpus	Without title	With title
France	-0.24 (504)	-0.01 (134)
Indonesia	0.03 (316)	0.28 (161)
Russia	-0.62 (618)	-0.03 (136)
South Africa	-0.50 (520)	0.03 (178)
Turkey	-0.58 (568)	-0.02 (124)
United States	-0.55 (563)	0.09 (180)
Overall	-0.45 (3089)	0.05 (913)

Table 6: Average stance and in brackets the absolute number of tweets without or with a title in their naming form.

Our analysis reveals a relation between the formality of names and the stance of tweets. More formal forms are significantly more frequent among positive tweets than less formal ones.

We thus confirm sociolinguistic claims that naming marks status and expresses respect that had not previously been investigated in a large, quantitative study, nor for social media texts. This study also represents the first approach to entity framing by providing evidence for a framing effect of naming.

Future work should investigate whether naming forms in address vs. reference impact stance differently, whether naming form usage differs depending on demographics and whether the naming trends found across the time span of our tweets can also be found across a longer time span. Also valuable would be a study of this effect in other languages and on different politician subgroups, such as female politicians. Studies such as Uscinski and Goren (2011) suggest that titles of female politicians are omitted more frequently and with different effect.

NLP work can use our corpus as further data for stance detection. Experiments in Mohammad et al. (2016) show that cross-target stance detection is very challenging. Our corpus can provide further training and testing data both for in-target and cross-target classification.

Acknowledgements

We thank the reviewers for their insightful comments. This research is funded by the Leibniz ScienceCampus Empirical Linguistics& Computational Language Modeling, supported by Leibniz Association grant no. SAS2015-IDS-LWC and by the Ministry of Science, Research, and Art of Baden-Wurttemberg.

References

David J Allerton. 1996. Proper names and definite descriptions with the same reference: A pragmatic choice for language users. *Journal of Pragmatics*, 25(5):621–633.

Enrique Amigó, Jorge Carrillo-de Albornoz, Irina Chugur, Adolfo Corujo, Julio Gonzalo, Edgar Meij, Maarten de Rijke, and Damiano Spina. 2014. Overview of RepLab 2014: Author profiling and reputation dimensions for online reputation management. In *Proceedings of the Fifth International Conference of the CLEF Initiative*, pages 307–322.

Enrique Amigó, Adolfo Corujo, Julio Gonzalo, Edgar Meij, Maarten de Rijke, et al. 2012. Overview of RepLab 2012: Evaluating online reputation management systems. In *CLEF 2012 Evaluation Labs and Workshop, Online Working Notes*.

Enrique Amigó, Jorge Carrillo De Albornoz, Irina Chugur, Adolfo Corujo, Julio Gonzalo, Tamara Martín, Edgar Meij, Maarten De Rijke, and Damiano Spina. 2013. Overview of RepLab 2013: Evaluating online reputation monitoring systems. In *Proceedings of the Fourth International Conference of the CLEF Initiative*, pages 333–352.

Christopher A Bail, Lisa P Argyle, Taylor W Brown, John P Bumpus, Haohan Chen, MB Fallin Hunzaker, Jaemin Lee, Marcus Mann, Friedolin Merhout, and Alexander Volfovsky. 2018. Exposure to opposing views on social media can increase political polarization. *Proceedings of the National Academy of Sciences*, 115(37):9216–9221.

Roger Brown and Marguerite Ford. 1961. Address in American English. *Journal of abnormal and social psychology*, 62(2):375–385.

Roger Brown and Albert Gilman. 1960. The pronouns of power and solidarity. In Thomas A Sebeok, editor, *Style in Language*, pages 253–276. MIT Press, Cambridge, MA.

Sven Buechel and Udo Hahn. 2017. Emobank: Studying the impact of annotation perspective and representation format on dimensional emotion analysis. In *Proceedings of the 15th Conference of the European Chapter of the Association for Computational Linguistics*, volume 2, pages 578–585.

Pete Burnap, Rachel Gibson, Luke Sloan, Rosalynd Southern, and Matthew Williams. 2016. 140 characters to victory? Using twitter to predict the UK 2015 General Election. *Electoral Studies*, 41:230–233.

Dallas Card, Amber E Boydstun, Justin H Gross, Philip Resnik, and Noah A Smith. 2015. The media frames corpus: Annotations of frames across issues. In *Proceedings of the 53rd Annual Meeting of the Association for Computational Linguistics and the 7th International Joint Conference on Natural Language Processing*, volume 2, pages 438–444.

Dallas Card, Justin Gross, Amber Boydstun, and Noah A Smith. 2016. Analyzing framing through the casts of characters in the news. In *Proceedings of the 2016 Conference on Empirical Methods in Natural Language Processing*, pages 1410–1420.

Linh Dang-Xuan, Stefan Stieglitz, Jennifer Wladarsch, and Christoph Neuberger. 2013. An investigation of influentials and the role of sentiment in political communication on Twitter during election periods. *Information, Communication & Society*, 16(5):795–825.

Eleanor Dickey. 1997. Forms of address and terms of reference. *Journal of linguistics*, 33(2):255–274.

Robert M Entman. 1993. Framing: Toward clarification of a fractured paradigm. *Journal of communication*, 43(4):51–58.

Susan Ervin-Tripp. 1972. On sociolinguistic rules: Alternation and co-occurrence. *Directions in sociolinguistics*, pages 213–250.

Anjalie Field, Doron Kliger, Shuly Wintner, Jennifer Pan, Dan Jurafsky, and Yulia Tsvetkov. 2018. Framing and agenda-setting in Russian news: a computational analysis of intricate political strategies. In *Proceedings of the 2018 Conference on Empirical Methods in Natural Language Processing*, pages 3570–3580.

Dean Fulgoni, Jordan Carpenter, Lyle Ungar, and Daniel Preotiuc-Pietro. 2016. An empirical exploration of moral foundations theory in partisan news sources. In *Proceedings of the Tenth International Conference on Language Resources and Evaluation*, pages 3730–3736.

Dirk Hovy, Taylor Berg-Kirkpatrick, Ashish Vaswani, and Eduard Hovy. 2013. Learning whom to trust with MACE. In *Proceedings of the 2013 Conference of the North American Chapter of the Association for Computational Linguistics: Human Language Technologies*, pages 1120–1130.

Long Jiang, Mo Yu, Ming Zhou, Xiaohua Liu, and Tiejun Zhao. 2011. Target-dependent twitter sentiment classification. In *Proceedings of the 49th Annual Meeting of the Association for Computational Linguistics: Human Language Technologies*, volume 1, pages 151–160.

Kenneth Joseph, Lisa Friedland, William Hobbs, David Lazer, and Oren Tsur. 2017. Constance: Modeling annotation contexts to improve stance classification. In *Proceedings of the 2017 Conference on Empirical Methods in Natural Language Processing*, pages 1115–1124.

Xinfan Meng, Furu Wei, Xiaohua Liu, Ming Zhou, Sujian Li, and Houfeng Wang. 2012. Entity-centric topic-oriented opinion summarization in twitter. In *Proceedings of the 18th ACM SIGKDD international conference on Knowledge discovery and data mining*, pages 379–387. ACM.

Saif Mohammad, Svetlana Kiritchenko, Parinaz Sobhani, Xiaodan Zhu, and Colin Cherry. 2016. Semeval-2016 task 6: Detecting stance in tweets. In *Proceedings of the 10th International Workshop on Semantic Evaluation (SemEval-2016)*, pages 31–41.

Brian L Ott. 2017. The age of Twitter: Donald J. Trump and the politics of debasement. *Critical Studies in Media Communication*, 34(1):59–68.

Nathaniel Persily. 2017. The 2016 US election: Can democracy survive the internet? *Journal of democracy*, 28(2):63–76.

Sara Rosenthal, Noura Farra, and Preslav Nakov. 2017. Semeval-2017 task 4: Sentiment analysis in Twitter. In *Proceedings of the 11th International Workshop on Semantic Evaluation (SemEval-2017)*, pages 502–518.

Allan M Siegal and William G Connolly. 1999. *The New York Times manual of style and usage*. Three Rivers Press (CA).

Swapna Somasundaran and Janyce Wiebe. 2010. Recognizing stances in ideological on-line debates. In *Proceedings of the NAACL HLT 2010 Workshop on Computational Approaches to Analysis and Generation of Emotion in Text*, pages 116–124.

Matt Taddy. 2013. Measuring political sentiment on Twitter: Factor optimal design for multinomial inverse regression. *Technometrics*, 55(4):415–425.

Oren Tsur, Dan Calacci, and David Lazer. 2015. A frame of mind: Using statistical models for detection of framing and agenda setting campaigns. In *Proceedings of the 53rd Annual Meeting of the Association for Computational Linguistics and the 7th International Joint Conference on Natural Language Processing (Volume 1: Long Papers)*, volume 1, pages 1629–1638. ACL.

Joseph E Uscinski and Lilly J Goren. 2011. What's in a name? Coverage of senator Hillary Clinton during the 2008 democratic primary. *Political Research Quarterly*, 64(4):884–896.

Brian E Weeks, Alberto Ardèvol-Abreu, and Homero Gil de Zúñiga. 2017. Online influence? Social media use, opinion leadership, and political persuasion. *International Journal of Public Opinion Research*, 29(2):214–239.

Identification, Interpretability, and Bayesian Word Embeddings

Adam M. Lauretig
Department of Political Science
Ohio State University
Columbus, OH
`lauretig.1@osu.edu`

Abstract

Social scientists have recently turned to analyzing text using tools from natural language processing like word embeddings to measure concepts like ideology, bias, and affinity. However, word embeddings are difficult to use in the regression framework familiar to social scientists: embeddings are are neither identified, nor directly interpretable. I offer two advances on standard embedding models to remedy these problems. First, I develop Bayesian Word Embeddings with Automatic Relevance Determination priors, relaxing the assumption that all embedding dimensions have equal weight. Second, I apply work identifying latent variable models to anchor the dimensions of the resulting embeddings, identifying them, and making them interpretable and usable in a regression. I then apply this model and anchoring approach to two cases, the shift in internationalist rhetoric in the American presidents' inaugural addresses, and the relationship between bellicosity in American foreign policy decision-makers' deliberations. I find that inaugural addresses became less internationalist after 1945, which goes against the conventional wisdom, and that an increase in bellicosity is associated with an increase in hostile actions by the United States, showing that elite deliberations are not cheap talk, and helping confirm the validity of the model.

1 Introduction

Important questions in the social sciences turn on the meanings of words used to express ideas like language change, emotion, and ideological affinity (Hamilton et al., 2016; Rheault et al., 2016; Pomeroy et al., 2018). One increasingly popular way to represent meaning, originating in natural language processing, is through the use of word embeddings. This class of models learns a set of coefficients which encode meaning by predicting a word given the surrounding words (Mikolov et al., 2013a,b). These coefficients are the *embeddings*, which can then be used to analyze word meanings.

Unfortunately, existing embedding models are not always appropriate for answering social scientists' questions. Embeddings are not identified, and the dimensions are not directly interpretable, which makes it difficult to perform statistical inference on the embeddings produced by standard models, for example, using them as covariates in a regression model.[1]

To resolve these issues, I cast word embeddings as a Bayesian latent variable model. Identifying multidimensional latent variable models is a known problem, and I draw on solutions proposed in the ideal point modeling literature (Rivers, 2003; Clinton et al., 2004) to render embeddings interpretable and usable in a regression framework. I demonstrate these results on two corpora: a collection of inaugural addresses, and a selection of declassified diplomatic documents from the *Foreign Relation of the United States*. In the inaugural addresses, I find rhetoric became more domestically-focused after 1945, a shift which existing social science approaches cannot detect. This finding stands in contrast to what existing theories of international relations would have us expect. In the *FRUS* documents, I find that more bellicose rhetoric results in more aggressive American foreign policy behavior, helping confirm that elite deliberation matters for shaping foreign policy, and that the measurements I create correlate with existing datasets, helping to establish the validity of the model results.

---

[1] This is because in a regression setup, the coefficient is the change in the dependent variable for a 1-unit increase in the independent variable. With embedding dimensions, it is not clear what a 1-unit increase in the independent variable means, nor does direction have any clear meaning.

Proceedings of the Third Workshop on Natural Language Processing and Computational Social Science, pages 7–17
Minneapolis, Minnesota, June 6, 2019. ©2019 Association for Computational Linguistics

2 Social Science and Embedding Models of Language

Traditional approaches to creating variables from text in the social sciences involve human coders, who assign documents to categories based on pre-defined criteria. However, this approach is expensive, and does not scale. Text as data techniques attempt to solve this problem through the use of natural language processing techniques to convert a corpus of text into numeric objects which makes inference possible (Grimmer and Stewart, 2013; Gentzkow et al., 2017). These techniques allow scholars to create variables and operationalize concepts in corpora that are too large for human coding, and investigate ideas which cannot be measured directly (unlike indicators like Gross Domestic Product or population).

While a variety of models have been proposed to create variables from political text, including scaling models (Lowe et al., 2011), and topic models (Blei et al., 2003; Grimmer, 2010; Roberts et al., 2016), these approaches focus on the document as the unit of analysis. Word embeddings, which have a long history in the natural language processing literature (see Turney and Pantel (2010) for an extensive review of pre-neural network models), have recently been embraced by social scientists for their potential for inference at the word level. Modern neural word embedding models learn a low-dimensional representation of a word as a dense vector by either factorizing a word co-occurrence matrix or predicting the co-occurrence of a pair of words using a single-layer neural network. Among the best known of these models is word2vec (Mikolov et al., 2013a,b), which proposed an efficient model for learning embeddings, framing embedding learning as a prediction task, rather than a factorization task.

For social scientists, word embeddings are a powerful tool because they can represent the meanings of individual words. Embeddings can help isolate patterns in corpora that are expensive to label, and make apparent latent phenomena not observable through simple document-feature counts such as patterns of semantic change, (Hamilton et al., 2016), cultural assumptions and biases (Caliskan et al., 2017; Kozlowski et al., 2018; Garg et al., 2018), and ideological affinity in international organizations (Pomeroy et al., 2018).

However, these embeddings can be problematic for social science research, where scholars care about both model identification and interpretable results. Embeddings are multidimensional latent variable models, which are not, by default, identified: a known problem with this class of model, where multiple permutations of latent dimensions can result in the same observed data (Rivers, 2003; Clinton et al., 2004; Aldrich et al., 2014). However, by anchoring points on these dimensions, it is possible to present identified and interpretable dimensions. In the ideal-point literature, these anchors represent ideological "endpoints," with theory guiding the selection of which legislators are most liberal and conservative. Choosing words as anchors with a large number of dimensions is more difficult than choosing legislators, however, I offer a solution below.

There have been multiple efforts at developing Bayesian word embeddings (Rudolph et al., 2016; Barkan, 2017; Ji et al., 2017; Havrylov and Titov, 2018), however, none of these have exploited the key advantage of Bayesian inference: the ability to quantify the uncertainty in parameter estimates, and use prior information to inform parameter estimates. The one approach that has incorporated both uncertainty and hypothesis testing is Han et al. (2018), who offer both measures of uncertainty, and a way to test the effect of metadata on the similarity of embeddings, however, this approach does not account for identification problems in the learned embeddings.

3 Bayesian Word Embeddings

In this section, I develop word embeddings as Bayesian latent variable models estimated with variational inference, following similar work for probabilistic principal components analysis (Bishop, 1999) and ideal-point models (Imai et al., 2016). I first discuss the embedding model setup, add Automatic Relevance Determination priors to the model, and then, present the variational updates to estimate the model.

Word embeddings predict the probability of a word-context pair co-occurring, and because the co-occurrence is a binary variable ($Y_{ij} = 1$ if w_i and w_j co-occur, 0 otherwise), I use a probit link function to model the probability of co-occurrence.

$$p(Y_{ij} = 1) =$$
$$(\mathbf{1}[z_{ij} > 0]\mathbf{1}[y_{ij} = 1] + \mathbf{1}[z_{ij} < 0]\mathbf{1}[y_{ij} = 0]) \quad (1)$$
$$\mathcal{TN}(z_{ij}|\boldsymbol{x}_i^\top \boldsymbol{\beta}_j, 1).$$

X and β are $K \times I$ (or $K \times J$, respectively) - dimensional matrices, Y is an $I \times J$ co-occurrence matrix, the corpus contains I words and J context words. Each embedding vector (x_i or β_j) has a K-dimensional multivariate normal prior.

Most existing approaches to word embeddings contain no measures of uncertainty, or the covariance between dimensions. This can be a problem during estimation, as the model attempts to put equal weight on all dimensions. To resolve this, I use Automatic Relevance Determination (ARD) priors, which place a separate gamma-distributed scalar (e.g. α_{X_k}) on the diagonal for each dimension of the covariance matrix (MacKay and Neal, 1994; Bishop, 1999). These priors penalize unnecessary model dimensions, improving model fit.

This specification results in the following likelihood:

$$
\begin{aligned}
p(Z,&X,\beta,\alpha_{\mathbf{X}},\alpha_\beta|\mathbf{Y}) \propto \\
&(\mathbf{1}[z_{ij} > 0]\mathbf{1}[y_{ij} = 1] + \mathbf{1}[z_{ij} < 0]\mathbf{1}[y_{ij} = 0]) \\
&\mathcal{TN}(z_{ij}|x_i^\top\beta_j, 1) \times \\
&\prod_i \mathcal{MVN}(x_i|0, \alpha_X^{-1}) \times \\
&\prod_i \mathcal{MVN}(\beta_j|0, \alpha_\beta^{-1}) \times \\
&\prod_k \mathrm{Gam}(\alpha_{X_k}|c_{X_0}, d_{X_0}) \times \\
&\prod_k \mathrm{Gam}(\alpha_{\beta_k}|c_{\beta_0}, d_{\beta_0}).
\end{aligned}
$$

$$(2)$$

For Bayesian models like this, the goal is to estimate posterior distributions of the parameters most likely to have produced the observed data. Given the joint density (probability of data and parameters), we want to calculate the conditional density of the parameters by evaluating the following integral (notation follows Bishop (1999)):

$$
P(\mathbf{Y}) = \int p(\mathbf{Y}, \theta) d\theta \tag{3}
$$

where $\theta = \{Z, X, \beta, \alpha_X, \alpha_\beta\}$. This integral is analytically intractable, so we transform the integral using Jensen's inequality:

$$
\begin{aligned}
\ln P(\mathbf{Y}) &= \ln \int p(\mathbf{Y}, \theta) d\theta \\
&= \ln \int \mathcal{Q}(\theta) \frac{P(\mathbf{Y}, \theta)}{\mathcal{Q}(\theta)} d\theta \\
&\geq \int \mathcal{Q}(\theta) \ln \frac{P(\mathbf{Y}, \theta)}{\mathcal{Q}(\theta)} d\theta \\
&= \mathcal{L}(Q)
\end{aligned} \tag{4}
$$

where $\mathcal{L}(Q)$ is evidence lower bound (ELBO).

The difference between the true model $P(Y)$ and variational approximation $\mathcal{L}(Q)$ can be represented is the Kullbeck-Leibler divergence:

$$
KL(Q\|P) = -\int \mathcal{Q}(\theta)\ln\frac{P(Y|\theta)}{\mathcal{Q}(\theta)} d\theta \tag{5}
$$

so we turn to a mean-field variational approximation to estimate the model, minimizing the Kullbeck-Leibler divergence (Wainwright and Jordan, 2008; Blei et al., 2017). This requires assuming that the approximation to the posterior can be factorized:

$$
\begin{aligned}
\mathcal{Q}(Z,&X,\beta,\alpha_X,\alpha_\beta) = \\
&\mathcal{Q}(Z), \mathcal{Q}(X), \mathcal{Q}(\beta), \mathcal{Q}(\alpha_X), \mathcal{Q}(\alpha_\beta)
\end{aligned} \tag{6}
$$

and that appropriate approximating distributions can be found. In this case, the requirement is met: z_{ij} is approximated with a truncated normal, x_i and β_j are approximated with multivariate normals, and α_{X_k} and α_{β_k} are approximated with gamma distributions. This factorization and approximation can be further factorized into the following parameter updates:

$$
z_{ij}^* = \mathbb{E}[x_i^\top]\mathbb{E}[\beta_j]
$$

$$
\mathbb{E}[q(z_{ij})] = \begin{cases} z_{ij}^* + \frac{\phi(z_{ij}^*)}{\Phi(z_{ij}^*)} & \text{if } y_{ij} = 1 \\ z_{ij}^* - \frac{\phi(z_{ij}^*)}{1-\Phi(z_{ij}^*)} & \text{if } y_{ij} = 0 \end{cases}
$$

$$
A = \left(\mathrm{diag}(\mathbb{E}[\alpha_X])^{-1} + \sum_j \mathbb{E}[\beta_j\beta_j^\top] \right)
$$

$$
a_i = \sum_j \mathbb{E}[\beta_j]\mathbb{E}[z_{ij}]
$$

$$
\mathbb{E}[q(x_i)] = A^{-1}a_i
$$

$$
B = \left(\mathrm{diag}(\mathbb{E}[\alpha_\beta])^{-1} + \sum_i \mathbb{E}[x_ix_i^\top] \right)
$$

$$
b_j = \sum_i \mathbb{E}[x_i]\mathbb{E}[z_{ij}]
$$

$$
\mathbb{E}[q(\beta_j)] = B^{-1}b_j
$$

$$
c_x = c_{x_0} + \frac{I}{2}
$$

$$
d_{x_k} = d_{x_0} + \frac{\|\mathbb{E}[x_k]\|^2}{2}
$$

$$
\mathbb{E}[q(\alpha_{X_k})] = \frac{c_x}{d_{x_k}}
$$

$$
c_\beta = c_{\beta_0} + \frac{J}{2}
$$

$$
d_{\beta_k} = d_{\beta_0} + \frac{\|\mathbb{E}[\beta_k]\|^2}{2}
$$

$$
\mathbb{E}[q(\alpha_{\beta_k})] = \frac{c_\beta}{d_{\beta_k}}
$$

$$(7)$$

where $c_{x_0}, d_{x_0}, c_{\beta_0}, d_{\beta_0}$ are hyperparameters set by the user. Convergence is monitored via change in the ELBO, and when change drops below a user-specified threshold, the model is considered converged. This model is implemented in the R package bwe.[2]

4 Identifying Model Output

The output from multidimensional latent variable models is not identified, as many possible permutations of latent values can produce the same observed data (Rivers, 2003). However, by fixing $K(K + 1)$ linearly independent values (anchors), users can guarantee the embedding matrix is identified (Rivers, 2003; Clinton et al., 2004; Bafumi et al., 2005). To determine these anchors in the ideal point modeling literature, theory drives the endpoint selection: Clinton et al. (2004) fix both points for Jesse Helms, Ted Kennedy, and Lincoln Chaffee as right, left, and center anchors, respectively, in a $K = 2$ model.

While theory should always motivate modeling choices, determining theoretically motivated anchors when K ranges from 50 to 300 can be difficult. I propose a solution: theory can motivate initial anchor selection, and then, for each additional anchor, the most cosine dis-similar word is chosen as the opposite anchor. This allows the analyst to specify theoretically motivated opposites as initial anchors, and then, resulting anchors are chosen from remaining words. I provide an implementation of this algorithm in the R package bwe.

5 Interpreting Model Output

Anchoring the embeddings ensures they are identified, however, they are still not in a format which allows for ready interpretability in the regression-based models social scientists are most familiar with. To transform embeddings so that they can be used in regression, I opt for a modification of the anchoring approach discussed above. For this approach, the user specifies a pair of endpoints for a dimension, where the endpoints of interest are set to 1 and -1. This can be applied to as many dimensions as necessary, and then the automatic, cosine-based anchoring is used for the rest of the dimensions. An affine transformation is then used to transform the embedding matrix relative to the chosen anchors.

---

[2] https://github.com/adamlauretig/bwe.

A key advantage of this approach is that because two anchors are supplied, words are scaled on this dimension. For example, while simply choosing "war" as an anchor results in the results words scaled according to their similarity with "war", setting "war" and "peace" as opposite anchors (1 and -1, respectively) allows for a measure of bellicosity in a corpus.

This method can be applied to as many words/concepts as the user is interested in (as the automated cosine similarity will handle the other dimensions), and, of note for social scientists, each of these word scalings, which are $I \times 1$, can be multiplied by a $D \times I$ document-term matrix: $D \times I * I \times 1$, scaling the documents in a corpus according to dimensions of interest. These document values can then we used in a regression, and the coefficients can be interpreted in a straightforward way.

6 Inaugurals and Internationalism

In an initial test of this model, I investigate whether the United States saw itself in a new, global role after 1945, as perceived in presidents' inaugural addresses. After 1945, the United States was the global hegemon, and international relations theory argues that this resulted in a shift in American attitudes towards the world (Mearsheimer, 2001). It has been shown that the public takes elite cues on various issues (Zaller, 1992; Druckman and Jacobs, 2015), and since foreign-policy is generally viewed as an elite-led phenomenon (Aldrich et al., 2006), I explore whether, after the second World War, inaugural addresses were more internationally focused than those before the war.

I use the corpus of inaugural addresses available in the quanteda R package (Benoit et al., 2018), which contains 58 speeches. I keep words which occur with frequency > 5, and then lowercase and tokenize the texts, resulting in 2705 words. I estimate the model with a context window of 9, with 5 negative samples for every positive sample, and and the number of dimensions $K = 50$. After fitting the model, I compare three possible anchorings: an un-anchored embedding, an embedding anchored on "american," and an embedding scaled with the first dimension anchored on "international" and "domestic;" the results are visible in Table 1. We see that changing the anchoring points changes the most similar words, however, anchoring helps make these embeddings more interpretable. To test whether there was a statistically significant difference between American perceptions of global roles before and after 1945, I multiply the document-term matrix by the embedding dimension anchored on "international" and "domestic," creating an "internationalism" scale for documents. I test this hypothesis using a one-sided Kolmogorov-Smirnov test, and reject the null hypothesis, that pre-1945 inaugural addresses are less internationalist than the post-1945 addresses at $p < .05$. This means pre-1945 addresses are more "internationalist" than the post-1945 addresses. I plot the differing distributions in Figure 1.

What explains this finding? One possibility, building on Herring (2008, ch. 1), is that the United States was not isolationist prior to 1945, that isolationism was largely a product of the 1920s and 1930s, however, the United States was more unilateral before 1945. Because the multilateral world order was a fact of life after 1945, it is possible presidents were less likely to comment on international affairs, international action was the norm, rather than the exception. Furthermore, the public played a larger role in shaping foreign policy action, particularly during the Vietnam War era, than it had previously (Aldrich et al., 2006), and this could lead to a blurring of the lines between foreign and domestic politics when presidents address the public.

I compare the results from Bayesian Word Embeddings to the results from a standard model used in the social sciences to analyze text, the structural topic model (Roberts et al., 2016)[3]. I find that "domestic" and "international" topics are not linked, the structural topic model captures no relationship between these words. I then investigate the change in "domestic" and "international" topics before and after 1945, and find no effect. There is ample belief and qualitative evidence of a change in American views about the world after 1945, which is not captured in the structural topic model. These differing results suggest that the embeddings are capable of recovering patterns in language that document-based topic models cannot.

7 Diplomacy and the Onset of War

Natural language processing and text as data methods offer the opportunity to quantify decision-

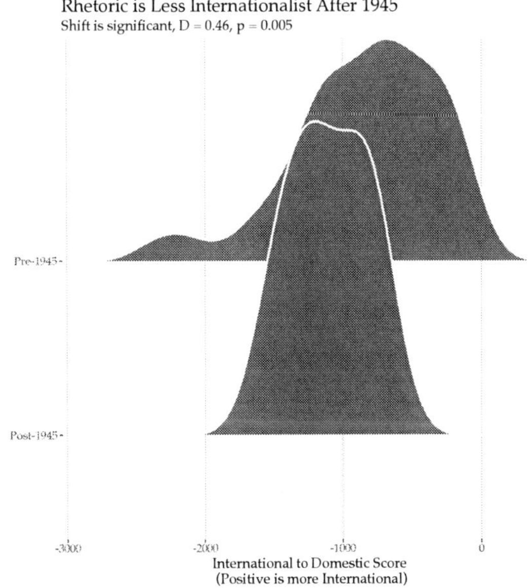

Figure 1: After 1945, rhetoric in inaugural addresses becomes less internationalist, and more domestic.

making and attitude among elites, which is notoriously difficult to measure, especially in times of conflict. Existing approaches to measuring elite attitudes often depend on survey or laboratory experiments (Feaver and Gelpi, 2006; LeVeck et al., 2014), however, I offer an alternative approach that allows us to examine elite decisions as they occur. Drawing on a novel corpus of recently digitized diplomatic cables, the *Foreign Relations of the United States* (FRUS), I investigate whether changes in the bellicosity of elite rhetoric precedes an escalation in US hostility. The FRUS dataset provides an exciting opportunity to investigate bellicosity among American foreign policy elites as events happened, as it contains primary source documents of private communications from the policymakers who develop and implement the United States' foreign policy. Among the sources for documents included in FRUS are "Presidential libraries, Departments of State and Defense, National Security Council, Central Intelligence Agency, Agency for International Development, and other foreign affairs agencies as well as the private papers of individuals involved in formulating U.S. foreign policy," with a focus on documents relevant to policy-making (State Department, 2017). When a FRUS volume is compiled, the compiler(s) first identify a set of themes, develop a list all relevant documents, and then select

---

[3]Results presented in the Appendix.

Word of Interest	Anchor: International, Domestic							
war	large	declarations	pay	carefully	choice	equal	this	greater
peace	practices	meeting	strife	inspiring	confederacy	advance	temple	objections
american	engagements	soil	cultivate	by	heroes	goes	pride	she
international	declare	path	honor	expression	speaking	where	vision	ignorance
national	temple	subject	learned	demand	advance	objections	principle	guard
	Anchor: American							
war	abroad	remedies	violate	slaves	violence	declarations	proposition	sectional
peace	army	plenty	victory	effort	resumption	front	regulation	agreement
american	regards	brief	instrumentality	execute	able	friendly	hands	friendship
international	assembly	european	continent	capable	various	canal	differing	affected
national	now	recognition	corporations	monetary	south	more	character	diversity
	Anchor: None							
war	made	had	peace	force	never	after	still	place
peace	world	nations	war	strength	prosperity	progress	just	security
american	through	opportunity	america	life	justice	right	individual	equal
international	maintain	lasting	fixed	beneficial	settlement	likely	relationship	intercourse
national	most	necessity	common	given	free	first	an	power

Table 1: The most similar words to "war," "peace," "american," "international," and "national," according to each of the anchoring choices, measured via cosine similarity. Choosing appropriate anchors leads to more interpretable embeddings than the unanchored model.

those with the greatest historical import. These are then redacted or declassified, typeset, compared to the original document, and printed and bound (McAllister et al., 2015).

To explore elite bellicosity, I investigate behavior during 1964-1966, the leadup to the Vietnam War, and the breakdown of the "Cold War Consensus" (Krebs, 2015). The era is particularly interesting because, while the United States increased its commitment to Vietnam, it also engaged in several other interventions around the world (Herring, 2008, ch. 16). Thus, we would expect to see that an increase in bellicosity in the FRUS corpus would be correlated with an increase in hostile actions by the United States.

I measure hostility using the Cline Center Historical Event Data, coded from the *New York Times* (Althaus et al., 2017). These data take the form *(DATE, STATE A, ACTION, STATE B)*, where *(STATE A, STATE B)* are directed dyads, *DATE* is the day the event was observed, and *ACTION* is one of five categories of action: neutral, verbal cooperation, verbal conflict, material cooperation, or material conflict (Norris et al., 2017). I select only those events where *STATE A* is the United States, and sum events at the biweekly level. I measure hostility using counts of material conflict events, and display the hostile event counts in Figure 2.

To calculate bellicosity, I first estimate a Bayesian Word Embedding model, with context window of 9, $K = 50$, keeping any word that occurs at least 40 times. I then anchor the embeddings on a "war-peace" dimension. I summarize the results of the anchoring using Uniform Manifold Approximation and Projection for Dimension Reduction (UMAP), which calculates a low dimensional number of components, similar to principal components analysis. Unlike PCA, UMAP calculates distance using cosine similarity, while balancing both global and local structure in the embeddings (Becht et al., 2019). I present results in Table 2, and the components reveal themes in the corpus, clustering by region and issue, helping highlight the face validity of the embeddings.

To estimate the bellicosity of a given document, I multiply the war-peace dimension by the document term matrix, averaging document bellicosity scores at the bi-weekly level. I plot the bi-weekly bellicosity scores in Figure 2.

To determine if there is a relationship between hostile events and bellicosity, I regress events on the lagged bellicosity (to account for a delay in policy implementation), using a Poisson generalized linear model, due to the count-distributed nature of the outcome.[4] I plot the regression line against the data in Figure 3, and find a positive and statistically significant effect.

This result suggests that bellicosity in elite deliberations, captured in diplomatic documents, results in an increase in conflictual events, which suggests that the documents in the *FRUS* corpus do not simply contain cheap talk, these deliberations ultimately shape policy. These findings also help establish the validity of the "bellicosity" scale, that is, it correlates with an entirely

---

[4]In the appendix, I remove outliers and high-leverage points from the dataset, and fit the model again. Results do not change.

iran	doubtful	communications	tam	bases	relatively	robertson	initials
iranian	blocked	relations	systematically	family	zambia	outflows	secretary
shah	sponsored	appreciably	north	leave	udi	payments	footnotes
aram	ultimatum	masses	hanoi	deployments	tran	liabilities	present
iranians	telecommunications	sites	recce	fixed	rhodesia	fowler	conflict
afghan	recommendation	overtures	drv	precondition	sr	banks	president
squadron	imminent	concurs	vinh	laotian	neighboring	tax	raymond
mnd	jet	harass	chau	reasons	continent	corporations	even

Table 2: The top words from a subset of components estimated from UMAP. Components include a variety of regional and substantive themes. These results help highlight the validity of the embeddings: semantically similar words are appearing near each other in cosine space.

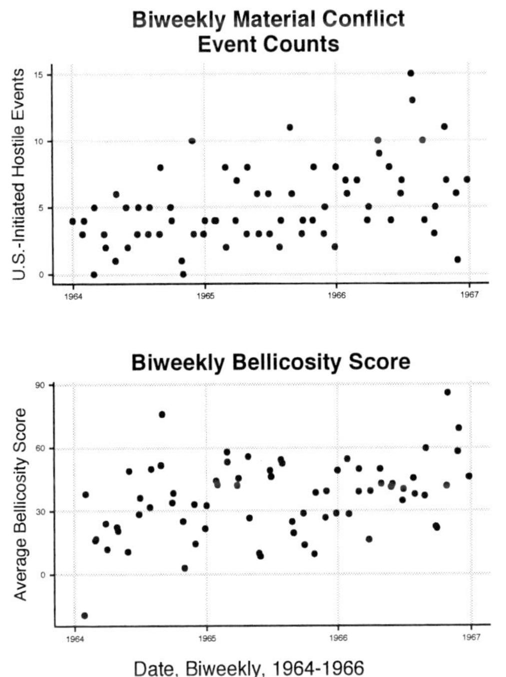

Figure 2: Plotting material conflict event counts and bellicosity scores over time aggregated at the bi-weekly level. Both bellicosity and the count of material conflict events increase with time, as the United States increased its involvement in the Vietnam War.

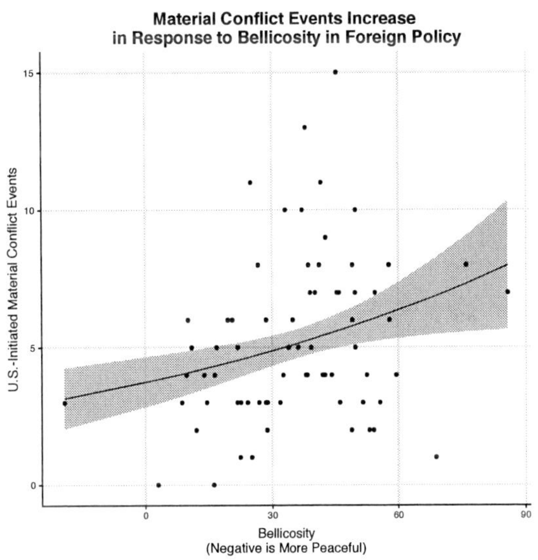

Figure 3: An increase in the previous bi-weekly period's bellicosity is associated with an increase in U.S.-initiated hostile events. The regression is from a Poisson generalized linear model, and uncertainty is displayed with 95% confidence intervals.

separate dataset, which captures a similar phenomena. All replication materials are available at `https://github.com/adamlauretig/bwe_application_naacl_2019`.

8 Conclusion

In this paper, I introduced Bayesian Word Embeddings, a method for estimating word embeddings which uses variational bayesian methods. I incorporated Automatic Relevance Determination priors on the embedding dimensions, relaxing the requirement that all dimensions have equal weight. Linking word embeddings to Bayesian latent variable models, I then discussed issues with identification, and solutions proposed in the ideal-point literature, as well as offering an alternative which allows for scaling along dimensions of interest, which creates model model that can then be used in a regression.

I applied Bayesian Word Embeddings to two cases: examining the change in American attitudes about the world before and after 1945 as captured in Presidential inaugural addresses, and then, testing whether an increase in the bellicosity of internal elite discussion (in diplomatic documents) results in an increase in American hostility. I found that there was a statistically significant different in the views of the world expressed in inaugural addresses, and that this shift was the opposite of what hypotheses generated from international relations theory would expect. When testing the effect of bellicosity on the hostility of American foreign policy, I that an increase in bellicosity resulted in an increase in hostility.

Overall, I have contributed a tool which can serve many purposes for social scientists. By building a probabilistic embedding model, I have constructed a tool which moves beyond document-based inferential approaches to text as data, allowing inference on individual words. This promises new reaches for social scientists, in particular, the promise of crossover with interpretivist work, building on Nelson (2017). Concepts such as securitization theory (Wæver, 1995) draw on the idea that language and word choice by elites shape the attitude of the public, and through the methods introduced above provide the opportunity to generate statistical tests for hypotheses derived from theories like securitization theory.

Future methodological work will follow three tracks. The first will build on Rudolph et al. (2016) and Han et al. (2018), one goal is incorporating document-level metadata into embedding estimation, allowing embeddings to vary according to document-specific attributes, and then, identifying the resulting embeddings. The second will take advantage of stochastic variational inference (Hoffman et al., 2013) to enable Bayesian Word Embeddings to scale to massive corpora. Finally, the third track for future word will involve tying the anchoring approach discussed above with the emerging literature on making casual claims from text (Fong and Grimmer, 2016; Mozer et al., 2018), and taking advantage of the word similarities to identify appropriate linguistic counterfactuals.

Acknowledgments

I would like to thank Bear Braumoeller, William Minozzi, and Gregory Smith, along with the three reviewers for valuable feedback on this project. I would like to thank Michael Neblo and the Institute for Democratic Engagement and Accountability at Ohio State for funding which helped support this project.

References

John H. Aldrich, Christopher Gelpi, Peter Feaver, Jason Reifler, and Kristin Thompson Sharp. 2006. Foreign policy and the electoral connection. *Annual Review of Political Science*, 9:477–502.

John H. Aldrich, Jacob M. Montgomery, and David B. Sparks. 2014. Polarization and ideology: Partisan sources of low dimensionality in scaled roll call analyses. *Political Analysis*, 22(4):435–456.

Scott Althaus, Joseph Bajjalieh, John F. Carter, Buddy Peyton, and Dan A. Shalmon. Cline center historical phoenix event data [online]. 2017.

Joseph Bafumi, Andrew Gelman, David K. Park, and Noah Kaplan. 2005. Practical issues in implementing and understanding bayesian ideal point estimation. *Political Analysis*, 13(2):171–187.

Oren Barkan. 2017. Bayesian neural word embedding. In *AAAI*, pages 3135–3143.

Etienne Becht, Leland McInnes, John Healy, Charles-Antoine Dutertre, Immanuel W.H. Kwok, Lai Guan Ng, Florent Ginhoux, and Evan W. Newell. 2019. Dimensionality reduction for visualizing single-cell data using umap. *Nature biotechnology*, 37(1):38.

Kenneth Benoit, Kohei Watanabe, Haiyan Wang, Paul Nulty, Adam Obeng, Stefan Müller, and Akitaka Matsuo. 2018. quanteda: An r package for the quantitative analysis of textual data. *Journal of Open Source Software*, 3(30):774.

CM Bishop. 1999. Variational principal components. In *Artificial Neural Networks, 1999. ICANN 99. Ninth International Conference on (Conf. Publ. No. 470)*, volume 1, pages 509–514. IET.

David M. Blei, Alp Kucukelbir, and Jon D. McAuliffe. 2017. Variational inference: A review for statisticians. *Journal of the American Statistical Association*, 112(518):859–877.

David M. Blei, Andrew Y. Ng, and Michael I. Jordan. 2003. Latent dirichlet allocation. *Journal of machine Learning research*, 3(Jan):993–1022.

Aylin Caliskan, Joanna J. Bryson, and Arvind Narayanan. 2017. Semantics derived automatically from language corpora contain human-like biases. *Science*, 356(6334):183–186.

Joshua Clinton, Simon Jackman, and Douglas Rivers. 2004. The statistical analysis of roll call data. *American Political Science Review*, 98(2):355–370.

James N. Druckman and Lawrence R. Jacobs. 2015. *Who Governs?: Presidents, Public Opinion, and Manipulation*. University of Chicago Press.

Peter D. Feaver and Christopher Gelpi. 2006. *Choosing your battles: American civil-military relations and the use of force*. Princeton University Press.

Christian Fong and Justin Grimmer. 2016. Discovery of treatments from text corpora. In *ACL (1)*.

Nikhil Garg, Londa Schiebinger, Dan Jurafsky, and James Zou. 2018. Word embeddings quantify 100 years of gender and ethnic stereotypes. *Proceedings of the National Academy of Sciences*, 115(16):E3635–E3644.

Matthew Gentzkow, Bryan T. Kelly, and Matt Taddy. 2017. Text as data. Technical report, National Bureau of Economic Research.

Justin Grimmer. 2010. A bayesian hierarchical topic model for political texts: Measuring expressed agendas in senate press releases. *Political Analysis*, pages 1–35.

Justin Grimmer and Brandon M. Stewart. 2013. Text as data: The promise and pitfalls of automatic content analysis methods for political texts. *Political Analysis*, page mps028.

William L. Hamilton, Jure Leskovec, and Dan Jurafsky. 2016. Diachronic word embeddings reveal statistical laws of semantic change. In *Proceedings of the 54th Annual Meeting of the Association for Computational Linguistics (Volume 1: Long Papers)*, volume 1, pages 1489–1501.

Rujun Han, Michael Gill, Arthur Spirling, and Kyunghyun Cho. 2018. Conditional word embedding and hypothesis testing via bayes-by-backprop. In *Proceedings of the 2018 Conference on Empirical Methods in Natural Language Processing*, pages 4890–4895.

Serhii Havrylov and Ivan Titov. 2018. Embedding words as distributions with a bayesian skip-gram model. In *Proceedings of the 27th International Conference on Computational Linguistics*, pages 1775–1789.

George C. Herring. 2008. *From colony to superpower: US foreign relations since 1776*. Oxford University Press.

Matthew D. Hoffman, David M. Blei, Chong Wang, and John Paisley. 2013. Stochastic variational inference. *The Journal of Machine Learning Research*, 14(1):1303–1347.

Kosuke Imai, James Lo, and Jonathan Olmsted. 2016. Fast estimation of ideal points with massive data. *American Political Science Review*, 110(4):631–656.

Geng Ji, Robert Bamler, Erik B. Sudderth, and Stephan Mandt. 2017. Bayesian paragraph vectors. *arXiv preprint arXiv:1711.03946*.

Austin C. Kozlowski, Matt Taddy, and James A. Evans. 2018. The geometry of culture: Analyzing meaning through word embeddings. *arXiv preprint arXiv:1803.09288*.

Ronald R. Krebs. 2015. How dominant narratives rise and fall: Military conflict, politics, and the cold war consensus. *International Organization*, 69(04):809–845.

Brad L LeVeck, D Alex Hughes, James H Fowler, Emilie Hafner-Burton, and David G Victor. 2014. The role of self-interest in elite bargaining. *Proceedings of the National Academy of Sciences*, 111(52):18536–18541.

Will Lowe, Kenneth Benoit, Slava Mikhaylov, and Michael Laver. 2011. Scaling policy preferences from coded political texts. *Legislative studies quarterly*, 36(1):123–155.

David J.C. MacKay and Radford M. Neal. 1994. Automatic relevance determination for neural networks. In *Technical Report*. Cambridge University.

William B. McAllister, Joshua Botts, Peter Cozzens, and Aaron W. Marrs. 2015. *Toward "Thorough, Accurate, and Reliable": A History of the Foreign Relations of the United States Series*. Government Printing Office.

John J. Mearsheimer. 2001. *The tragedy of great power politics*. WW Norton & Company.

Tomas Mikolov, Ilya Sutskever, Kai Chen, Greg S Corrado, and Jeff Dean. 2013a. Distributed representations of words and phrases and their compositionality. In *Advances in neural information processing systems*, pages 3111–3119.

Tomas Mikolov, Wen-tau Yih, and Geoffrey Zweig. 2013b. Linguistic regularities in continuous space word representations. In *NAACL-HLT*, volume 13, pages 746–751.

Reagan Mozer, Luke Miratrix, Aaron Russell Kaufman, and L Jason Anastasopoulos. 2018. Matching with text data: An experimental evaluation of methods for matching documents and of measuring match quality. *arXiv preprint arXiv:1801.00644*.

Laura K. Nelson. 2017. Computational grounded theory: A methodological framework. *Sociological Methods & Research*, page 0049124117729703.

Clayton Norris, Philip Schrodt, and John Beieler. 2017. Petrarch2: Another event coding program. *The Journal of Open Source Software*, 2(9).

Caleb Pomeroy, Niheer Dasandi, and Slava Jankin Mikhaylov. 2018. Multiplex communities and the emergence of international conflict. *arXiv preprint arXiv:1806.00615*.

Ludovic Rheault, Kaspar Beelen, Christopher Cochrane, and Graeme Hirst. 2016. Measuring emotion in parliamentary debates with automated textual analysis. *PloS one*, 11(12):e0168843.

Douglas Rivers. 2003. Identification of multidimensional spatial voting models. *Typescript. Stanford University*.

Margaret E. Roberts, Brandon M. Stewart, and Edoardo M. Airoldi. 2016. A model of text for experimentation in the social sciences. *Journal of the American Statistical Association*, (just-accepted):1–49.

Maja Rudolph, Francisco Ruiz, Stephan Mandt, and David Blei. 2016. Exponential family embeddings. In *Advances in Neural Information Processing Systems*, pages 478–486.

State Department. About the foreign relations of the united states series [online]. 2017.

Peter D. Turney and Patrick Pantel. 2010. From frequency to meaning: Vector space models of semantics. *Journal of artificial intelligence research*, 37:141–188.

Ole Wæver. 1995. Securitization and desecuritization. In *On Security*, pages 46–86. Columbia University Press.

Martin J. Wainwright and Michael I. Jordan. 2008. Graphical models, exponential families, and variational inference. *Foundations and Trends® in Machine Learning*, 1(1–2):1–305.

John R. Zaller. 1992. *The nature and origins of mass opinion*. Cambridge university press.

A Comparing BWE to STM

Unlike the results from the Bayesian Word Embedding, the structural topic model detects no difference in topics before and after 1945. The top words, as determined by FREX score, are visible in 3.

International Topic	Domestic Topic
representative	pacific
civilization	territory
making	question
international	whilst
tax	importance
popular	constitution
concern	slavery
supreme	domestic

Table 3: Top eight words from structural topic model for international and domestic topics, by FREX score.

B Inauguration Robustness Check

One concern with the role of internationalism in inaugural addresses is that by splitting at 1945, the "internationalism" of the pre-1945 sample is due to World War Two, and the Roosevelt presidency. To account for this, I re-estimate the Kolmogorov-Smirnov test from above, excluding the Roosevelt

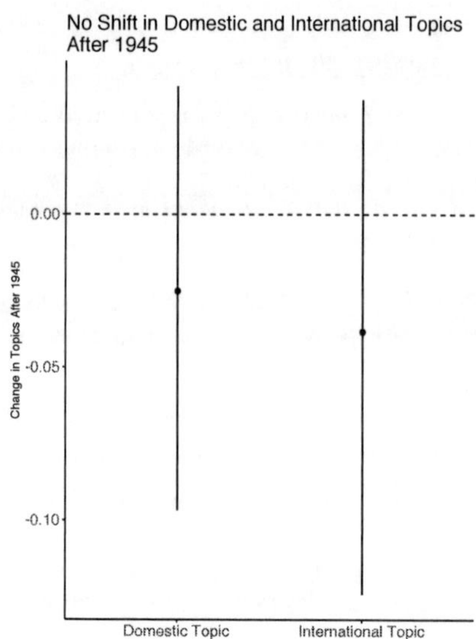

Figure 4: There is no significant difference between foreign and international topics before and after 1945, uncertainty is displayed with 95% confidence intervals.

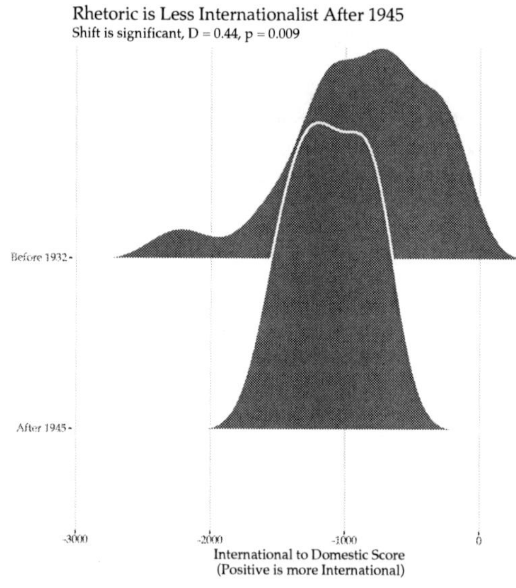

Figure 5: Even excluding the Roosevelt administration, when only examining inaugural addresses from before 1932 and after 1945, the pre-1932 inaugural addresses are more internationalist than the post-1945 addresses.

inaugural addresses, and present the results in 5. This compares inaugurals from before 1932 to those after 1945, and the substantive results do not change.

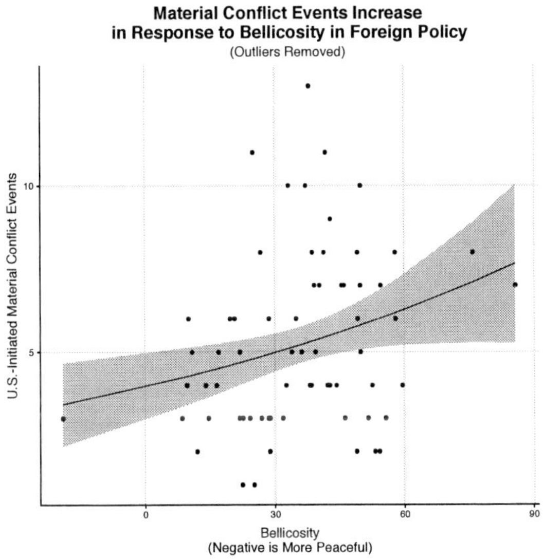

Figure 6: An increase in bellicosity is associated with an increase in U.S.-initiated hostile events. The regression is from a Poisson generalized linear model, and uncertainty is displayed with 95% confidence intervals.

C GLM without Outliers

To ensure that the results presented in Figure 3 were not the results of outliers, I removed any outliers and high-leverage points, and re-fit the model. The results were the same, as visible in Figure 6.

Tweet Classification without the Tweet:
An Empirical Examination of User versus Document Attributes

Veronica E. Lynn[1], Salvatore Giorgi[2],
Niranjan Balasubramanian[1] and H. Andrew Schwartz[1]
[1]Stony Brook University, [2]University of Pennsylvania
{velynn, niranjan, has}@cs.stonybrook.edu, sgiorgi@sas.upenn.edu

Abstract

NLP naturally puts a primary focus on leveraging document language, occasionally considering user attributes as supplemental. However, as we tackle more social scientific tasks, it is possible user attributes might be of primary importance and the document supplemental. Here, we systematically investigate the predictive power of user-level features alone versus document-level features for *document*-level tasks. We first show user attributes can sometimes carry more task-related information than the document itself. For example, a tweet-level stance detection model using only 13 user-level attributes (i.e. features that did not depend on the specific tweet) was able to obtain a higher F1 than the top-performing SemEval participant. We then consider multiple tasks and a wider range of user attributes, showing the performance of strong document-only models can often be improved (as in stance, sentiment, and sarcasm) with user attributes, particularly benefiting tasks with stable "trait-like" outcomes (e.g. stance) most relative to frequently changing "state-like" outcomes (e.g. sentiment). These results not only support the growing work on integrating user factors into predictive systems, but that some of our NLP tasks might be better cast primarily as user-level (or human) tasks.

1 Introduction

Natural language processing is increasingly tackling new tasks over microblogs and social media, such as stance detection, sarcasm detection, and variations of sentiment analysis. Building on techniques used for traditional NLP, it is natural to attempt such tasks with inputs based solely on the content of the document (e.g. tweet) in question. We present an empirical argument for why this text-only scope may be a limiting view which inflates the value of document-only solutions.

Our work aims to answer the following questions: 1) What and how much information do user attributes alone carry for different social media tasks, particularly for predictive tasks that are more about the user than the document (e.g. stance)? 2) When are user attributes useful and what do language features contribute in these cases? While there are multiple works that show that adding user attributes is useful for different prediction tasks (Hovy, 2015; Zamani and Schwartz, 2017; Lynn et al., 2017), there is no single systematic study that answers these questions.

To this end we conduct a systematic evaluation of user attribute-only models on multiple tasks including stance detection, sarcasm detection, sentiment analysis, and prepositional phrase attachment. We evaluate the impact of user attribute-only models through a range of features derived from publicly available information about the users including: written profile bio, inferred demographics and personality, self-reported location, profile picture, who one follows in a social network, and a background of users' past language. The evaluations show that user attributes can have a large impact and, depending on the nature of the task, even outperform document-only features — *inference on a document without even looking at its contents!*

We conduct further evaluations comparing document contributions to an inference task relative to user-level features. Recent research has explored *how user-level attributes add value **on top of** document-level language* (Volkova et al., 2013; Hovy, 2015; Lynn et al., 2017; Zamani et al., 2018). Instead we quantify how well user attributes **alone** can predict and then what document-level language can uniquely add, identifying cases where the document is essential.

Contributions. Our specific contributions are three-fold: **(1)** We show that the stance of a

Proceedings of the Third Workshop on Natural Language Processing and Computational Social Science, pages 18–28
Minneapolis, Minnesota, June 6, 2019. ©2019 Association for Computational Linguistics

tweet can be predicted with state-of-the-art F1 scores (better than all participant systems of the SemEval-2016 stance task) without even looking at the given tweet, suggesting such tasks might be better case as user-level (we outperform tweet-specific models that use thousands of features or complex neural networks using only 13 easily-derived features). **(2)** We put forth a theory that tasks which capture more "trait-like" human attributes (those that are stable over time, e.g. stance) benefit more from user-level information as compared to "state-like" attributes (frequently changing, e.g. sentiment). We evaluate this theory by looking at the role of user attributes across different predictive tasks. **(3)** We provide a set of considerations and metrics, for task participants and designers alike, for the inclusion of user information within new social science-related tasks.

2 Background

Recent work has shown that considering language within the context of user attributes can improve classification accuracy (Volkova et al., 2013; Bamman et al., 2014; Yang and Eisenstein, 2015; Hovy, 2015; Kulkarni et al., 2016; Lynn et al., 2017). Other work has used network or other meta data, such as in Bamman and Smith (2015); Johnson and Goldwasser (2016); Joseph et al. (2017); Khattri et al. (2015). In a sense these trail-blazing works might be viewed as case studies on user attributes — identifying particular pieces of information for particular tasks where user information has lead to an advantage. We believe this is the first systematic study on the extent to which tasks are more easily achieved with user information or by combining user attributes with document language. In addition, prior work has explored what user attributes add on top of language, whereas we focus primarily on user attributes, with the contributions from document-level features being secondary.

Models designed specifically to put language within the context of human factors, such as demographics or location, have led to improvements on a variety of NLP tasks. For example, Hovy (2015) improved on three types of text classification tasks by learning age- and gender-specific word embeddings. Similarly, Yang and Eisenstein (2015) found that sentiment analysis benefited from learning community-specific embeddings from social networks. Lynn et al. (2017)

proposed a method to adapt language to user factors by composing the factors with language features in a domain adaptation-like formulation, demonstrating improvements on multiple tasks; this technique was expanded upon by Zamani et al. (2018). Still, even simple methods for incorporating these factors provide predictive power and should not be overlooked; our paper examines this in-depth.

Some work in stance detection has focused on document context and discourse structure (Walker et al., 2012a,b; Sridhar et al., 2015), though user attributes have been considered as well. When predicting stance for debates, Thomas et al. (2006) and Hasan and Ng (2013) benefited from enforcing the constraint that multiple statements from the same person should receive the same predicted stance, making the assumption that stance is unlikely to change over the course of a single conversation. Johnson and Goldwasser (2016), who predict the stance of Twitter *users* as opposed to individual tweets, consider both temporal activity and political party affiliation in their models. Chen and Ku (2016) learned user embeddings for stance detection and found that the inclusion of such embeddings significantly improved model performance. Going in a somewhat different direction, Joseph et al. (2017) found that the amount and type of user attributes, such as political party affiliation or Twitter profile description, provided to annotators of a stance detection dataset significantly impacted annotation quality, suggesting that considering user attributes is important not just during classification but also during dataset creation.

User attributes and other contextual information has proven useful beyond stance detection. Bamman and Smith (2015) extensively evaluate the effects of extralinguistic information, including *author*, *audience*, and *environment* features, in the context of sarcasm detection. They observe an almost 10 point increase in performance when adding extralinguistic features to the text-only model and find such features perform well even without the textual features. Although their work is similar to ours, we explore more tasks and a different set of extralinguistic features, including inferred factors; we see our work as complementary to — and expanding on — theirs.

Amir et al. (2016) outperformed Bamman and Smith (2015) on the same dataset by incorporating user embeddings, learned from users' past tweets, into a deep sarcasm model. Khattri et al. (2015) use past tweets to improve sarcasm detection by comparing the sentiment expressed towards an entity in the target tweet to that expressed in historical tweets. Martin et al. (2016) found that, when predicting retweet count, a user's past success (measured as the average number of retweets received for other tweets in the past) was nearly as predictive as a model using all features they tried, including those drawn from the tweet itself. Jurgens et al. (2017) find that they are able to accurately predict the attributes of a user based on communications targeted at them (as opposed to written by them), emphasizing that a person's social network is itself an important source of user-level information. Finally, Hovy and Fornaciari (2018) demonstrate that user attributes can be used to improve the quality of author embeddings via retrofitting.

3 Prediction Models

This paper seeks to systematically and empirically understand the role of user attributes within the context of social media tasks. To that end, we consider a variety of user-level features and evaluate their importance for four tweet-level prediction tasks.

3.1 Tasks

The following section provides details for the systems and datasets used for analysis. Development sets were used for hyperparameter tuning. Statistics for each task are given in Table 1.

Stance. For stance detection we use the SemEval-2016 dataset (Mohammad et al., 2016), which contains tweets annotated as being *in favor of*, *against*, or *neutral toward* one of five targets: atheism, climate change as a real concern, feminism, Hillary Clinton, and legalization of abortion. Note that *neutral* does not indicate "neither for nor against", but rather not enough information to say either way (for example, "I know who I'm voting for!" would be *neutral* towards Hillary Clinton). Similar to the top baseline system in this task, we train a logistic regression classifier on character n-grams of size two to five and word n-grams of size one to three. We preserve the train/test split of the original dataset. For evaluation purposes, we obtain the predictions from the top participating system, MITRE (Zarrella and Marsh, 2016), and subset them to our test set.

Sarcasm. Sarcasm detection replicates the work of Bamman and Smith (2015) by using the tweet features described in the paper (e.g n-grams, sentiment scores, Brown clusters) and evaluating on their dataset using a logistic regression classifier via ten-fold cross validation. The folds are split such that no user appears in both the training and testing sets. Bamman and Smith (2015)'s dataset was constructed by sampling tweets that did or did not contain hashtags indicating sarcasm (e.g. *I love when it snows #sarcastic*); these hashtags were removed during preprocessing.

Sentiment. Message-level sentiment annotations indicating *positive*, *negative*, and *neutral* are available from the SemEval-2013 dataset (Nakov et al., 2013). We mostly replicate the top-performing system on this task (Mohammad et al., 2013) by training a linear SVM on character n-grams, word n-grams, and features from multiple sentiment and emotion lexicons (Hu and Liu, 2004; Wilson et al., 2005; Mohammad and Turney, 2010, 2013; Mohammad et al., 2013; Kiritchenko et al., 2014). The train/test split of the original dataset was used for evaluation.

PP-Attachment. A prepositional-phrase attachment dataset for Twitter was constructed by combining annotated data from Tweebank (Kong et al., 2014) and Lynn et al. (2017). Candidate heads are ranked using an SVM-Rank (Joachims, 2006) model trained on n-gram, WordNet, and Treebank features similar to those used in Belinkov et al. (2014). Cross validation is used for evaluation.

Task	Tweets	Users	Instances
Stance	3021	2349	3021
Sarcasm	17084	10966	17084
Sentiment	10339	9917	10339
PP-Attachment	1319	1319	2365

Table 1: Number of tweets, users, and instances represented in each task.

3.2 User Attribute Features

Each user's name, location, description, and picture were extracted from their Twitter profile. We also collected up to 200 of their tweets, excluding retweets and those included in the task data. Finally, we collected a list of every account that each user follows. Features were derived from this data as described below. We excluded tweets for which no user information was available; as a result, the test and training datasets were typically smaller than the originals[1].

One concern with using predicted user attributes such as age, gender, or personality is that they are prone to noise. However, one can look at it as a way of reducing large quantities of text to a single feature that happens to correlate well with some external quantity. Because we were interested in what a person's language says about themselves, any discrepancies between a user's predicted and actual attribute may provide additional predictive power: a 50-year-old whose writing style is more typical of a 20-year-old is likely better represented using their predicted age (20) than their actual age (50).

Demographics & Personality. Real-valued estimates of these attributes were obtained by applying pre-existing predictive lexica to each user's past tweets. Age and gender were obtained from the models of Sap et al. (2014). For personality, we used Park et al. (2015) to predict each of the Big Five traits: openness, conscientiousness, extroversion, agreeableness, and neuroticism.

Political Ideology. Using the dataset from Preoţiuc-Pietro et al. (2017), we train a ridge regression model on topic and n-gram features to predict real-valued political ideology scores between 1 (*very conservative*) and 7 (*very liberal*) from each user's tweets. This model achieved a Pearson $r = .374$ through cross validation of the training data.

User Embeddings. Five-dimensional latent factors were derived from each user's prior tweets using the generative factor analysis approach proposed by Kulkarni et al. (2017). Factors obtained using this method have been shown to correlate with outcomes such as income and IQ.

Profile Name. We used the Demographer package (Knowles et al., 2016) to predict gender from the profile name. We also used NamePrism (Ye et al., 2017) to predict scores for six ethnicities and thirty-nine nationalities.

Profile Description & Location. Character 2- to 5-grams and word 1- to 3-grams were extracted from the users' description and location fields.

Profile Picture. Borrowing from a popular method in transfer learning, we used a pre-trained image classification model, Inception-v3 (Szegedy et al., 2016), to obtain 2048-dimensional embeddings from the next-to-last layer of the model.

Followees. For each task, we identified the top 5000 Twitter accounts that were followed by the users in our dataset. Each of the 5000 accounts corresponded to a binary feature indicating if the user followed that account or not. We chose this representation for simplicity, though alternative methods such as network embeddings (e.g. Yang and Eisenstein (2015)) may be used instead.

4 Stance of a Tweet without the Tweet

We look first at the task of stance detection, as stance is typically seen more as a *trait* (attributable to a user) than a *state* (attributable to a point in time, such as a single message).

Table 2 compares stance prediction results for models trained only on tweet features to those trained only on user attribute features. Here, we only directly consider the *favor* and *against* classes so as to be consistent with the SemEval competition, which used an F1 measure that is an unweighted average of just these two classes. Note that `Inferred Factors` is a combination of `Demographics`, `Personality`, `Political Ideology`, and `User Embeddings`.

Stance without tweet is better than tweet only: Two of the user attribute types, `Followee` and `Inferred Factors`, perform better than the best tweet-based system that participated in SemEval-2016. `Location` also performs better than the most frequent class baseline. As we show next, if we consider the performance on the *neutral* class, we find that user attributes can do even better. We expect user attributes to carry some stance related information but it is surprising that they can compete with or outperform state-of-the-art models despite using a simpler model and/or fewer features.

Table 3 shows results when considering the full three-way classification task, where we evaluate performance on the *favor*, *against*, and *neutral* classes by taking the weighted average of F1 in all three classes. The table compares against the most frequent class (MFC) baseline to illustrate how much stance-related information is contained in each of the user attributes.

User attributes carry useful information for all stance prediction tasks as shown in Table 3. `Profile Description` and `Location` are

---

[1]The SemEval Top Participant result in Table 2 was restricted to our test set users to allow direct comparisons.

	SemEval F1
Most Frequent Class	67.0
Tweet Features Only	
SemEval Top Participant	68.4
User Attributes Only	
Name	66.5
Profile Description	64.5
Profile Picture	55.7
Location	67.8
Followees	72.3†‡
Inferred Factors	68.6
All User Attributes	69.5

Table 2: Comparison of different models for predicting the stance of a tweet. Models trained only on user attribute features perform as well as — or better than — models trained on features extracted from the tweet itself. SemEval F1 is the unweighted average between $F_{against}$ and F_{favor}. This version, which is the official metric used for evaluating SemEval participants, does not directly include the performance of the models on the *neutral* stance class. Statistical significance ($p < 0.05$) is indicated in comparison with the MFC (†) and the SemEval Top Participant (‡).

useful in four of the five tasks, excepting Climate. `Followees` and `Inferred Factors` are useful in all tasks, with `Followees` being more useful in three tasks and `Inferred Factors` more useful in two tasks.

User attributes, with the exception of `Name` and `Profile Picture`, predict stance better than MFC on average. For every target there is some user attribute that predicts stance better than MFC.

User attributes improve all targets: `Profile Description`, `Location`, and `Followee` information all provide improvements over the MFC for all targets. `Name`, which encodes inferred information about the ethnicity, nationality, and gender of the users, shows improvements for Hillary. The `Profile Picture` features carry some information for Feminism, Hillary and Abortion targets. These show that publicly available information about the users carry useful signals about the users' stances.

Inferred factors versus other features: We see substantial gains with `Inferred Factors` for Atheism, Feminism, and Abortion (at least 5 points in F1) but only minor gains for the Climate and Hillary targets. No single factor provides consistent gains across all targets. For instance,

`Personality` is useful for Atheism and Feminism but not for Abortion, whereas `Political Ideology` is useful for Atheism and Abortion but not for Feminism. These show the importance of considering multiple factors.

We can drill deeper into personality factors and consider the correlations of personality dimensions with stances. Figure 1 provides the correlations of each dimension with stance. As can be seen in the figure, Atheism has the strongest correlations which explains the big prediction gains we see on that target. Although Climate and Feminism have a similar range of correlations, we don't see gains for Climate while we do for Feminism. This is likely due to the extreme class imbalance for Climate; the *against* class only made up 6% of tweets in the test set, and indeed few participants of the SemEval competition were able to beat the MFC for this target (Mohammad et al., 2016).

Overall, inferred factors perform better for Feminism and Abortion targets, while direct user attributes perform better for Atheism, Climate, and Hillary. These results suggest that stances on some targets correlate with psychological attributes such as personality and political orientation, whereas others are more correlated with demographic factors such as location.

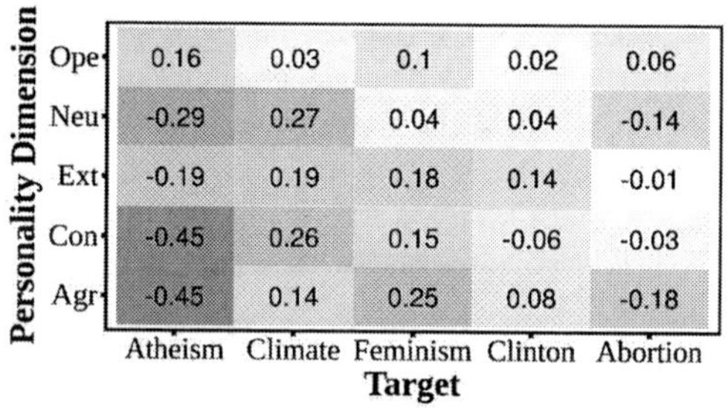

Figure 1: Pearson R correlation matrix for personality and stance.

Figure 2 shows the probability distribution of stances for Atheism over demographic variables. Age by itself has different distributions in *favor* and *against* populations, whereas there is no difference in the gender score distributions. Together, age and gender show stark contrasts in the distributions. Also note that for both gender and age, the *neutral* class distributions seem to capture a fairly symmetric split of *favor* and *against*. This may be related to the idea that stance is more of a user-level attribute than a message-level one, in that the *neutral* population actually contains users whose "real" stances are *favor* or *against* but

	F1					
	Atheism	*Climate*	*Feminism*	*Hillary*	*Abortion*	*All (Avg.)*
Most Frequent Class	61.7	60.8	45.8	47.0	55.8	54.2
User Attributes Only						
Name	61.7	59.1	46.1	48.8	55.5	54.2
Profile Description	64.3	58.6	**53.8†**	56.0†	59.6	58.5†
Profile Picture	58.5	57.6	47.0	50.1	57.3	54.1
Location	64.9	51.8	51.0	53.1†	**61.1†**	56.4
Followees	**73.2†**	**67.1**	52.4	**58.3†**	58.0	**61.8†**
Inferred Factors Only						
Demographics	61.9	60.5	49.6	46.8	55.8	54.9
Personality	**69.3†**	59.8	53.1†	47.0	55.8	57.0†
Political Ideology	65.8†	60.8	44.1	47.0	60.7†	55.7†
User Embeddings	64.5	59.0	43.5	47.9	56.0	54.2
All Inferred	67.5	**61.5**	**55.2†**	**48.9**	**63.4†**	**59.3†**

Table 3: Performance of stance prediction models trained only on user attributes, shown here for each of the different stance targets. Bold indicates best in column for user attributes and inferred factors. The weighted F1 is shown for each target and the last column is the unweighted average across all targets. † indicates statistical significance at the 0.05 level compared to the MFC baseline.

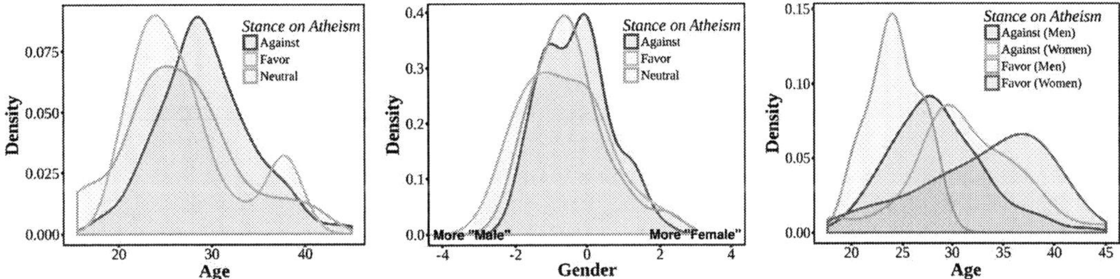

Figure 2: The first two graphs show the probability density of age (left) and gender (middle) for each of the three stance classes on the Atheism target. The rightmost graph shows the probability density of users' ages for Atheism, broken down by gender and class label (excluding *neutral*). There is a clear relationship between age, gender, and stance, demonstrating the need for user attributes.

which aren't expressed in the tweet itself. Overall, the plots show the degree to which stances can be separated simply by demographics but also suggest that one might benefit from variables capturing a combination of age and gender.

5 When is the Tweet Useful?

Tweets provide the most direct expression of a user's intent. However, the amount of task-related information in a tweet and the ability of tweet-derived features to model it reliably vary with the task. Table 4 compares tweet features and user attributes for stance, sarcasm, sentiment, and PP-attachment.

Overall, combining user attributes with tweet-derived features provides the best results for stance, sarcasm and sentiment.

<u>Stance:</u> Even though user attributes outperform tweet features when only considering *favor* and *against* classes, we find that tweet features turn out to be better when considering all three classes including the *neutral* class. The average F1 across all three classes for the tweet-only baseline is higher than any of the user attribute-only models (+1 point in average F1 over `Followees`, the best user attribute feature).

A closer look reveals why this is the case. For any given user, their positive or negative stance towards a target seldom changes. What may change instead is whether they express their stance or remain neutral when writing a particular tweet.

		F1		**Acc.**
		Stance	*Sarcasm*	*Sentiment*	*PP-Attach.*
Baselines	MFC	54.2	51.2	28.0	64.4*
	Tweet Only	62.8	74.1	69.2	**71.0**
No Tweet	Name	54.2	59.0†	38.9†	64.4
	Profile Description	58.5†	64.7†	40.3†	64.4
	Profile Picture	54.1	61.4†	40.7†	64.4
	Location	56.4	58.3†	38.7†	64.4
	Followees	61.8†	73.1†	42.3†	64.4
	Inferred Factors	59.3†	71.9†	41.4†	64.4
	All User Attributes	60.8†	74.4†	42.5†	64.4
With Tweet	Name + Tweet	62.9†	74.9†‡	69.4†	71.0
	Profile Description + Tweet	63.5†	73.4†	68.9†	71.0
	Profile Picture + Tweet	62.2†	71.1†	68.7†	71.0
	Location + Tweet	64.1†	74.0†	68.9†	71.0
	Followees + Tweet	**65.9†‡**	**78.6†‡**	**69.5†**	71.0
	Inferred Factors + Tweet	65.1†‡	77.3†‡	69.3†	71.0
	All User Attributes + Tweet	63.8†	76.8†‡	67.4†	71.0

Table 4: Using user attributes to predict stance, sarcasm, sentiment, and PP-attachment. Bold indicates best in column. Statistical significance ($p < 0.05$) is indicated in comparison with the MFC (†) and the tweet-only model (‡). *MFC computed by training a model only on the distance between the preposition and the candidate head.

Thus, while user attributes are better at predicting a user's overall stance, the tweet features provide a better indication of whether there is an expression of it in the specific tweet. Indeed, combining tweet features and user attributes yields additional gains in most cases: Profile Description (+0.7 points), Location (+1.3), Inferred Factors (+2.3), and Followees (+3.1). When combining Followees with tweet features, we see an 18.4 point improvement for $F_{neutral}$ on average over using Followees alone.

There can be non-linear interactions between the user attributes and the tweet features. For instance, we find that with a random forest classifier we can obtain a baseline performance of 65.0 F1 for the tweet-only features, which increases to 66.4 when combined with all user attributes. This exploration is beyond the scope of our work; here we only intend to show that even a simple combination can provide gains.

Sarcasm: Tweet features are no better than the combined set of user attributes for sarcasm, showing once again the extent of predictive power in user information.

Inferred Factors and Followees are the strongest user attributes and boost performance when combined with the tweet features, provid-ing roughly 3.2 and 4.5 point gains respectively. Name embeddings which carry nationality, ethnicity, and gender information provide a 0.8 point gain. The other features provide no gains when combined with tweet features. Combining all user attributes performs worse than using Followees or Inferred Factors alone, presumably due to pushing the bounds in terms of total number of features given limited observations.

Sentiment: User attributes appear far less useful than tweet features for sentiment. While users can lean positive or negative overall, sentiments are contextual and are best inferred from expressions in the tweet. Still, combining user attributes with tweet features yields minor gains.

PP-Attachment: The user attributes provide no useful predictive value. They do not do better than even the simple MFC baseline[2] and combining with text doesn't provide any improvements, reflecting the idea that this task is closer to something purely linguistic. Even so, prior work suggests user attributes can still benefit PP-attachment when using more sophisticated approaches like user-factor adaptation (Lynn et al., 2017).

---

[2] For PP-attachment, the MFC is computed by training the model only on the distance between the preposition and the candidate head.

5.1 Trait versus State

Overall, we see that stance and sarcasm benefit most from user attributes, sentiment benefits a little, and PP-attachment not at all. Supported by these results, we theorize that outcomes which are more "trait-like" benefit more from user attributes than those that are more "state-like". Trait-like outcomes are those that tend to be stable over time, such as stance; while the exact expression may vary from tweet to tweet, a person's overall stance is likely to remain relatively unchanged across many messages. State-like outcomes, on the other hand, are those that change frequently, such as sentiment. Sarcasm is somewhere in between — trait-like, in that a person can have a predisposition for being sarcastic, but the expression at message level still largely depends on context. PP-attachment is a state-like outcome as it depends entirely on the syntactic structure of the tweet.

6 Discussion

We found: (1) state-of-the-art tweet stance detection can be achieved without even using the tweet and instead using user attributes; (2) user attributes have varying predictive utility depending on the target of stance (e.g. atheism versus abortion); (3) different types of user attributes are valuable for different tasks — out of those we considered, followees on Twitter were most valuable; and (4) adding the tweet content back in on top of user attributes yields even greater performance.

The fact that user attributes predict stance better than tweet attributes may be surprising considering that the gold-standard labels were done by human annotators who were not privy to user attributes of the tweet author (Mohammad et al., 2016). Annotators were in fact trying to guess what the user's stance was from their tweet. They were instructed to "infer from the tweet that the tweeter [supports|is against|has a neutral stance] towards the target" (or that it was not possible to tell). However, our predictive models without the tweet were not even seeing the same information as these humans they were trying to mimic, and yet these tweetless models predicted just as well as models that did see the tweet. This raises interesting questions about whether the tweet-based models are unable to reliably use the information in text or whether the annotators used implicit signals in tweets to infer user attitudes towards the target. Joseph et al. (2017) raise a similar issue with systematic errors in stance annotation according to the context provided to human annotators.

This raises a counterpoint to the standard framing of social media tasks as making inferences over text alone. These results, combined with the fact that similar patterns were replicated with sarcasm and sentiment, speak to the question: **How much merit is there in attempting social media tasks agnostic to user attributes?**

For applications of stance, sarcasm, and sentiment tasks, such as tracking changes over time (stance, sentiment), or identifying particular tweets to interpret differently (sarcasm), it would certainly be less than ideal to simply predict the same outcome for every tweet from a given user as our *tweetless* models would do. Thus, we can at least say that there is value in the tweet or individual document itself, so the question is how to integrate user attributes and the tweet. Prior work on user-factor adaptation (Lynn et al., 2017) and use of residualized models (Zamani and Schwartz, 2017; Zamani et al., 2018) provide interesting avenues for exploration.

The results provide some insights into designing future social media tasks. First, given the strong impact of user attributes on these tasks, it becomes readily apparent that the diversity of the user base is a key consideration in designing these tasks. Consider a training sample of tweets that is drawn only from users with certain attributes. Not only will the test performance on other users suffer, we also lose the opportunity to leverage strong user-level correlations in making predictions. A secondary implication is that when considering performance of user attributes on these tasks, care must be taken to see whether there is a representative diversity in the training sample before dismissing the value of the attribute.

We also propose that shared tasks consider user attribute baselines, mirroring the idea of "controls" in social scientific studies, whereby the goal is to predict above and beyond such attributes or leverage both most effectively. Setups like this have been done for some user-level tasks, such as providing age and gender estimates for mental health prediction (Coppersmith et al., 2015) or socioeconomic information for assessing community life satisfaction (Schwartz et al., 2013) or market prices (Zamani and Schwartz, 2017). However, for document-level tasks like those Twitter tasks we explore, a comparison to user attributes has usually been restricted to case studies such as those we mentioned in Section 2.

Still, it can be challenging to determine what user attributes to include as a baseline. Other fields, such as psychology, suggest always controlling for basic human traits — such as age and gender — as well as theoretically-related variables such as socioeconomic variables or, perhaps, political ideology in the case of stance detection (Gazzaniga and Heatherton, 2015). Another approach could be to consider what other information is readily available — those we have included here are typically available if one's documents are tweets but, for example, one also might often find location, demographics, and years of experience available for news or scientific articles.

7 Conclusion

More and more natural language processing tasks focus on social media. With advances in incorporating user information it has become increasingly clear that many tasks are best framed in user and social contexts. This work emphasizes the increasingly prominent role for user attributes in language tasks. We have shown state-of-the-art performance in tweet stance detection without the tweet itself, and shown that stance classification, sarcasm detection, and sentiment analysis models can be significantly improved with user factors. We find variance in utility of different user attribute features across tasks and raise important practical considerations for designing future social media tasks and their solutions.

References

Silvio Amir, Byron C Wallace, Hao Lyu, Paula Carvalho, and Mário J Silva. 2016. Modelling context with user embeddings for sarcasm detection in social media. *CoNLL 2016*, page 167.

David Bamman, Jacob Eisenstein, and Tyler Schnoebelen. 2014. Gender identity and lexical variation in social media. *Journal of Sociolinguistics*, 18(2):135–160.

David Bamman and Noah A Smith. 2015. Contextualized sarcasm detection on Twitter. In *Ninth International AAAI Conference on Web and Social Media*.

Yonatan Belinkov, Tao Lei, Regina Barzilay, and Amir Globerson. 2014. Exploring compositional architectures and word vector representations for prepositional phrase attachment. *TACL*, 2:561–572.

Wei-Fan Chen and Lun-Wei Ku. 2016. Utcnn: a deep learning model of stance classificationon on social media text. In *Proceedings of COLING: Technical Papers*, pages 1635–1645.

Glen Coppersmith, Mark Dredze, Craig Harman, Kristy Hollingshead, and Margaret Mitchell. 2015. Clpsych 2015 shared task: Depression and ptsd on twitter. In *CLPsych @ North American Association for Computational Linguistics*, pages 31–39.

Michael Gazzaniga and Todd Heatherton. 2015. *Psychological Science: Fifth International Student Edition*. WW Norton & Company.

Kazi Saidul Hasan and Vincent Ng. 2013. Stance classification of ideological debates: Data, models, features, and constraints. In *IJCNLP*, pages 1348–1356.

Dirk Hovy. 2015. Demographic factors improve classification performance. In *Proceedings of ACL*.

Dirk Hovy and Tommaso Fornaciari. 2018. Increasing in-class similarity by retrofitting embeddings with demographic information. In *Proceedings of the 2018 Conference on Empirical Methods in Natural Language Processing*, pages 671–677.

Minqing Hu and Bing Liu. 2004. Mining and summarizing customer reviews. In *Proceedings of the tenth ACM SIGKDD international conference on Knowledge discovery and data mining*, pages 168–177. ACM.

Thorsten Joachims. 2006. Training linear SVMs in linear time. In *Proceedings of KDD*, pages 217–226. ACM.

Kristen Johnson and Dan Goldwasser. 2016. "All I know about politics is what I read in Twitter": Weakly supervised models for extracting politicians' stances from Twitter. In *Proceedings of COLING*, pages 2966–2977.

Kenneth Joseph, Lisa Friedland, William Hobbs, David Lazer, and Oren Tsur. 2017. Constance: Modeling annotation contexts to improve stance classification. In *Proceedings of the 2017 Conference on Empirical Methods in Natural Language Processing*, pages 1126–1135.

David Jurgens, Yulia Tsvetkov, and Dan Jurafsky. 2017. Writer profiling without the writers text. In *International Conference on Social Informatics*, pages 537–558. Springer.

Anupam Khattri, Aditya Joshi, Pushpak Bhattacharyya, and Mark Carman. 2015. Your sentiment precedes you: Using an authors historical tweets to predict sarcasm. In *Proceedings of the 6th workshop on computational approaches to subjectivity, sentiment and social media analysis*, pages 25–30.

Svetlana Kiritchenko, Xiaodan Zhu, and Saif M Mohammad. 2014. Sentiment analysis of short informal texts. *Journal of Artificial Intelligence Research*, 50:723–762.

Rebecca Knowles, Josh Carroll, and Mark Dredze. 2016. Demographer: Extremely simple name demographics. In *EMNLP Workshop on NLP and Computational Social Science*, pages 108–113. Association for Computational Linguistics.

Lingpeng Kong, Nathan Schneider, Swabha Swayamdipta, Archna Bhatia, Chris Dyer, and Noah A. Smith. 2014. A dependency parser for tweets. In *Proceedings of EMNLP*.

Vivek Kulkarni, Margaret L Kern, David Stillwell, Michal Kosinski, Sandra Matz, Lyle Ungar, Steven Skiena, and H Andrew Schwartz. 2017. Latent human traits in the language of social media: An open-vocabulary approach. *arXiv preprint arXiv:1705.08038*.

Vivek Kulkarni, Bryan Perozzi, and Steven Skiena. 2016. Freshman or fresher? Quantifying the geographic variation of language in online social media. In *Tenth International AAAI Conference on Web and Social Media*.

Veronica E. Lynn, Youngseo Son, Vivek Kulkarni, Niranjan Balasubramanian, and H. Andrew Schwartz. 2017. Human centered NLP with user-factor adaptation. In *Empirical Methods in Natural Language Processing*, pages 1146–1155.

Travis Martin, Jake M Hofman, Amit Sharma, Ashton Anderson, and Duncan J Watts. 2016. Exploring limits to prediction in complex social systems. In *Proceedings of the 25th International Conference on World Wide Web*, pages 683–694. International World Wide Web Conferences Steering Committee.

Saif M. Mohammad, Svetlana Kiritchenko, Parinaz Sobhani, Xiaodan Zhu, and Colin Cherry. 2016. SemEval-2016 task 6: Detecting stance in tweets. In *Proceedings of SemEval-2016*, volume 16.

Saif M. Mohammad, Svetlana Kiritchenko, and Xiaodan Zhu. 2013. NRC-Canada: Building the state-of-the-art in sentiment analysis of tweets. In *Proceedings of SemEval-2013*.

Saif M Mohammad and Peter D Turney. 2010. Emotions evoked by common words and phrases: Using mechanical turk to create an emotion lexicon. In *Proceedings of the NAACL HLT 2010 workshop on computational approaches to analysis and generation of emotion in text*, pages 26–34. Association for Computational Linguistics.

Saif M Mohammad and Peter D Turney. 2013. Crowdsourcing a word–emotion association lexicon. *Computational Intelligence*, 29(3):436–465.

Preslav Nakov, Zornitsa Kozareva, Alan Ritter, Sara Rosenthal, Veselin Stoyanov, and Theresa Wilson. 2013. SemEval-2013 task 2: Sentiment analysis in Twitter.

Gregory Park, H. Andrew Schwartz, Johannes C. Eichstaedt, Margaret L. Kern, Michal Kosinski, David J. Stillwell, Lyle H. Ungar, and Martin E. P. Seligman. 2015. Automatic personality assessment through social media language. *Journal of Personality and Social Psychology*, 108(6):934.

Daniel Preoţiuc-Pietro, Ye Liu, Daniel Hopkins, and Lyle Ungar. 2017. Beyond binary labels: political ideology prediction of Twitter users. In *Proceedings of the 55th Annual Meeting of the Association for Computational Linguistics (Volume 1: Long Papers)*, volume 1, pages 729–740.

Maarten Sap, Gregory J. Park, Johannes C. Eichstaedt, Margaret L. Kern, David Stillwell, Michal Kosinski, Lyle H. Ungar, and Hansen Andrew Schwartz. 2014. Developing age and gender predictive lexica over social media. In *Proceedings of EMNLP*.

H Andrew Schwartz, Johannes C Eichstaedt, Margaret L Kern, Lukasz Dziurzynski, Megha Agrawal, Gregory J Park, Shrinidhi K Lakshmikanth, Sneha Jha, Martin EP Seligman, and Lyle Ungar. 2013. Characterizing geographic variation in well-being using tweets. In *International Conference on Web blogs and Social Media*.

Dhanya Sridhar, James Foulds, Bert Huang, Lise Getoor, and Marilyn Walker. 2015. Joint models of disagreement and stance in online debate. In *Proceedings of the 53rd Annual Meeting of the Association for Computational Linguistics and the 7th International Joint Conference on Natural Language Processing (Volume 1: Long Papers)*, volume 1, pages 116–125.

Christian Szegedy, Vincent Vanhoucke, Sergey Ioffe, Jon Shlens, and Zbigniew Wojna. 2016. Rethinking the inception architecture for computer vision. In *Proceedings of the IEEE Conference on Computer Vision and Pattern Recognition*, pages 2818–2826.

Matt Thomas, Bo Pang, and Lillian Lee. 2006. Get out the vote: Determining support or opposition from Congressional floor-debate transcripts. In *Proceedings of EMNLP*, pages 327–335.

Svitlana Volkova, Theresa Wilson, and David Yarowsky. 2013. Exploring demographic language variations to improve multilingual sentiment analysis in social media. In *Proceedings of EMNLP*.

Marilyn A Walker, Pranav Anand, Robert Abbott, and Ricky Grant. 2012a. Stance classification using dialogic properties of persuasion. In *Proceedings of the 2012 Conference of the North American Chapter of the Association for Computational Linguistics: Human Language Technologies*, pages 592–596. Association for Computational Linguistics.

Marilyn A Walker, Jean E Fox Tree, Pranav Anand, Rob Abbott, and Joseph King. 2012b. A corpus for research on deliberation and debate. In *LREC*, pages 812–817.

Theresa Wilson, Janyce Wiebe, and Paul Hoffmann. 2005. Recognizing contextual polarity in phrase-level sentiment analysis. In *Proceedings of the conference on human language technology and empirical methods in natural language processing*, pages 347–354. Association for Computational Linguistics.

Yi Yang and Jacob Eisenstein. 2015. Putting things in context: Community-specific embedding projections for sentiment analysis. *CoRR*, abs/1511.06052.

Junting Ye, Shuchu Han, Yifan Hu, Baris Coskun, Meizhu Liu, Hong Qin, and Steven Skiena. 2017. Nationality classification using name embeddings. In *CIKM*, pages 1897–1906.

Mohammadzaman Zamani, H Andrew Schwartz, Veronica E Lynn, Salvatore Giorgi, and Niranjan Balasubramanian. 2018. Residualized factor adaptation for community social media prediction tasks. *arXiv preprint arXiv:1808.09479*.

Mohammadzaman Zamani and Hansen Andrew Schwartz. 2017. Using twitter language to predict the real estate market. In *EACL 2017: European Association for Computational Linguistics*, page 28.

Guido Zarrella and Amy Marsh. 2016. Mitre at semeval-2016 task 6: Transfer learning for stance detection. *Proceedings of SemEval*, pages 458–463.

Geolocating Political Events in Text

Andrew Halterman
Department of Political Science
Massachusetts Institute of Technology
ahalt@mit.edu

Abstract

This work introduces a general method for automatically finding the locations where political events in text occurred. Using a novel set of 8,000 labeled sentences, I create a method to link automatically extracted events and locations in text. The model achieves human level performance on the annotation task and outperforms previous event geolocation systems. It can be applied to most event extraction systems across geographic contexts. I formalize the event–location linking task, describe the neural network model, describe the potential uses of such a system in political science, and demonstrate a workflow to answer an open question on the role of conventional military offensives in causing civilian casualties in the Syrian civil war.

1   Introduction

Researchers in social science, and especially in comparative politics and security studies, are increasingly turning toward micro-level data, with subnational variation at very fine resolutions becoming a major source of empirical puzzles and evidence in these fields. At the same time, text data is becoming one of the most important sources of new data in social science. I develop and describe a method that enables researchers to connect these two trends, automatically linking events extracted from text to the specific locations where they are reported to occur.

Specifically, I develop a method that, given a sentence and an event's verb in the sentence, will return the place names from the sentence where the event took place. Formulated as a general task, this is an unsolved problem in both political science and computer science. Drawing on a set of 8,000 hand-labeled sentences, I train a recurrent neural network that draws on a rich set of linguistic features to label a sequence of text with la-

bels for whether the word is a location word corresponding to a specified verb. Measured by token, the model produces precision and recall scores of over 0.83, compared with a rule-based model's 0.25–0.29. A software implementation and example workflow is provided.

I provide an example application, creating a new dataset on the locations of military offensives in Syria and contributing to an ongoing debate in conflict studies on the causes of civilian casualties in civil war. The model is general enough for applied researchers to use in other contexts, including the study of protests, political mobilization, political violence, and electoral politics. The new shared dataset will enable other researchers in NLP to contribute to this task and the wider research project of better extracting political relationships from text.

2   Task and Formulation

Event–location linking sits within a larger set of techniques for extracting information on political events from text, including entity extraction and toponym resolution.

Event extraction is the process of recognizing defined event types in text (e.g. "attack" or "protest") and extracting and classifying the actors involved in the events. Many approaches to this task exist in both political science and NLP, using both rule-based and machine learning coders (Schrodt, Davis, and Weddle 1994; O'Connor, Stewart, and Smith 2013; Schrodt, Beieler, and Idris 2014; Boschee et al. 2015; Beieler 2016; Beieler et al. 2016; Hanna 2017; Keith et al. 2017).

To be useful in subnational research, these events require information on the location where they occurred. A second related information extraction task is "geoparsing", the process of rec-

29

Proceedings of the Third Workshop on Natural Language Processing and Computational Social Science, pages 29–39
Minneapolis, Minnesota, June 6, 2019. ©2019 Association for Computational Linguistics

ognizing place names in text ("toponym recognition") and resolving them to their coordinates or gazetteer entry ("toponym resolution"). Some work on geoparsing, also referred to as "georeferencing" or "toponym resolution" exists (Leidner 2008; Hill 2009; Speriosu and Baldridge 2013; Berico Technologies, n.d.; D'Ignazio et al. 2014; Gritta et al. 2017; Halterman 2017; Avvenuti et al. 2018). Performing this task requires disambiguating place names using heuristics or a model (in a particular document, is "Prague" the capital of the Czech Republic or the town in Oklahoma?).

The task that this paper addresses sits between the two: given an extracted event in a sentence, which of place name is the location where the event occurred? Consider the following sentence as a running example:

> After establishing a foothold in the northern Aleppo towns of Tadif and Al-Bab, the Turkish Army and allied Syrian rebels launched an offensive on its neighbouring town of Bza'a, a spokesperson for Ankara said today.

An event extraction system may identify events such an "establish foothold" event or a "launch offensive" event. A geoparser would be concerned with recognizing the place names in the text ("Aleppo", "al-Bab", "Bza'a") and resolving them to their correct coordinates (made difficult by "Aleppo" being the governorate here, not the city). An event–location linking system of the kind introduced here would associate the "establish foothold" event with "al-Bab" and the "launch offensive" event with "Bza'a".

The task can be formalized as follows. Consider $X = \{w_1, ... w_n\}$, a sentence of n tokens. Given an event e_k, the location where event e_k occurred is defined as a set of tokens $G_k = \{g_1, ..., g_j\}$. For $e_1 =$ "establish a foothold", $G_1 = \{\text{Tadif, Al-Bab}\}$.

Because a sentence can contain multiple events, the set of event locations G_k and $G_{k'}$ are not equivalent for $k \neq k'$. For $e_2 =$ "launch an offensive", $G_2 = \{\text{Bza'a}\}$. G_k can have zero elements, one, or several elements. Thus, for $e_3 =$ "said", $G_3 = \{\}$, as the "said" event is not associated with a specific place.

Each token $w_i \in X$ is given a label $y_i^{(k)}$, where

$$y_i^{(k)} = \begin{cases} 1 \text{ if } w_i \text{ is where event } k \text{ occurred} \\ 0 \text{ otherwise} \end{cases}$$

To make the estimation of $\hat{y}^{(k)}$ tractable, I make several assumptions.

First, in order to condition on the event e_k, I assume that the information provided by the verb v_k of the event e_k is sufficient.[1] Thus, $y^{(k)} = f(X, e_k) := f(X, v_k)$. This assumption, that events are "anchored" by a verb, is a common assumption in semantic role labeling, a closely related task to event–location linking (Palmer, Gildea, and Kingsbury 2005; White et al. 2016; Marcheggiani and Titov 2017).[2]

Second, I assume that an adequate representation of each word w_i is $\phi(w_i)$, where ϕ is a feature-making function that maps w_i from a high dimensional one-hot vector to a lower dimensional dense encoding, drawing on the context of the word in the sentence. Applied to a sentence,

$$\Phi(X) = \{\phi(w_1), \ldots, \phi(w_n)\}.$$

Thus,

$$\hat{y}^{(k)} = \hat{f}(\Phi(X), v_k).$$

Finally, I assume that the event location status $y_i^{(k)}$ of word w_i is conditionally independent of other words' labels $y_{j \neq i}^{(k)}$ after conditioning on the matrix of sentence context $\Phi(X)$. Making this assumption greatly simplifies estimation, as the task of assigning labels can be decomposed into a set of independent tasks:

$$\hat{y}^{(k)} = \hat{f}(\Phi(X), v_k)$$
$$= \{\hat{f}(\phi(w_1), v_k), ..., \hat{f}(\phi(w_n), v_k)\}$$

This assumption only carries costs if words' labels affect each other through a mechanism outside of X. The assumption seems warranted here,

---

[1] By "verb" I mean the highest verb on the dependency tree that is uniquely part of event e_k. In dictionary-based event coding methods, this is in practice the lexical "trigger" word for the event, though the event–location linking method is agnostic to how the event is coded.

[2] Though consider the phrase "After the riots in Gujarat...". This sentence reports a "riot" event but without a verb. These clausal mentions of events are rarely coded by event extraction systems, both because of difficulty in coding and because they often describe historical, rather than contemporary events, meaning the decision to require a verb has little practical difference.

though, because of the binary nature of the classification task.[3]

3 Previous work

Many existing open source geolocated event datasets, including GDELT and Phoenix, make no effort to explicitly link events and locations, simply returning a top location from a sentence, without using information on the extracted event to inform the geolocation step, which has also been used in NLP (Aone and Ramos-Santacruz 2000).[4] Two recently proposed models do attempt to find events' locations, however (Imani et al. 2017; Lee, Liu, and Ward 2018). Both make a major simplifying assumption, that returning the correct location does not depend on conditioning on an event of interest: $G_k = G_{k'}$ for all e_k, e'_k. The advantage of this assumption is that each model can use a simple bag-of-words model that does not account for word order or grammatical information, but it means that the labels they produce for text with multiple events and locations will be incorrect for at least some events.

Imani et al. (2017) propose a method for finding the "primary focus location" of a story, which they define as "the place of occurrence of the event" (1956). Their method makes the simplifying assumption that documents have one single, fixed "focus location" that is invariant to different potential events in the document. During training and testing, they eliminate all documents with multiple events and multiple "focus locations." Their model discards word order information, representing each sentence as a weighted average of pretrained word embedding, and use this feature vector as an input to an SVM that predicts which sentence contains the "focus location." Then, the most frequent place name in the "focus sentence" is the "focus location."

Lee, Liu, and Ward (2018) also make several other restrictive assumptions. The implementation of their model is only able to located events to the governorate/province (ADM1) level, and finds locations based on a dictionary search of known place names: $y_i = 0$ for any w_i that is not present in the list of place names. This limits the maximum accuracy to a relatively coarse level, and prevents the method from recognizing places that are not on a relatively short list of place names, which is unlikely to contain more rural or obscure places. Any findings will be biased toward more populated areas, a known problem in political violence research (Kalyvas 2004; Douglass and Harkness 2018). Second, they learn a different f for different event types, requiring documents to be classified into event types before geolocation, requiring a training round with labeled data for each event type and preventing parameters from being shared across models for different event types.

Other work, in natural language processing, is related but not directly applicable. Existing semantic role labeling and event extraction tasks sometimes include location slots for events (e.g. Doddington et al. 2004), but none are precisely suited to a general system focused on political events. FrameNet (Baker, Fillmore, and Lowe 1998) events have highly specific slots for different event types, while PropBank (Palmer, Gildea, and Kingsbury 2005) defines locations in a broad way that includes non-tangible places ("keep in our *thoughts*). A more specific literature on spatial information in text also exists. For instance, the SpaceEval task (Pustejovsky et al. 2015) provides a comprehensive ontology of spatial relations in text. These relations are focused on entities, rather than events, and provide more detail than is desirable in a application-oriented model. The task as I have formulated it thus seeks to be much more general, in that it attempts to locate any type of event, but also more limited, in that it focuses solely on where events occurred, rather than a larger set of spatial relations between entities.

The closest existing work in NLP is Chung et al. (2017). They attempt to find both explicit and implicit event locations in text, using a corpus of 48 documents. They use a rule-based system built on top of word embedding similarity and existing gold standard OntoNotes grammatical information to infer the locations of events. While the system shows good performance and is able to geolocate events even when the location information is not

---

[3]This conditional independence of labels assumption is generally not made in part of speech tagging, dependency parsing, or named entity recognition. In these tasks, each word can be assigned one of many possible labels, and past labels dramatically change label probabilities. (For example, if a word is predicted to have the part-of-speech label VERB, the following word cannot be labeled be VERB if the sentence is to be grammatical). These tasks required more sophisticated beam search or shift-reduce models (Goldberg 2017; Jurafsky and Martin 2018).

[4]ICEWS uses a proprietary system to link events and locations that is not documented or accessible to researchers (Lautenschlager, Starz, and Warfield 2017).

provided directly in the sentence, it relies on access to gold standard dependency parse information in a single domain of text.

4 Data

Implementing an automated procedure for geolocating events required collecting a novel set of data. I created a new dataset of around 8,000 labeled sentences in English, each of which is annotated with an event verb and its corresponding location or locations (if any).[5] Sentences may have multiple annotations corresponding to different verbs of interest. Sentences were selected from a range of sources to maximize the applicability of models trained on the data. The text is drawn from a wide range of sources, including an assortment of international papers and news wires (50%), a selection of local English-language media from Syria (35%), and non-news sources such as Wikipedia, atrocity monitoring reports, or press releases (15%). Annotation consisted of selecting a verb, either using a dictionary of specified verbs that focused on territorial capture-type events, or using verbs automatically detected using spaCy with the exception of "to be" to ensure the generalizability of the data. The verbs were not filtered through an event extraction system to keep the set as general as possible. Annotators then selected the tokens representing the event locations for the verb, if any. Around 5,000 annotations were provided by a research assistant and 5,000 were annotated by me. After annotation, each sentence looks something like the following:

> He was speaking a day after Ankara [launched $_{\text{VERB}}$] an offensive in the Syrian towns of [Jarablus $_{\text{EVENT\_LOC}}$] and [Kobane $_{\text{EVENT\_LOC}}$].

Annotations consist of the most specific named place or places, in contrast to previous approaches that were limited to the city (Imani et al. 2017) or the governorate/province (Lee, Liu, and Ward 2018). Events can have no reported event, a single event with multiple location tokens ("New York"), or multiple event locations ("New York and Washington"). The modal number of locations is one (49%), followed by no locations (47%), and multiple locations comprise the remainder (3%). Most locations consist of a single token (69%), 19% are

two tokens, and the remaining 12% are three or more. Sentences have a large number of verbs, and thus a potentially large number of events. The average number of verbs per sentences is 3.6, after excluding auxiliary verbs. Only 9% contain a single non-auxiliary verb, and 21% contain five or more verbs.

5 Model

I develop two neural network models to perform the event–location linking task. I also describe a rule-based baseline model, along with existing models from the literature as comparisons.

I use as a baseline model a rule-based event–location linker that locates an event to the automatically recognized location word in closest linear proximity to the event's verb. This model provides per-event locations, unlike existing models, and incorporates a minimal sentence distance feature.

Neural networks are now the dominant approach to most of natural language processing (Goldberg 2017; Jurafsky and Martin 2018) so they are the models adopted here. Determining the event locations in a sentence using neural networks requires a language representation that preserves word order and useful grammatical information in the sentence. I preprocess the sentence by representing each word as a concatenation of the following information generated by the spaCy NLP library (Honnibal and Montani 2017) pretrained GloVe vector, dependency label, named entity label, part-of-speech tag, an indicator for whether the word is the event verb of interest, the (signed) distance between the word and the indicated verb, and the distance between the verb and the token on the dependency tree. I use the same features for two neural network models. Both of the neural net models below look at a token, along with its context, and make a binary prediction for whether the token is an event location for the specified event.

The first neural network model uses a series of stacked convolutional layers. Some research suggests that convolutional neural networks (CNNs) perform equivalently to recurrent neural networks on sequence modeling tasks with lower computational cost (Bai, Kolter, and Koltun 2018). Each convolution looks at three inputs (words) at once, and slides down the sentence one token at a time. By stacking layers on top of each other, the ele-

---

ments of the final output of the final convolutional layer includes information from across the sentence. I use residual layers (He et al. 2016), which are now the state-of-the-art on image recognition tasks. Residual layers help prevent the "vanishing/exploding gradient" problem that deep neural networks often encounter, and speed the model's fitting. A CNN with residual layers empirically outperformed a model of similar depth and structure without residual blocks, and is theoretically justified because they allow me to train a deeper network with lower demands on my limited pool of input data. After training and evaluating several dozen models, the best performing CNN model used 7 residual layers with 64 hidden nodes in each, followed by two dense layers with 512 nodes each with a dropout of 0.4 and ReLU activation.

The second class models is recurrent neural network (RNN), specifically a long short-term memory (LSTM) network (Hochreiter and Schmidhuber 1997), which explicitly models the sequential nature of their input data (see Figure 1). RNNs are the dominant approach to sequence modeling tasks in natural language processing and achieve state-of-the-art results on many tasks (Goldberg 2017). LSTMs store an internal state at each step of the input data in the form of a hidden vector. In contrast to vanilla RNNs, LSTMs can learn when to add information from their current input step to the hidden state and when to "forget" information from the hidden state. In theory, this allows LSTMs to learn much longer relationships than they would otherwise be able to. Bidirectional LSTMs are the standard extension to LSTMs when the model has access to the "future", and compute two state vectors for each input step: one from the left and one from the right. These two vectors are concatenated and used as input to the rest of the model. The best LSTM network I trained used a bidirectional LSTM with a hidden size of 128 and 0.2 recurrent dropout, followed by a dense layer of 128 with ReLu and 0.5 dropout, and a final binary output node for each time step.

All models were trained in Keras with a Tensorflow backend on a multicore CPU.[6]

In addition to my baseline and neural network models, I also perform comparisons with three existing approaches. First, PropBank is included as a point of comparison. The PropBank includes an ArgM-LOC label in Palmer, Gildea, and Kingsbury (2005). The framing of the location task in PropBank is quite different than the generalized event–location linking task I introduce, as I describe above, but the performance of the baseline model in Palmer, Gildea, and Kingsbury (2005) on the task serves as another baseline. Second, I modify Profile (Imani et al. 2017) to accept new text and compare its performance on my new labeled data. Third, I report the best-case values from Chung et al. (2017).

Finally, I estimate the expected real-world performance of a human annotator by comparing an annotator's performance to a "gold standard" set of annotations. To produce the gold set, I randomly selected sentences annotated by the research assistant. I reannotated them, skipping ambiguous sentences. Sentences with the same annotations in the two periods were included in the gold evaluation set totalling 500 sentences. I could then compare RA performance with a "gold" measure of performance.

6 Evaluation

I evaluate these and several existing models on the task and the English-language dataset I introduce. To evaluate the performance of each model, I assess accuracy on both a per-token and per-sentence basis. For per-token accuracy, I take a common approach of calculating the precision and recall in the evaluation sentences. Each model is evaluated on how well it can can produce, for each token $w_i \in X$ whether w_i is an event location for event k. This evaluation approach allows "partial credit" for models that that may miss or falsely include a single token and is a common approach to evaluating sequence labeling tasks (Strötgen and Gertz 2016). I also include a second measure that more closely matches real-word accuracy. This measure reports the proportion of documents for which the annotation produced by the method exactly matches the correct label for each token in the document: $\hat{y}_i^{(k)} = y_i^{(k)} \forall i \in X$. The results for the word distance baseline measure, existing approaches, expected human performance, and the two models I develop are reported in Table 1.[7]

---

[6]The models are are available in Mordecai, an open-source document geoparser: `https://github.com/openeventdata/mordecai`

[7]Results are not reported for the method developed by Lee, Liu, and Ward (2018). Unlike the other approaches, this method only geolocates to the province/ADM1 level, which is much coarser than these other techniques. It can only find place names on a provided whitelist of names, and models are customized to specific countries and events, making it unsuit-

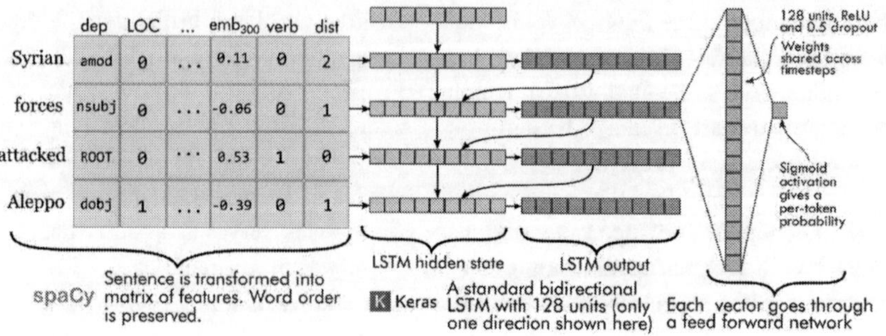

Figure 1: High-level schematic of LSTM model

Model	Prec	Rec	F1	Sentence
Baseline	0.29	0.25	0.27	0.28
Profile	0.54	0.29	0.37	0.51
PropBank[8]	*0.61*	*0.39*	*0.47*	-
CNN	0.70	0.54	0.61	-
Chung et al.[9]	*0.74*	*0.62*	*0.62*	-
Annotator	**0.88**	0.65	0.74	0.73
LSTM	0.85	**0.83**	**0.84**	**0.77**

Table 1: Per-token precision, recall, and F1 scores, and full-sentence accuracy for the word distance baseline model, expected human performance, existing results from the literature, and new model-based approaches.

The word distance baseline model, which locates an event to the closest recognized place name in the text, performs the worst of any model, perhaps due to the unreliability of the distance heuristic itself, errors in the NER system, and the model missing places when multiple correct locations are present.

Profile (Imani et al. 2017) performs next worst, with an token-level F1 score of 0.37. The model is unable to to vary its location prediction by event type, meaning that it will correctly locate at best one event's location in a multi-event, multi-location sentence. Profile also returns only one location per sentence, lowering its accuracy on events that occur in multiple locations. Profile's intended use case is on longer pieces of text: its

poor performance on this task should be taken only as an indication of its ability to geolocate events in text, not on its ability to find the primary "focus" (D'Ignazio et al. 2014) location of a piece of text.

PropBank is included as a point of comparison. The PropBank values are reported for the ArgM-LOC label in Palmer, Gildea, and Kingsbury (2005). The framing of the location task in PropBank is quite different than the generalized event–location linking task I introduce, as I describe above. The reported F1 score of 0.47 can be taken as a reasonable baseline performance on an event–location linking task. Chung et al's (2017) accuracy on their dataset and version of the task is the best of any prior model.

The LSTM model performs much better than the CNN model, even after extensive tuning for the CNN model. Inspection of the CNN model's output (not included) indicates that the model seems to not learn long-distance relationships well, and failed to appropriately change probability weights when the verb of interest changed. The LSTM model, in contrast, performs very well and is very sensitive to changes in the input verb: the same sentence with two different flagged verbs of interest will produce quite different results for those events' location. The LSTM and CNN are comparable in training time.

Notably, the LSTM also outperforms an estimate of expected human performance on the event–location linking task. While humans are able to pick up on nuance and deal with grammatical complexity that machines still cannot handle, humans are also unsuited to the tedium of labeling thousands of sentences and may be susceptible to drift in their definitions or understanding of the task. Not only is the automated method vastly cheaper and faster than a human process, it does so with accuracy at least as good.

---

able for this more general task of linking arbitrary locations and events. Finally, the replication code provided is not easily applicable to new datasets, only to run the initial experiments.

[8]These numbers are performance on the PropBank dataset, not on the dataset I create.

[9]Performance of Chung et al's model on their corpus of 48 OntoNotes documents. The maximum values achieved for precision, recall, and F1 across their models are reported here. Note that the results on my model report per-token precision and recall, while they report per-location precision and recall.

6.1 Ablation test

Figure 2 shows the results of an ablation process on the best performing LSTM model, revealing that some features are more important than others across several random partitions and retrainings of the model.

The ablation test reveals several interesting findings. First, the variability in feature importance across different train-test splits of the data prevents overly strong claims. With that in mind, the named entity label returned by spaCy would seem to be a useful feature in a task that requires picking one of potentially several place names. In fact, removing it leaves the accuracy unchanged, perhaps because the labeled data skews toward Arabic place names, which spaCy's model struggles to recover. The two distance features, one encoding distance from each word to the verb of interest and the other encoding the length of the shortest dependency path between them, both seem marginally helpful. Surprisingly, the part-of-speech feature is more useful than the dependency label. This may be because the tree structure of the dependency parse is not being incorporated, only its labels. Finally, the pretrained GloVe embedding feature is helpful (second to the right column), but it is by no means sufficient on its own (rightmost column). While some of the literature on neural networks for NLP simply starts from pretrained word or character embeddings and learns useful representations from those, these results indicate that wider feature inclusion is very helpful for the model's accuracy. The result is not driven solely by place names being out-of-vocabulary, as GloVe contains embeddings for 78% of the place names in the corpus.

Qualitative inspection of miscoded sentences also reveals that the model often fails to select the more specific location when one is available. Performing the geoparsing step first, and then incorporating that information into the event linking step could reduce this mode of failure. Future work could also replace categorical features, such as POS and dependency labels, with embeddings (see, e.g. Nguyen and Grishman 2015).

7 Application: Geolocating offensives in Syria

To demonstrate the usefulness of this approach, I use it to create a dataset of Syrian military offensives in 2016 by automatically coding military offensive events from text and geolocating them.

I collected 15,000 news stories on Syria covering 2016 from four sources: Al-Masdar news, Middle East Eye, Ara News, and news put out by the opposition National Coalition. To recognize the events themselves in the text, I created a one-off event coder that performs a dependency parse of the documents in the corpus and compares different grammatical parts of the sentence with a hand-specified set of terms to describe military offensives.

After recognizing an event in the text, I then use my event geoparsing method to find the location(s) in the text linked to the event's verb. In order to produce final usable event data, I also perform the final step of resolving the event location or locations to their geographical coordinates. To do so I use the Mordecai text geoparser (Halterman 2017), which uses a neural network trained on several thousand gold-standard resolved place names to infer the country of a location mention, then performs a fuzzy-string search over the Geonames gazetteer (Wick and Boutreux 2011) and selects the best location among the locations returned from the search.

When combined with geolocated data on civilian deaths in Syria (Halterman 2018), the geolocated offensives allow us to determine that around 7% of civilian deaths in Syria occurred within one day and 1 kilometer of an announced military operation. This new dataset contributes to a growing literature on violence against civilians in civil war, showing that even in a conventional civil war like Syria's, only a relatively small number of casualties are plausibly related to collateral damage from military operations. Figure 3 shows the geographic distribution of new offensives. This ability to create a dataset of when and where conventional fighting is occurring paves the way for better understanding of the patterns of violence against civilians in civil wars.

8 Conclusion

This paper introduces a state-of-the-art technique for linking events and locations in text with performance as good as humans. It proposes a new conceptualization of this task, focusing more on broad applicability than previous approaches in natural language processing, but more carefully accounting for grammar and the potential multiplicity of events than previous work in political science. It

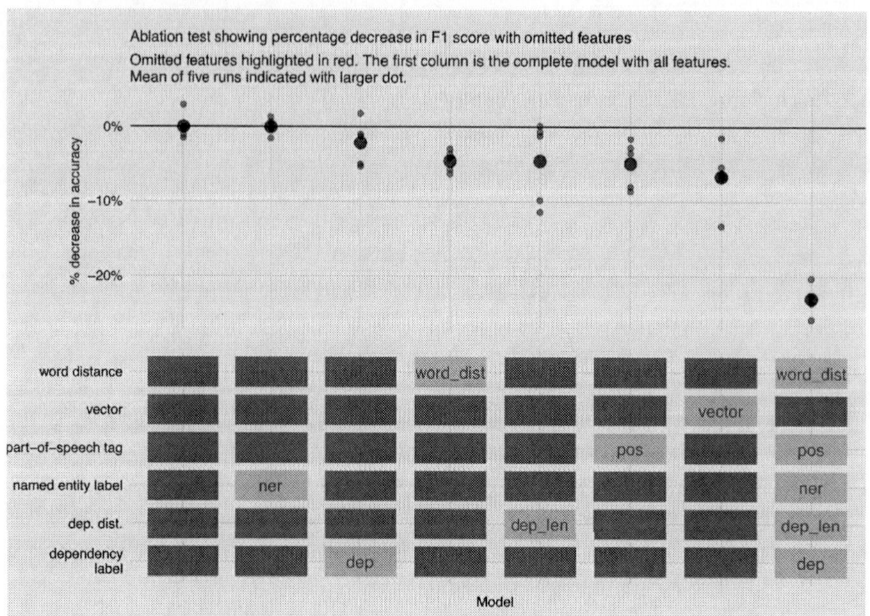

Figure 2: Ablation test showing decrease in F1 score with omitted features on a test set. Full model includes dependency labels, pre-trained GloVe embeddings, part-of-speech tags, named entity labels, the (signed) distance from the word to the verb, and the length of the dependency path from the word to the verb. All conditions used the same neural net model, with the best performing model on a validation set applied to held out test set.

Figure 3: Locations of reported offensives in Syria in 2016

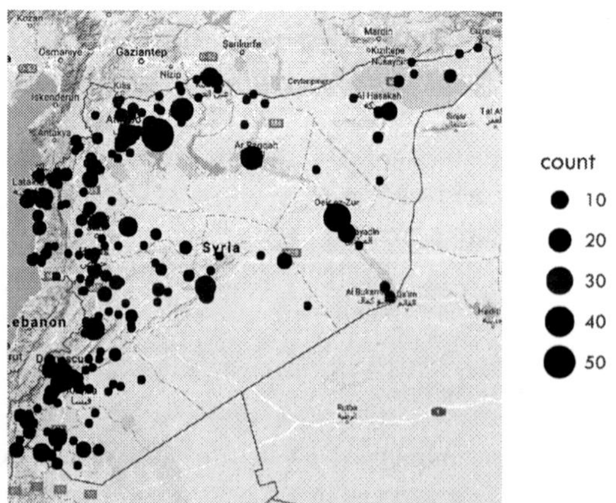

introduces a new labeled corpus of events and their locations, making the task accessible to other NLP researchers. The trained model achieves an F1 score of 0.82, making it accurate enough for researchers to begin to use.

In the social sciences, the availability of a model that can link events and locations in text should greatly increase the utility of event-type data for subnational researchers. Event data research on police violence in the United States (Keith et al. 2017), protest mobilization (Hanna 2017), political violence (Hammond and Weidmann 2014), and instability forecasting (Ward et al. 2013) could all be greatly improved by better techniques for automatically geolocating events. Researchers' understandings of many of these social phenomena are limited by the availability of very fine-grained geographic data.

Future NLP work could improve accuracy by integrating the "toponym resolution" and event–location linking steps to improve accuracy, and could extend the model beyond a single sentence to increase the range of event types that the method can be applied to.

More broadly, this work builds on a growing body of research at the intersection of NLP and social science that attempts to extract information from text, rather than summarizing or categorizing documents. Text also holds a great deal of factual information and new techniques are needed to allow researchers to extract political information from text. The technique introduced here will improve researchers' ability to incorporate information extracted from text into research studies that rely on geographically fine-grained data.

9 Acknowledgements

For valuable feedback on stages of this paper, I thank John Beieler, Fotini Christia, In Song Kim, Rich Nielsen, David Smith, Brandon Stewart, Rachel Tecott, and two very helpful anonymous reviewers. Emily Young provided excellent assistance in annotating training data. I gratefully acknowledge the support of a National Science Foundation Graduate Research Fellowship. For support in developing Mordecai (https://github.com/openeventdata/mordecai) and for creating annotated text data, I thank the National Science Foundation under award number SBE-SMA-1539302, the Defense Advanced Research Project Agency's XDATA program, and the U.S. Army Research Laboratory and the U.S. Army Research Office through the Minerva Initiative under grant number W911NF-13-0332. Any opinions, findings, and conclusions or recommendations expressed in this material are those of the author and do not necessarily reflect the views of the National Science Foundation or the Department of Defense.

10 References

Aone, Chinatsu, and Mila Ramos-Santacruz. 2000. "REES: A Large-Scale Relation and Event Extraction System." In *Proceedings of the Sixth Conference on Applied Natural Language Processing*, 76–83. Association for Computational Linguistics.

Avvenuti, Marco, Stefano Cresci, Leonardo Nizzoli, and Maurizio Tesconi. 2018. "GSP (Geo-Semantic-Parsing): Geoparsing and Geotagging with Machine Learning on Top of Linked Data." *Extended Semantic Web Conference (ESWC)*.

Bai, Shaojie, J. Zico Kolter, and Vladlen Koltun. 2018. "An Empirical Evaluation of Generic Convolutional and Recurrent Networks for Sequence Modeling." *arXiv Preprint arXiv:1803.01271*.

Baker, Collin F, Charles J Fillmore, and John B Lowe. 1998. "The Berkeley FrameNet Project." In *Proceedings of the 17th International Conference on Computational Linguistics-Volume 1*, 86–90. Association for Computational Linguistics.

Beieler, John. 2016. "Generating Politically-Relevant Event Data." *CoRR*. http://arxiv.org/abs/1609.06239.

Beieler, John, Patrick T Brandt, Andrew Halterman, Erin Simpson, and Philip A Schrodt. 2016. "Generating Political Event Data in Near Real Time: Opportunities and Challenges." In *Data Analytics in Social Science, Government, and Industry*, edited by R. Michael Alvarez. Cambridge University Press.

Berico Technologies. n.d. "CLAVIN: Cartographic Location and Vicinity Indexer."

Boschee, Elizabeth, Jennifer Lautenschlager, Sean O'Brien, Stephen M Shellman, James Starz, and Michael D Ward. 2015. "ICEWS Coded Event Data." In *Harvard Dataverse, V9, http://dx.doi.org/10.7910/DVN/28075*.

Chung, Jin-Woo, Wonsuk Yang, Jinseon You, and Jong C Park. 2017. "Inferring Implicit Event Locations from Context with Distributional Similarities." In *IJCAI*, 979–85.

Doddington, George R, Alexis Mitchell, Mark A Przybocki, Lance A Ramshaw, Stephanie Strassel, and Ralph M Weischedel. 2004. "The Automatic Content Extraction (ACE) Program-Tasks, Data, and Evaluation." In *LREC*, 2:1.

Douglass, Rex W, and Kristen A Harkness. 2018. "Measuring the Landscape of Civil War: Evaluating Geographic Coding Decisions with Historic Data from the Mau Mau Rebellion." *Journal of Peace Research*.

D'Ignazio, Catherine, Rahul Bhargava, Ethan Zuckerman, and Luisa Beck. 2014. "CLIFF-CLAVIN: Determining Geographic Focus for News." *NewsKDD: Data Science for News Publishing, at KDD* 2014.

Goldberg, Yoav. 2017. *Neural Network Methods for Natural Language Processing*. Synthesis Lectures on Human Language Technologies. Morgan & Claypool Publishers.

Gritta, Milan, Mohammad Taher Pilehvar, Nut Limsopatham, and Nigel Collier. 2017. "What's Missing in Geographical Parsing?" *Language Resources and Evaluation*. Springer, 1–21.

Halterman, Andrew. 2017. "Mordecai: Full Text Geoparsing and Event Geocoding." *The Journal of Open Source Software* 2 (9).

doi:10.21105/joss.00091.

———. 2018. "Violence Against Civilians in Syria's Civil War." *MIT Political Science Department Research Paper.*

Hammond, Jesse, and Nils B Weidmann. 2014. "Using Machine-Coded Event Data for the Micro-Level Study of Political Violence." *Research & Politics* 1 (2).

Hanna, Alex. 2017. "MPEDS: Automating the Generation of Protest Event Data." *SocArXiv Https://Osf. Io/Preprints/Socarxiv/Xuqmv.*

He, Kaiming, Xiangyu Zhang, Shaoqing Ren, and Jian Sun. 2016. "Deep Residual Learning for Image Recognition." In *Proceedings of the Ieee Conference on Computer Vision and Pattern Recognition*, 770–78.

Hill, Linda L. 2009. *Georeferencing: The Geographic Associations of Information.* MIT Press.

Hochreiter, Sepp, and Jürgen Schmidhuber. 1997. "Long Short-Term Memory." *Neural Computation* 9 (8). MIT Press: 1735–80.

Honnibal, Matthew, and Ines Montani. 2017. "SpaCy 2: Natural Language Understanding with Bloom Embeddings, Convolutional Neural Networks and Incremental Parsing." *To Appear.*

Imani, Maryam Bahojb, Swarup Chandra, Samuel Ma, Latifur Khan, and Bhavani Thuraisingham. 2017. "Focus Location Extraction from Political News Reports with Bias Correction." In *Big Data (Big Data), 2017 IEEE International Conference on*, 1956–64. IEEE.

Jurafsky, Dan, and James H Martin. 2018. *Speech and Language Processing.* 3rd ed. draft. draft: https://web.stanford.edu/ jurafsky/slp3/.

Kalyvas, Stathis N. 2004. "The Urban Bias in Research on Civil Wars." *Security Studies* 13 (3). Taylor & Francis: 160–90.

Keith, Katherine A, Abram Handler, Michael Pinkham, Cara Magliozzi, Joshua McDuffie, and Brendan O'Connor. 2017. "Identifying Civilians Killed by Police with Distantly Supervised Entity-Event Extraction." *arXiv Preprint arXiv:1707.07086.*

Lautenschlager, Jennifer, James Starz, and Ian Warfield. 2017. "A Statistical Approach to the Subnational Geolocation of Event Data." In *Advances in Cross-Cultural Decision Making*, 333–43. Springer.

Lee, Sophie J, Howard Liu, and Michael D Ward. 2018. "Lost in Space: Geolocation in Event Data." *Political Science Research and Methods*, 1–18.

Leidner, Jochen L. 2008. *Toponym Resolution in Text: Annotation, Evaluation and Applications of Spatial Grounding of Place Names.* Universal-Publishers.

Marcheggiani, Diego, and Ivan Titov. 2017. "Encoding Sentences with Graph Convolutional Networks for Semantic Role Labeling." *arXiv Preprint arXiv:1703.04826.*

Nguyen, Thien Huu, and Ralph Grishman. 2015. "Relation Extraction: Perspective from Convolutional Neural Networks." In *Proceedings of the 1st Workshop on Vector Space Modeling for Natural Language Processing*, 39–48.

O'Connor, Brendan, Brandon Stewart, and Noah A Smith. 2013. "Learning to Extract International Relations from Political Context." *Proceedings of the 51st Annual Meeting of the Association for Computational Linguistics (Volume 1: Long Papers)* Vol. 1.

Palmer, Martha, Daniel Gildea, and Paul Kingsbury. 2005. "The Proposition Bank: An Annotated Corpus of Semantic Roles." *Computational Linguistics* 31 (1). MIT Press: 71–106.

Pustejovsky, James, Parisa Kordjamshidi, Marie-Francine Moens, Aaron Levine, Seth Dworman, and Zachary Yocum. 2015. "SemEval-2015 Task 8: SpaceEval." In *Proceedings of the 9th International Workshop on Semantic Evaluation (Semeval 2015)*, 884–94.

Schrodt, Philip A, John Beieler, and Muhammed Idris. 2014. "Three's a Charm?: Open Event Data Coding with EL:DIABLO, PETRARCH, and the Open Event Data Alliance."

Schrodt, Philip A, Shannon G Davis, and Judith L Weddle. 1994. "Political Science: KEDS—a Program for the Machine Coding of Event Data." *Social Science Computer Review* 12 (4): 561–87.

Speriosu, Michael, and Jason Baldridge. 2013. "Text-Driven Toponym Resolution Using Indirect Supervision." In *ACL (1)*, 1466–76.

Strötgen, Jannik, and Michael Gertz. 2016. "Domain-Sensitive Temporal Tagging." *Synthesis Lectures on Human Language Technologies* 9 (3). Morgan & Claypool Publishers: 1–151.

Ward, Michael D, Nils W Metternich, Cassy L Dorff, Max Gallop, Florian M Hollenbach, Anna Schultz, and Simon Weschle. 2013. "Learning from the Past and Stepping into the Future: Toward a New Generation of Conflict Prediction."

International Studies Review 15 (4): 473–90.

White, Aaron Steven, Drew Reisinger, Keisuke Sakaguchi, Tim Vieira, Sheng Zhang, Rachel Rudinger, Kyle Rawlins, and Benjamin Van Durme. 2016. "Universal Decompositional Semantics on Universal Dependencies." In *Proceedings of the 2016 Conference on Empirical Methods in Natural Language Processing*, 1713–23. Austin, Texas: Association for Computational Linguistics.

Wick, Marc, and C Boutreux. 2011. "GeoNames." *GeoNames Geographical Database*.

Neural Network Prediction of Censorable Language

Kei Yin Ng Anna Feldman Jing Peng Chris Leberknight
Montclair State University
Montclair, New Jersey, USA
{ngk2,feldmana,pengj,leberknightc}@montclair.edu

Abstract

Internet censorship imposes restrictions on what information can be publicized or viewed on the Internet. According to Freedom House's annual Freedom on the Net report, more than half the world's Internet users now live in a place where the Internet is censored or restricted. China has built the world's most extensive and sophisticated online censorship system. In this paper, we describe a new corpus of censored and uncensored social media tweets from a Chinese microblogging website, Sina Weibo, collected by tracking posts that mention 'sensitive' topics or authored by 'sensitive' users. We use this corpus to build a neural network classifier to predict censorship. Our model performs with a 88.50% accuracy using only linguistic features. We discuss these features in detail and hypothesize that they could potentially be used for censorship circumvention.

1   Introduction

Free flow of information is absolutely necessary for any democratic society. Unfortunately, political censorship exists in many countries, whose governments attempt to conceal or manipulate information to make sure their citizens are unable to read or express views that are contrary to those in power. One such example is Sina Weibo, a Chinese microblogging website. It was launched in 2009 and became the most popular social media platform in China. Sina Weibo has over 431 million monthly active users[1]. In cooperation with the ruling regime, Weibo sets strict control over the content published under its service. According to Zhu et al. (2013), Weibo uses a variety of strategies to target censorable posts, ranging from keyword list filtering to individual user monitoring. Among all posts that are eventually censored,

---

[1] https://www.investors.
com/news/technology/
weibo-reports-first-quarter-earnings/

nearly 30% of them are censored within 5–30 minutes, and nearly 90% within 24 hours (Zhu et al., 2013).Research shows that some of the censorship decisions are not necessarily driven by the criticism of the state (King et al., 2013), the presence of controversial topics (Ng et al., 2018a,b), or posts that describe negative events. Rather, censorship is triggered by other factors, such as for example, the collective action potential (King et al., 2013). The goal of this paper is to compare censored and uncensored posts that contain the same sensitive keywords and topics. Using the linguistic features extracted, a neural network model is built to explore whether censorship decision can be deduced from the linguistic characteristics of the posts.

2   Previous Work

There have been significant efforts to develop strategies to detect and evade censorship. Most work, however, focuses on exploiting technological limitations with existing routing protocols (Leberknight et al., 2012; Katti et al., 2005; Levin et al., 2015; McPherson et al., 2016; Weinberg et al., 2012). Research that pays more attention to linguistic properties of online censorship in the context of censorship evasion include, for example, Safaka et al. (2016) who apply linguistic steganography to circumvent censorship. Lee (2016) uses parodic satire to bypass censorship in China and claims that this stylistic device delays and often evades censorship. Hiruncharoenvate et al. (2015) show that the use of homophones of censored keywords on Sina Weibo could help extend the time a Weibo post could remain available online. All these methods rely on a significant amount of human effort to interpret and annotate texts to evaluate the likeliness of censorship, which might not be practical to carry out for common Internet users in real life. There has also been research that uses linguistic and content

Proceedings of the Third Workshop on Natural Language Processing and Computational Social Science, pages 40–46
Minneapolis, Minnesota, June 6, 2019. ©2019 Association for Computational Linguistics

clues to detect censorship. Knockel et al. (2015) and Zhu et al. (2013) propose detection mechanisms to categorize censored content and automatically learn keywords that get censored. King et al. (2013) in turn study the relationship between political criticism and chance of censorship. They come to the conclusion that posts that have a Collective Action Potential get deleted by the censors even if they support the state. Bamman et al. (2012) uncover a set of politically sensitive keywords and find that the presence of some of them in a Weibo blogpost contribute to higher chance of the post being censored. Ng et al. (2018b) also target a set of topics that have been suggested to be sensitive, but unlike Bamman et al. (2012), they cover areas not limited to politics. Ng et al. (2018b) investigate how the textual content as a whole might be relevant to censorship decisions when both the censored and uncensored blogposts include the same sensitive keyword(s).

3 Tracking Censorship

Tracking censorship topics on Weibo is a challenging task due to the transient nature of censored posts and the scarcity of censored data from well-known sources such as FreeWeibo[2] and Weibo-Scope[3]. The most straightforward way to collect data from a social media platform is to make use of its API. However, Weibo imposes various restrictions on the use of its API[4] such as restricted access to certain endpoints and restricted number of posts returned per request. Above all, Weibo API does not provide any endpoint that allows easy and efficient collection of the target data (posts that contain sensitive keywords) of this paper. Therefore, an alternative method is needed to track censorship for our purpose.

4 Data Collection

4.1 Web Scraping

4.2 Decoding Censorship

According to Zhu et al. (2013), the unique ID of a Weibo post is the key to distinguish whether a post has been censored by Weibo or has been instead removed by the author himself. If a post has been censored by Weibo, querying its unique ID through the API returns an error message of "permission denied" (system-deleted), whereas a user-removed post returns an error message of "the post does not exist" (user-deleted). However, since the Topic Timeline (the data source of our web scraper) can be accessed only on the front-end (i.e. there is no API endpoint associated with it), we rely on both the front-end and the API to identify system- and user-deleted posts. It is not possible to distinguish the two types of deletion by directly querying the unique ID of all scraped posts because, through empirical experimentation, uncensored posts and censored (system-deleted) posts both return the same error message – "permission denied"). Therefore, we need to first check if a post still exists on the front-end, and then send an API request using the unique ID of post that no longer exists to determine whether it has been deleted by the system or the user. The steps to identify censorship status of each post are illustrated in Figure 1. First, we check whether a scraped post is still available through visiting the user interface of each post. This is carried out automatically in a headless browser 2 days after a post is published. If a post has been removed (either by system or by user), the headless browser is redirected to an interface that says "the page doesn't exist"; otherwise, the browser brings us to the original interface that displays the post content. Next, after 14 days, we use the same methods in step 1 to check the posts' status again. This step allows our dataset to include posts that have been removed at a later stage. Finally, we send a follow-up API query using the unique ID of posts that no longer exist on the browser in step 1 and step 2 to determine censorship status using the same decoding techniques proposed by Zhu et al. as described above (2013). Altogether, around 41 thousand posts are collected, in which 952 posts (2.28%) are censored by Weibo.

topic	censored	uncensored
cultural revolution	55	66
human rights	53	71
family planning	14	28
censorship & propaganda	32	56
democracy	119	107
patriotism	70	105
China	186	194
Trump	320	244
Meng Wanzhou	55	76
kindergarten abuse	48	5
Total	**952**	**952**

Table 1: Data collected by scraper for classification

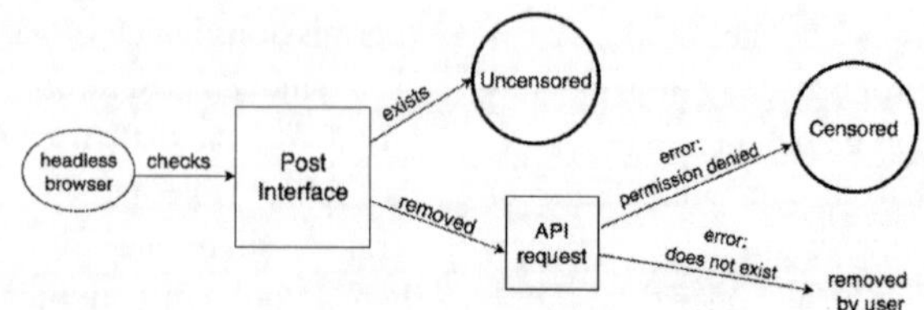

Figure 1: Logical flow to determine censorship status

4.3 Pre-existing Corpus

Zhu et al. (2013) collected over 2 million posts published by a set of around 3,500 sensitive users during a 2-month period in 2012. We extract around 20 thousand text-only posts using 64 keywords across 26 topics (which partially overlap with those of scraped data, see Table 3) and filter all duplicates. Among the extracted posts, 930 (4.63%) are censored by Weibo as verified by Zhu et al. (2013) The extracted data from Zhu et al.(2013)'s are also used in building classification models.

dataset	N	H	features	accuracy
baseline				49.98
human baseline (Ng et al., 2018b)				63.51
scraped	500	50,50,50	Seed 1	80.36
scraped	800	60,60,60	Seed 1	80.2
Zhu et al's	800	50,7	Seed 1	87.63
Zhu et al's	800	30,30	Seed 1	86.18
both	800	60,60,60	Seed 1	75.4
both	500	50,50,50	Seed 1	73.94
scraped	800	30,30,30	all except LIWC	72.95
Zhu et al's	800	60,60,60	all except LIWC	70.64
both	500	40,40,40	all except LIWC	84.67
both	800	20,20,20	all except LIWC	88.50
both	800	30,30,30	all except LIWC	87.04
both	800	50,50,50	all except LIWC	87.24

Table 2: MultilayerPerceptron classification results. N = number of epochs, H = number of nodes in each hidden layer

5 Feature Extraction

We extract features from both our scraped data and Zhu et al.'s dataset. While the datasets we use are different from that of Ng et al. (2018b), some of the features we extract are similar to theirs. We include CRIE features (see below) and the number of followers feature that are not extracted in Ng et al. (2018b)'s work.

topic	censored	uncensored
cultural revolution	19	29
human rights	16	10
family planning	4	4
censorship & propaganda	47	38
democracy	94	53
patriotism	46	30
China	300	458
Bo Xilai	8	8
brainwashing	57	3
emigration	10	11
June 4th	2	5
food & env. safety	14	17
wealth inequality	2	4
protest & revolution	4	5
stability maintenance	66	28
political reform	12	9
territorial dispute	73	75
Dalai Lama	2	2
HK/TW/XJ issues	2	4
political dissidents	2	2
Obama	8	19
USA	62	59
communist party	37	10
freedom	12	11
economic issues	31	37
Total	**930**	**930**

Table 3: Data extracted from Zhu et al. (2013)'s dataset for classification

5.1 Linguistic Features

We extract 4 sets of linguistic features from both datasets – the LIWC features, the CRIE features, the semantics features, and the number of followers feature. We are interested in the LIWC and CRIE features because they are purely linguistic, which aligns with the objective of our study. Also, some of the LIWC features extracted from Ng et al. (2018a)'s data have shown to be useful in classifying censored and uncensored tweets.

LIWC features The English Linguistic Inquiry and Word Count (LIWC) (Pennebaker et al., 2017, 2015) is a program that analyzes text on a word-by-word basis, calculating percentage of words that match each language dimension, e.g., pronouns, function words, social processes, cognitive processes, drives, informal language use etc. LIWC builds on previous research establishing strong links between linguistic patterns and personality/psychological state. We use a version of LIWC developed for Chinese by Huang et al. (2012) to extract the frequency of word categories. Altogether we extract 95 features from LIWC. One important feature of the LIWC lexicon is that categories form a tree structure hierarchy. Some features subsume others.

CRIE features We use the Chinese Readability Index Explorer (CRIE) (Sung et al., 2016), a text analysis tool developed for the simplified and traditional Chinese texts. CRIE outputs 50 linguistic features (see Appendix A.1), such as word, syntax, semantics, and cohesion in each text or produce an aggregated result for a batch of texts. CRIE can also train and categorize texts based on their readability levels. We use the textual-features analysis for our data and derive readability scores for each post in our data. These scores are mainly based on descriptive statistics.

Sentiment features We use BaiduAI[5] to obtain a set of sentiment scores for each post. It outputs a positive sentiment score and a negative sentiment score which sum to 1.

Semantic features We use the Chinese Thesaurus (同义词词林) developed by Mei (1984) and extended by HIT-SCIR[6] to extract semantic features. The structure of this semantic dictionary is similar to WordNet, where words are divided into 12 semantic classes and each word can belong to one or more classes. It can be roughly compared to the concept of word senses. We derive a semantic ambiguity feature by by dividing the number of words in each post by the number of semantic classes in it.

5.1.1 Frequency & readability

We compute the average frequency of characters and words in each post using Da (2004)[7]'s work and Aihanyu's CNCorpus [8] respectively. For words with a frequency lower than 50 in the reference corpus, we count it as 0.0001%. It is intuitive to think that a text with less semantic variety and more common words and characters is relatively easier to read and understand. We derive a

Readability feature by taking the mean of character frequency, word frequency and word count to semantic classes described above. It is assumed that the lower the mean of the 3 components, the less readable a text is. In fact, these 3 components are part of Sung et al. (2015)'s readability metric for native speakers on the word level and semantic level.

Followers The number of followers of the author of each post is recorded and used as a feature for classification.

6 Classification

A balanced corpus is created. The uncensored posts of each dataset are randomly sampled to match with the number of their censored counterparts (see Table 1 and Table 3). All numeric values have been standardized before classification. We use the MultilayerPerceptron function of Weka for classification. A number of classification experiments using different combinations of features are carried out. Best performances are achieved using the combination of CRIE, sentiment, semantic, frequency, readability and follower features (i.e. all features but LIWC) (see Table 2).

We also apply the Weka RandomSubset filter using Seed 1 to 8 to randomly select features for classification. The 77 randomly selected features of Seed 1, which is a mix of all features, perform consistently well across the datasets (see Appendix A.1 for the full list of features).

We vary the number of epochs and hidden layers. The rest of the parameters are set to default – learning rate of 0.3, momentum of 0.2, batch size of 100, validation threshold of 20. Classification experiments are performed on 1) both datasets 2) scraped data only 3) Zhu et al.'s data only. Each experiment is validated with 10-fold cross validation. We report the accuracy of each model in Table 2. It is worth mentioning that using the LIWC features only, or the CRIE features only, or all features excluding the CRIE features, or all features except the LIWC and CRIE features all result in poor performance of below 54%.

7 Discussion and Conclusion

Our best results are about 30% higher than the baseline. We also compare our classifiers to the human baseline reported in Ng et al. (2018b). The accuracies of our models are about 25 % higher than the human baseline, which shows that our

---

⁵https://ai.baidu.com

⁶Harbin Institute of Technology Research Center for Social Computing and Information Retrieval.

⁷http://lingua.mtsu.edu/chinese-computing/statistics/

⁸http://www.aihanyu.org/cncorpus/index.aspx

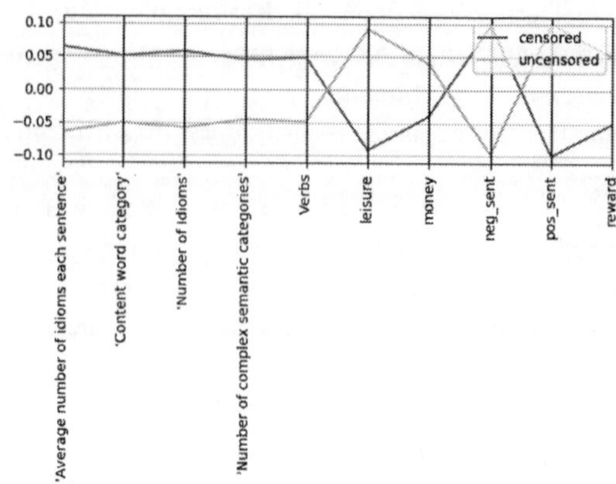

Figure 2: Parallel Coordinate Plots of the top 10 features that have the greatest difference in average values

classifier has a greater censorship predictive ability compared to human judgments. The classification on both datasets together tends to give higher accuracy using at least 3 hidden layers. However, the performance does not improve when adding additional layers (other parameters being the same). Since the two datasets were collected differently and contain different topics, combining them together results in a richer dataset that requires more hidden layers to train a better model. It is worth noting that classifying both datasets using seed 1 features decreases the accuracy, while using all features but LIWC improves the classification performance. The reason for this behavior could be an existence of consistent differences in the LIWC features between the datasets. Since the seed 1 LIWC features (see Appendix A.1) consist of mostly word categories of different genres of vocabulary (i.e. grammar and style agnostic), it might suggest that the two datasets use vocabularies differently. Yet, the high performance obtained excluding the LIWC features shows that the key to distinguishing between censored and uncensored posts seems to be the features related to writing style, readability, sentiment, and semantic complexity of a text.

To gain further insight into what might be the best features that contribute to distinguishing censored and uncensored posts, we compare the mean of each feature of the two classes. The 6 features distinguish censored from uncensored are 1) negative sentiment 2) average number of idioms in each sentence 3) number of idioms 4) number of complex semantic categories 5) verbs 6) number of content word categories. On the other hand, the

4 features that distinguish uncensored from censored are 1) positive sentiment 2) words related to leisure 3) words related to reward 4) words related to money (see Figure 2) This might suggest that the censored posts generally convey more negative sentiment and are more idiomatic and semantically complex in terms of word usage. On the other hand, the uncensored posts might be in general more positive in nature (positive sentiment) and include more content that talks about neutral matters (money, leisure, reward).

To conclude, our work shows that there are linguistic fingerprints of censorship and it is possible to use linguistic properties of a social media post to automatically predict if it is going to be censored. It will be interesting to explore if the same linguistic features can be used to predict censorship on other social media platforms and in other languages.

Acknowledgments

We thank the anonymous reviewers for their careful reading of this article and their many insightful comments and suggestions. This work is supported by the National Science Foundation under Grant No.: 1704113, Division of Computer and Networked Systems, Secure Trustworthy Cyberspace (SaTC).

References

David Bamman, Brendan O'Connor, and Noah A. Smith. 2012. Censorship and deletion practices in Chinese social media. *First Monday*, 17(3).

Jun Da. 2004. A corpus-based study of character and bigram frequencies in chinese e-texts and its implications for chinese language instruction. In *The studies on the theory and methodology of the digitalized Chinese teaching to foreigners: Proceedings of the Fourth International Conference on New Technologies in Teaching and Learning Chinese.*, pages 501–511. Beijing: Tsinghua University Press.

Chaya Hiruncharoenvate, Zhiyuan Lin, and Eric Gilbert. 2015. Algorithmically Bypassing Censorship on Sina Weibo with Nondeterministic Homophone Substitutions. In *Ninth International AAAI Conference on Web and Social Media*.

Chin-Lan Huang, Cindy Chung, Natalie K. Hui, Yi-Cheng Lin, Yi-Tai Seih, Ben C.P. Lam, Wei-Chuan Chen, Michael Bond, and James H. Pennebaker. 2012. The development of the chinese linguistic inquiry and word count dictionary. *Chinese Journal of Psychology*, 54(2):185–201.

S. Katti, D. Katabi, and K. Puchala. 2005. Slicing the onion: Anonymous routing without pki. Technical report, MIT CSAIL Technical Report 1000.

Gary King, Jennifer Pan, and Margaret E Roberts. 2013. How Censorship in China Allows Government Criticism but Silences Collective Expression. *American Political Science Review*, 107(2):1–18.

J. Knockel, M. Crete-Nishihata, J.Q. Ng, A. Senft, and J.R. Crandall. 2015. Every rose has its thorn: Censorship and surveillance on social video platforms in china. In *Proceedings of the 5th USENIX Workshop on Free and Open Communications on the Internet.*

Christopher S. Leberknight, Mung Chiang, and Felix Ming Fai Wong. 2012. A taxonomy of censors and anti-censors: Part i-impacts of internet censorship. *International Journal of E-Politics (IJEP)*, 3(2).

S. Lee. 2016. Surviving online censorship in china: Three satirical tactics and their impact. *China Quarterly*.

D. Levin, Y. Lee, L.Valenta, Z. Li amd V. Lai, C. Lumezanu, N. Spring, and B. Bhattacharjee. 2015. Alibi routing. In *Proceedings of the 2015 ACM Conference on Special Interest Group on Data Communication.*

Richard McPherson, Reza Shokri, and Vitaly Shmatikov. 2016. Defeating image obfuscation with deep learning. arXiv preprint arXiv:1609.00408.

jiā jū Méi. 1984. *The Chinese Thesaurus*.

Kei Yin Ng, Anna Feldman, and Chris Leberknight. 2018a. Detecting censorable content on sina weibo: A pilot study. In *Proceedings of the 10th Hellenic Conference on Artificial Intelligence*. ACM.

Kei Yin Ng, Anna Feldman, Jing Peng, and Chris Leberknight. 2018b. Linguistic Characteristics of Censorable Language on SinaWeibo. In *Proceedings of the 1st Workshop on NLP for Internet Freedom held in conjunction with COLING 2018*.

James W. Pennebaker, Roger Booth, and M.E. Francis. 2017. *Linguistic Inquiry and Word Count (LIWC2007)*.

James W. Pennebaker, Ryan L. Boyd, Kayla Jordan, and Kate Blackburn. 2015. The development and psychometric the development of psychometric properties of liwc. Technical report, University of Texas at Austin.

Iris Safaka, Christina Fragouli, , and Katerina Argyraki. 2016. Matryoshka: Hiding secret communication in plain sight. In *6th USENIX Workshop on Free and Open Communications on the Internet (FOCI 16). USENIX Association*.

Yao-Ting Sung, Tao-Hsing Chang, Wei-Chun Lin, Kuan-Sheng Hsieh, and Kuo-En Chang. 2016. Crie: An automated analyzer for chinese texts. *Behavior Research Methods*, 48(4):1238–1251.

Y.T. Sung, T.H. Chang, W.C. Lin, K.S. Hsieh, and K.E. Chang. 2015. Crie: An automated analyzer for chinese texts. *Behavior Research Method*.

Zachary Weinberg, Jeffrey Wang, Vinod Yegneswaran, Linda Briesemeister, Steven Cheung, Frank Wang, and Dan Boneh. 2012. Stegotorus: A camouflage proxy for the tor anonymity system. *Proceedings of the 19th ACM conference on Computer and Communications Security*.

T. Zhu, D. Phipps, A. Pridgen, JR Crandall, and DS Wallach. 2013. The velocity of censorship: high-fidelity detection of microblog post deletions. arXiv:1303.0597 [cs.CY].

A Appendices

A.1 Appendix I

Full List of CRIE features

*CRIE Readability 1.0
*SVM readability prediction 1.0
Paragraphs
Average paragraph length
*Characters
*Words
Adverbs
*Verbs
Type-token ratio
Difficult words
*Low-stroke characters
*Intermediate-stroke characters
*High-stroke characters
*Average strokes
*Two-character words
*Three-character words
*Sentences
*Average sentence length
*Simple sentence ratio
modifiers per NP
Np ratio
*Average propositional phrase
*Sentences with complex structure
Parallelism
Average number of idioms each sentence
*Content words
*Negatives
*Sentences with complex semantic categories
*Number of complex semantic categories
*Intentional words
*Noun word density
*Content word frequency in logarithmic
*Average frequency of content word in domain in
Logarithmic
Number of Idioms
*Pronouns
*Personal pronouns
*First personal pronouns
Third personal pronouns
*conjunctions
positive conjunctions
*negative conjunctions
*adversative conjunctions
*causal conjunctions
hypothesis conjunction
condition conjunction
*purpose conjunctions
*figure of speech (simile)

*Content word category

*feature that is included in Seed 1

Seed 1 LIWC features

WC
WPS
persconc
ppron
we
shehe
they
ipron
quanunit
specart
focuspast
progm
modal pa
general pa
interrog
quant
anx
family
friend
female
differ
see
feel
sexual
drives
achieve
power
risk
motion
work
home
netspeak
assent
Comma
Colon
Exclam
Parenth

Seed 1 semantic, sentiment, and follower features

neg sent
char freq
wc over semantic classes
readability
followers

Modeling performance differences on cognitive tests using LSTMs and skip-thought vectors trained on reported media consumption.

Maury Courtland[†], **Aida Davani**[‡], **Melissa Reyes**[*], **Leigh Yeh**[‡],
Jun Leung[*], **Brendan Kennedy**[‡], **Morteza Dehghani**[*‡], and **Jason Zevin**[*†]

[†] Department of Linguistics
[‡] Department of Computer Science
[*] Department of Psychology
University of Southern California
{landerpo, mostafaz, reyesmel, leighyeh,
junyenle, btkenned, mdehghan, zevin}@usc.edu

Abstract

Cognitive tests have traditionally resorted to standardizing testing materials in the name of equality and because of the onerous nature of creating test items. This approach ignores participants' diverse language experiences that potentially significantly affect testing outcomes. Here, we seek to explain our prior finding of significant performance differences on two cognitive tests (reading span and SPiN) between clusters of participants based on their media consumption. Here, we model the language contained in these media sources using an LSTM trained on corpora of each cluster's media sources to predict target words. We also model semantic similarity of test items with each cluster's corpus using skip-thought vectors. We find robust, significant correlations between performance on the SPiN test and the LSTMs and skip-thought models we present here, but not the reading span test.

1 Introduction

Generalization of experimental results crucially relies on the validity and representativeness of the experiment to study the phenomenon of interest. Researchers therefore invest considerable resources in experimental design, particularly in controlling for systematic confounds. When experiments rely on language samples for stimuli, this issue is further complicated because participants bring their complex and diverse language histories into the lab. When participants' language experiences differ systematically and the experiment does not control for this, a confound arises that compromises experimental validity and leads to systematic bias. This is the case for many cognitive tests that standardize language materials in the name of equality, whereas a more equitable approach would be to normalize test difficulty for individuals based on their experience.

One of the primary reasons for the traditional standardization approach over a normalization approach is that creating stimuli that are natural and free from confounds is a difficult laborious undertaking (e.g. as attested by Cutler (1981); Kalikow et al. (1977); Calandruccio and Smiljanic (2012)). The time required to create language stimuli is made worse by the fact that experiments can typically only use each target word or phrase once over the course of the experiment, meaning each stimulus must be uniquely created. In addition to the effort required, experimenter bias and error possibly significantly affect results (Forster, 2000).

While previous automation attempts have reduced experimenter bias, error, and workload (e.g. Lahl and Pietrowsky (2006); van Casteren and Davis (2007), vs. Hauk and Pulvermller (2004)'s manual selection) the process still relies on language statistics calculated from corpora unrepresentative of many participants' language experiences (e.g. Coltheart (1981); Linguistic Data Consortium (1996); Kucera and Francis (1967); Thorndike (1944), etc.). This mismatch between the language statistics used to generate test items and participants' actual language experiences represents a persistent confound detracting from experimental validity and perpetuating testing bias.

Our method allows participants to report for themselves the language they are comfortable with and regularly consume. Allowing participants to define their own language experiences ensures stimulus representativeness, increases fairness, and captures individual variability. This moves away from a model that gives researchers the power to define which language materials are representative across all participants (e.g. *Black Beauty* and *Little Women*: Thorndike (1944)) and moves towards a model that empowers participants to define their own language variety. To this end, we develop a method for evaluating lan-

Proceedings of the Third Workshop on Natural Language Processing and Computational Social Science, pages 47–53
Minneapolis, Minnesota, June 6, 2019. ©2019 Association for Computational Linguistics

guage experience's effect on cognitive test performance. In this work, we examine the relationship between the language that participants report consuming in media and their performance on two language-based cognitive tasks. We predict that participants' greater familiarity with the particular language variety of test items (as measured by semantic similarity and statistical predictability) will decrease test difficulty, resulting in higher scores.

Our previous results showed that participants cluster into distinct populations based on media consumption habits (Courtland et al., 2019). We determined media consumption habits by administering a self-report survey, asking participants what media content they currently consume in a variety of categories (Movies, Books, TV, etc.) as well as what they consumed in their formative years. K-means clustering identified two main clusters of participants based on the media sources they share in common. These clusters differ significantly in their performance on a test of verbal working memory (Daneman and Carpenter, 1980) and test of functional hearing (Kalikow et al., 1977). This is especially noteworthy considering we found the clusters to be orthogonal to (i.e. evenly distributed across) the traditionally used demographic variables we elicited at the end of the survey (e.g. Race, Socioeconomic Status, etc.). Here, we pursue a linguistic explanation for this performance difference by modeling the language comprising the sources participants reported consuming and examining its relationship to their performance on the behavioral tests.

To accomplish this, we use neural network language models to learn the joint probability function of word appearances in a corpus. Learning the probability of a word appearing at a certain position in a sentence can be difficult due to sparse representation in the training corpus. However, we choose these models based on their ability to capture long-distance statistical dependencies within a sentence: an advantage they enjoy over n-grams (Bengio et al., 2003). We examine a vanilla long short-term memory (LSTM) model and an attention-based model (Bahdanau et al., 2014). Both are based on recurrent neural networks and are designed to exploit semantic information distributed throughout a sentence to model the probability distribution of vocabulary words appearing as the sentence-final word (Sundermeyer et al., 2012). In addition to modeling the predictability of sentence-final words, we also use a recurrent neural network based encoder to capture sentence-level semantics (Kiros et al., 2015). We use this model to examine whether semantic familiarity affects participants' performances. We model semantics by embedding test items and corpus sentences in a high dimensional vector space and observing the distances between each item and its neighbors from the corpus. We predict that greater semantic similarity and greater sentence-final word predictability as captured by these models will correlate with participants' performance on our cognitive tasks.

2   Methods

2.1   Corpora and Behavioral Data

Participants were recruited from the USC undergraduate population (N=70) and on a local community college campus (L.A. Trade-Tech, N=25). To test language ability, participants complete the reading span task developed to assess verbal working memory (Daneman and Carpenter, 1980) and the speech perception in noise task (SPiN) developed to assess functional hearing (Kalikow et al., 1977). In the reading span task, participants read sets of sentences aloud while remembering the last word of each sentence. At the end of a set, they report the full sequence of sentence-final words in the set (with no partial credit). Set size increases (from 2 to 7) every three sets until participants cannot correctly recall any set at that length, at which point the task is terminated. The SPiN task presents spoken sentences over headphones masked with 12 talker babble (a combination of 6 male and 6 female voices speaking continuously). At the end of the sentence, participants are asked to report the final word of the sentence. We present the SPiN at +6dB SNR based on pilot results. We chose these tests for the important, yet often unacknowledged, role language processing is likely to play in both.

To capture participants' diverse language experiences, we use a proxy measure: the language materials they choose to consume regularly. Participants report these sources by completing an online survey of their current and formative media consumption habits. Using their responses, we aggregate the language data contained in these sources into corpora. We collect the sources for the corpora from *Springfield! Springfield!* and *YIFY Subtitles*, online repositories of television scripts and movie subtitles. In total, we collect 1027 scripts of complete series (e.g. all episodes of *Futurama*) and 194 movie subtitles. We then clean the sources by removing information that does not reach viewers (e.g. stage directions, parenthetical notes, etc.). Each corpus is then tokenized into sentences for model training.

2.2 Neural Cloze Model

Cloze probability refers to the probability of encountering the last word of a sentence given the sequence of words that precede it (i.e. all non-final words of that sentence). That is, given a sentence of words w_1 through w_n, the cloze probability is expressed by: $P(w_n|w_1...w_{n-1})$. This conditional probability is a particularly important metric for our purposes because of the privileged position sentence-final words enjoy in scoring both of our behavioral tasks (cf. Duffy and Giolas (1974)'s effect of predictability on task performance). Both our behavioral tasks place participants in a condition of increased cognitive burden (either using adverse listening conditions or simultaneous verbal storage and processing demands) and then ask them to identify or remember the last word of a sentence (Daneman and Carpenter, 1980; Kalikow et al., 1977). If these words are predictable for a given participant, top-down processing can alleviate the cognitive burden of online language processing, making the task easier (Winn, 2016). If participants systematically differ in their ability to predict these sentence-final words, as might be caused by different language experiences, the task would effectively be easier for one group of participants, leading to higher scores.

To test whether performance differences on our tasks were due to cloze probability differences, we trained a vanilla LSTM and LSTM with attention on each cluster's corpus to predict the last word of a sentence given all the previous words. The attention-based LSTM model is composed of a layer of LSTM cells that capture the hidden representation of the sequence of words from the beginning of the sentence up to the last word. The final representation for sentence i is shown by H_i (eq. 3, below) and is generated by applying attention weights (α_{ij}, eq. 2) to the LSTM's hidden states, h_{ij}, corresponding to each word j in sentence i of length n. W_s, W_t, u_s, b_s and b_t are learned simultaneously during back propagation (Wang et al., 2016).

$$u_{ij} = tanh(W_s h_{ij} + b_s) \qquad (1)$$

$$\alpha_{ij} = \frac{exp(u_s u_{ij})}{\sum_{k=0}^{n-1} exp(u_s u_{ik})} \qquad (2)$$

$$H_i = \sum_{j=0}^{n-1} (\alpha_{ij} * h_{ij}) \qquad (3)$$

Using a fully connected and a softmax layer, we then calculate the probability of each word w in the vocabulary appearing immediately after the sequence as p_w (i.e. at the end of that sentence).

$$v_{iw} = W_t H_i + b_t \qquad (4)$$

$$p_w = \frac{exp(v_{iw})}{\sum_{k=0}^{|vocabulary|} exp(v_{ik})} \qquad (5)$$

For the experiment, we use a vocabulary consisting of the 10k most frequent words in the corpus. The hidden size of the LSTM and attention vectors are set to 100. We use 300-dimensional GloVe word embeddings as the semantic representation of the words (Pennington et al., 2014).

2.3 Skip-thought Vectors

To obtain a quantitative measure of semantic similarity, we embed test items and sentences from each cluster's corpus in a high dimensional vector space and measure the distance of each test item to neighboring items from the corpus. To encode target and corpus items into vectors, we use combine-skip-thought vectors as detailed in Kiros et al. (2015). These encode sentences using RNNs with GRU into a 4800-dimensional vector which is the concatenation of a 2400-dimensional uni-directional encoder and a 2400-dimensional bi-directional encoder (1200 dimensions for backwards and forwards each). Results from the original paper show that these vectors capture a high degree of sentence-level semantics, particularly as it relates to encoding similarity as vector-space distance: the closer two sentences are in the embedded vector space, the more semantically related they are. We therefore take the distances in this embedded vector space to be indicative of how typical a test item's semantics are given the corpus of a participant's cluster.

We measure each test item's mean distance from all corpora items using the Taxicab distance (L^1 norm, eq. 6) and standardized Euclidean distance (eq. 7):

$$\sum_{i=1}^{n} |u_i - v_i| \qquad (6)$$

$$\sqrt{\sum_{i=1}^{n} (u_i - v_i)^2 / V[x_i]} \qquad (7)$$

	Cluster 1		Cluster 2	
	SPiN	span	SPiN	span
Vanilla LSTM	.39	-.03	.46	-.15
Attn. LSTM	.31	.02	.29	-.03
Taxicab	.486	.075	.519	-.022
Std. Euclid.	.408	-.048	.440	.092

Table 1: Mean behavioral performance on SPiN target items is significantly rank correlated to both LSTM activations and skip-thought distances for both clusters. We find no significant correlations with the span test for either cluster.

where $V[x_i]$ is the variance vector over the components of all vectors.

We also measure the mean distance to the closest 100 corpus neighbors in the event that similarity to all corpus items proves less informative than similarity to the closest matches from the corpus.

3 Results

3.1 Neural Cloze Model

For each test item, we correlate each cluster's LSTM activation of the sentence-final word with that cluster's mean behavioral performance (i.e. the percent of the cluster's participants who answered that item correctly). We use rank correlation as we are uncertain of how linear the mapping between predictability and performance benefit will be.

We observe significant rank correlations between the activation of both clusters' vanilla LSTMs and their respective mean performances on the SPiN items ($\rho(48) = .39, p < .01$ for cluster 1, $\rho(48) = .46, p < .005$ for cluster 2). We observe weaker but still significant correlations between the attention-based LSTM activations and mean performances on SPiN items ($\rho(48) = .31, p < .05$ for cluster 1, $\rho(48) = .29, p = .05$ for cluster 2). This poorer performance of the more complex model is noteworthy. We observe no significant rank correlations between any model's activations and performance on the corresponding span task item (see Table 1).

3.2 Skip-thought Vectors

For each cluster, we test for a correlation between the distance from all its corpus items to a given test item and the mean performance of its participants on that item. Given uncertainty of whether the distance-performance relationship will be linear, we use rank correlation. Using the distance metrics in eqs. (6) and (7), we observe significant rank correlations between vector-space distances and performances on the SPiN task (see Table 1 for test statistics, all $\rho(48), p < .005$) but not the span task. In addition to the mean distance of all

items, we calculated the distance to the closest 100 neighboring corpus items and obtained similar results.

4 Discussion

Language models tailored to the media consumption of different "clusters" of English speakers predict performance at the item level on a test of functional hearing (SPiN). In particular, LSTM models, which are perhaps the most natural way to model a task in which the predictability of the final word in a sentence has a strong influence on performance, correctly predict accuracy for each cluster. For the reading span task, in contrast, neither type of model correctly predicted performance. It is possible that the models are not capturing the relevant linguistic information for reading span or that reading span simply depends less on language (and language experience) overall than SPiN. An alternative explanation, however, comes from the difficulty in handling span performance data and its scoring. In the span task, items are presented in a fixed order, and difficulty increases from trial to trial as participants are required to maintain more items in working memory. This makes scoring at the item level difficult to interpret. Given these complications with the scoring procedure, it is possible that item-level analysis of the reading span is uninformative and invalid compared to the straight-forward scoring procedure of the SPiN.

Regarding the SPiN task, the robustness of the correlation between skip-thought vector mean-neighbor distances and participant performance is curious, however. The interesting aspect of this relationship is the direction of the correlation: that as the distance from corpus neighbors increases, performance on the item *increases*. This implies that unusual items are scored better on than familiar ones. This finding is not necessarily at odds with the finding of the neural cloze models: that increased predictability of the last word positively correlates with performance on that sentence. The two models differ in several key aspects which may explain their differences. Firstly, skipthought distances do not capture statistical predictability but rather semantic similarity, so while the last word (or in fact the sentence as a whole) may be semantically odd, it also may be relatively easy to predict the last word from the rest of the sentence. Secondly, skipthoughts operate at the level of the entire sentence rather than at the level of just the last word, which means that all of the words contributing to their embedding but the sentence-final one do not directly factor into the scoring of behavioral performance. This means that the majority of the linguistic information they encode is uninformative for capturing predictability of the last word, which is a direct correlate to how the task is scored. Lastly, skipthoughts are capturing the semantic novelty of a sentence. It is possible that the increased attentional resources these items demand above overly typical items actually causes participants to perform better on these items rather than worse. This must be tested further before concrete conclusions can be drawn, but it represents an interesting future direction for study.

We believe the results obtained here are an initial step toward taking participants' self-reported language experience into account in interpreting their performance on cognitive tests. In light of the evidence that a connection likely exists, we support the approach of normalizing, rather than standardizing, the language of cognitive tests. We predict normalization will produce tests that are simultaneously more fair and more valid. Regarding increased validity, the use of dynamically generated corpora would afford a significant benefit over static corpora by reducing sampling error. Every corpus necessarily contains idiosyncratic sampling error affecting results (Clark, 1973). The repeated use of norms generated from a single corpus (e.g. as was traditionally taken from Kucera and Francis (1967) or Thorndike (1944)) amplifies this noise and its role in experimental results. The construction of dynamic corpora we are planning will mitigate this effect by providing multiple samples across which real statistical regularities are likely to replicate, while sample noise is not (like bootstrapping: Efron (1979)).

While the eventual goal of this work is to generate valid and fair stimuli *ex nihilo* given people's language models, the evaluation of existing stimuli materials represents a necessary first step taken here. The development of models capturing linguistic features that predict behavioral performance provides the possibility for using these models to identify or synthesize fair test items. Modeling the relationship between language experience and task performance allows rapid prototyping and evaluation of stimuli sets with previously unfeasible speed. This allows a much larger set of candidate stimuli to be evaluated affording new levels of rigor to the test creation process. This speed also opens the door for individual personalization of test items, a task far too labor-intensive to perform manually. Our future work will test our models' ability to create test stimuli equitable across diverse language communities.

These methods for promoting equity are likely relevant to education where equality vs. equity is debated as the difference between equal access to educational resources vs. access to resources leading to equal outcomes (e.g. Green (1983); Stromquist (2005); Espinoza (2007)). Language-based cognitive testing and access to education share several features in common. Both are moderated by the complex individual variability of personal experience. Those with the worst outcomes in both are underrepresented among those setting policy and creating tests (National Science Foundation, 2013; Thaler and Jones-Forrester, 2013; Thaler et al., 2015). And most importantly, both also determine relevant real-world outcomes for test takers: the tests we consider here are used clinically to diagnose aphasia (Caspari et al., 1998), Alzheimer's disease (Kempler et al., 1998), schizophrenia (Stone et al., 1998), and age-related cognitive decline (Salthouse and Kersten, 1993). Many cognitive tests use linguistic stimuli to assess other cognitive functions; by identifying specific ways in which individuals' language variety influences their performance, we can start to tease apart potential educationally and clinically meaningful deficits from social and cultural differences between participant groups.

Acknowledgments

This work was supported by the NIH (5R21DC017018-02). Behavioral data used were collected under USC IRB #UP-18-00006.

References

Dzmitry Bahdanau, Kyunghyun Cho, and Yoshua Bengio. 2014. Neural machine translation by jointly learning to align and translate. *arXiv preprint arXiv:1409.0473*.

Yoshua Bengio, Réjean Ducharme, Pascal Vincent, and Christian Jauvin. 2003. A neural probabilistic language model. *Journal of machine learning research*, 3(Feb):1137–1155.

Lauren Calandruccio and Rajka Smiljanic. 2012. New Sentence Recognition Materials Developed Using a Basic Non-Native English Lexicon. *Journal of Speech, Language, and Hearing Research*, 55(5):1342–1355.

Isabelle Caspari, Stanley R. Parkinson, Leonard L. LaPointe, and Richard C. Katz. 1998. Working Memory and Aphasia. *Brain and Cognition*, 37(2):205–223.

Maarten van Casteren and Matthew H. Davis. 2007. Match: A program to assist in matching the conditions of factorial experiments. *Behavior Research Methods*, 39(4):973–978.

Herbert H. Clark. 1973. The language-as-fixed-effect fallacy: A critique of language statistics in psychological research. *Journal of Verbal Learning and Verbal Behavior*, 12(4):335–359.

Max Coltheart. 1981. The MRC Psycholinguistic Database. *The Quarterly Journal of Experimental Psychology Section A*, 33(4):497–505.

Maury Courtland, Aida Davani, Melissa Reyes, Leigh Yeh, Jun Leung, Brendan Kennedy, Morteza Dehghani, and Jason Zevin. 2019. Subtle differences in language experience moderate performance on language-based cognitive tests. In *Proceedings of the 41st Annual Conference of the Cognitive Science Society*, Austin, Texas. Cognitive Science Society.

Anne Cutler. 1981. Making up materials is a confounded nuisance, or: Will we able to run any psycholinguistic experiments at all in 1990? *Cognition*, 10(1):65–70.

Meredyth Daneman and Patricia A. Carpenter. 1980. Individual differences in working memory and reading. *Journal of Verbal Learning and Verbal Behavior*, 19(4):450–466.

Joseph R. Duffy and Thomas G. Giolas. 1974. Sentence Intelligibility as a Function of Key Word Selection. *Journal of Speech and Hearing Research*.

B. Efron. 1979. Bootstrap Methods: Another Look at the Jackknife. *The Annals of Statistics*, 7(1):1–26.

Oscar Espinoza. 2007. Solving the equityequality conceptual dilemma: a new model for analysis of the educational process. *Educational Research*, 49(4):343–363.

Kenneth I. Forster. 2000. The potential for experimenter bias effects in word recognition experiments. *Memory & Cognition*, 28(7):1109–1115.

Thomas F. Green. 1983. Excellence, Equity, and Equality.

O Hauk and F Pulvermller. 2004. Effects of word length and frequency on the human event-related potential. *Clinical Neurophysiology*, 115(5):1090–1103.

D. N. Kalikow, K. N. Stevens, and L. L. Elliott. 1977. Development of a test of speech intelligibility in noise using sentence materials with controlled word predictability. *The Journal of the Acoustical Society of America*, 61(5):1337–1351.

Daniel Kempler, Amit Almor, Lorraine K. Tyler, Elaine S. Andersen, and Maryellen C. MacDonald. 1998. Sentence Comprehension Deficits in Alzheimer's Disease: A Comparison of Off-Line vs. On-Line Sentence Processing. *Brain and Language*, 64(3):297–316.

Ryan Kiros, Yukun Zhu, Ruslan Salakhutdinov, Richard S. Zemel, Antonio Torralba, Raquel Urtasun, and Sanja Fidler. 2015. Skip-Thought Vectors. *arXiv:1506.06726 [cs]*. ArXiv: 1506.06726.

Henry Kucera and Winthrop Nelson Francis. 1967. *Computational analysis of present-day American English*. Dartmouth Publishing Group.

Olaf Lahl and Reinhard Pietrowsky. 2006. EQUIWORD: A software application for the automatic creation of truly equivalent word lists. *Behavior Research Methods*, 38(1):146–152.

Linguistic Data Consortium. 1996. *CELEX2*. OCLC: 1023487640.

National Science Foundation. 2013. Women, Minorities, and Persons with Disabilities in Science and Engineering: 2013: (558442013-001). Technical report, American Psychological Association. Type: dataset.

Jeffrey Pennington, Richard Socher, and Christopher Manning. 2014. Glove: Global vectors for word representation. In *Proceedings of the 2014 conference on empirical methods in natural language processing (EMNLP)*, pages 1532–1543.

Timothy A. Salthouse and Alan W. Kersten. 1993. Decomposing adult age differences in symbol arithmetic. *Memory & Cognition*, 21(5):699–710.

Maria Stone, John D. E. Gabrieli, Glenn T. Stebbins, and Edith V. Sullivan. 1998. Working and strategic memory deficits in schizophrenia. *Neuropsychology*, 12(2):278–288.

Nelly Stromquist. 2005. Comparative and International Education: A Journey toward Equality and Equity. *Harvard Educational Review*, 75(1):89–111.

Martin Sundermeyer, Ralf Schlüter, and Hermann Ney. 2012. Lstm neural networks for language modeling. In *Thirteenth annual conference of the international speech communication association*.

Nicholas S. Thaler and Sharon Jones-Forrester. 2013. IQ Testing and the Hispanic Client. In *Guide to Psychological Assessment with Hispanics*, pages 81–98. Springer, Boston, MA.

Nicholas S. Thaler, April D. Thames, Xavier E. Cagigas, and Marc A. Norman. 2015. IQ Testing and the African American Client. In Lorraine T. Benuto and Brian D. Leany, editors, *Guide to Psychological Assessment with African Americans*, pages 63–77. Springer New York, New York, NY.

Edward L. Thorndike. 1944. *The teacher's word book of 30,000 words*. New York :.

Yequan Wang, Minlie Huang, Li Zhao, et al. 2016. Attention-based lstm for aspect-level sentiment classification. In *Proceedings of the 2016 conference on empirical methods in natural language processing*, pages 606–615.

Matthew B. Winn. 2016. Rapid Release From Listening Effort Resulting From Semantic Context, and Effects of Spectral Degradation and Cochlear Implants. *Trends in Hearing*, 20:233121651666972.

Using time series and natural language processing to identify viral moments in the 2016 U.S. Presidential Debate

Josephine Lukito[1], Prathusha K Sarma[2], Jordan Foley[3] and Aman Abhishek[4]

[1], [3], [4] School of Journalism and Mass Communication, UW-Madison
[2] Electical and Computer Engineering, UW-Madison
{jlukito,kameswarasar,jfoley5,aabhishek}@wisc.edu

Abstract

This paper proposes a method for identifying and studying viral moments or highlights during a political debate. Using a combined strategy of time series analysis and domain adapted word embeddings, this study provides an in-depth analysis of several key moments during the 2016 U.S. Presidential election. First, a time series outlier analysis is used to identify key moments during the debate. These moments had to result in a long-term shift in attention towards either Hillary Clinton or Donald Trump (i.e., a transient change outlier or an intervention, resulting in a permanent change in the time series). To assess whether these moments also resulted in a discursive shift, two corpora are produced for each potential viral moment (a pre-viral corpus and post-viral corpus). A domain adaptation layer learns weights to combine a generic and domain specific (DS) word embedding into a domain adapted (DA) embedding. Words are then classified using a generic encoder+classifier framework that relies on these word embeddings as inputs. Results suggest that both Clinton and Trump were able to induced discourse-shifting viral moments, though the former is much better at producing a topically-specific discursive shift.

1 Introduction

Though research across disciplines tends to analyze language cross-sectionally, or synchronically, we know that language use is temporally dependent. In other words, discourse about a subject can ebb and flow dynamically over time, peaking at salient moments or dropping when attention to that subject is low. This feature is especially noticeable on social media platforms during media storms. Here, "media storm" is defined as "an explosive increase in news coverage of a specific item (event or issue) constituting a substantial share of the total news agenda during a certain time" (Boydstun et al., 2014). Media storms can be unplanned, such as the coverage of a scandal (Walgrave et al., 2017), or planned, like presidential debates (Dayan and Katz, 1994).

Three components are important to Boydstun's definition: news coverage must be explosive, all-consuming ("constituting a substantial share" of media attention), and long-lasting. Presidential debates fulfill all three conditions of a media storm because they are explosive (attention to the debate explodes when it begins, large (a debate consume most media attention until it is over) and can be long-lasting (post-debate spin ensures that coverage of the debate lasts for longer than 24 hours) (Fridkin et al., 2008).

Though news media are obviously important to media storms, the modern hybrid media ecology ensures that what appears in news media is likely to also appear on social media platforms. After all, if media storms concentrate news media attention towards one news events, social media attention likely becomes concentrated as well. This is particularly true on Twitter, which journalists rely on for their professional work (McGregor and Molyneux, 2016). As a result, Twitter has become an essential platform for the sharing of news information, and for public discussion of media storm events.

The purpose of this study is to explore the temporal and linguistic dynamics of viral moments during the first 2016 U.S. Presidential Debate, between Donald J. Trump and Hillary R. Clinton. In a media storm, viral moments constitute important peaks of attentionthe most discussed moments in an event that already garners significant media

Proceedings of the Third Workshop on Natural Language Processing and Computational Social Science, pages 54–64
Minneapolis, Minnesota, June 6, 2019. ©2019 Association for Computational Linguistics

scrutiny. Our study relies on an inductive, three-step approach to identifying and studying these viral moments during a debate.

2 Related Work on Debates and Viral Moment

Previous studies of political debates using computational methods have largely focused on candidates' rhetoric and topic shifts. For example a candidate who is able to shift topics during a debate is perceived to have greater relative power, which increases their ranks compared to other candidates (Prabhakaran et al., 2014). A handful of studies have also analyzed social media in tandem with debates, acknowledging the increasing role of second-screens. In these studies, social media is used to asses debate performance in real time (Diakopoulos and Shamma, 2010; Pond, 2016). We deviate somewhat from these analysis by focusing specifically on key viral moments, rather than overall sentiment or topic shifts.

"Going viral" constitutes a process of quickly becoming popular on one or multiple (digital) platforms (Hong et al., 2011). Many things can "go viral", including hashtags (Bastos et al., 2013) and people (Pancer and Poole, 2016). A "viral moment", therefore, is a moment in time where a person, place, or thing "goes viral". Because we are focused on debates, we are primarily interested in viral moments induced by candidates in the debate, and not (for example) by social media discourse occurring independently from the debate.

In a debate, candidates are likely to try inducing viral moments to garner and sustain attention during a highly publicized discursive spar. They may do so by making salient comments or gestures that received widespread attention for their deviance. These moments are important to candidates, as they can garner attention and "produce memorable and highly referenced moments" (Shah et al., 2016). Previous studies have found that these moments tend to be gaffs (misspoken statements) and zingers (insults) (Freelon and Karpf, 2015).

One unique feature of debates in the digital age is the popularity of "second-screening", whereby audiences watching something on one screen (the "first" screen) interact with a "second" screen, sometimes to enhance their overall viewing experience (Schirra et al., 2014). The most common example of this is live-tweeting when one watches television. Given the televised nature of political debates, many viewers enjoy live-tweeting and discussing the debate in real-time, often on a platform like Twitter. This creates a unique media consumption experience that did not exist in the 1960's or 1970's (Chadwick et al., 2017).

Within a media storm, particularly salient moments in time come to represent the media storm as a whole. These "highlights"or viral momentsare important to post-election spin. For example, citizens who did not watch the full debate may still seek out highlights to get the "main gist" of the event. This is not unlike news coverage of other planned media events, which tends to focus on that events key moments (Fridkin et al., 2007).

Furthermore, because of ability for the viewing audienceeveryday citizens, journalists, influencers, and celebrities alike, aka the "viewertariat" (Anstead and OLoughlin, 2011)to engage with discourse, the audience becomes especially meaningful to the production of viral moments. No longer are news media the gatekeepers of determining what is or is not an important debate moment. Rather, this can now be gaged through social media interaction and commentary.

Previous studies of these moments have largely been inductive (Shah et al., 2016; Freelon and Karpf, 2015). In other words, these moments are typically identified through an assessment made by the researchers, with varying levels of specificity regarding what constitutes or does not constitute a viral moment. There are a handful of exceptions; for example, one study looks at what content media will highlight from a debate (Tan et al., 2018). They find that many feature sets (including emotion, contrast, personal pronouns, and superlatives) increase the likelihood of a statement being highlighted. However, this analysis does not consider the role of social media.

This study contributes to ongoing information communication research by proposing a more quantitatively-driven, context-free strategy that can be applied to study highlights across many planned events. More specifically, we posit that viral moments during media storms (like this debate) are likely to have both temporal qualities and discursive properties that makes such a moment unique relative to the rest of a media storm.

3 Methodology

This study relies on a combination of time series models and Natural Language Processing (NLP) strategies to explore a set of possible viral moments induced by the debates candidates (see Figure 1).

Two primary data are used: the first is a corpus of English-language tweets about Hillary Clinton or Donald Trump at the time of the debate. This corpus was purchased through Gnip, a social media API aggregation company that is owned by Twitter. Through Gnip, Twitter sells historic "firehose" data (a census of tweets using a keyword search within a given time frame); the cost of this data varies with the number of tweets in the search. We purchased all the tweets within the debates 90-minute window using the following keyword search: ((clinton OR hillary) - (trump OR donald)) OR ((trump OR donald) - (clinton OR hillary)).

For the time series analysis, counts of tweets referencing either Clinton or Trump were aggregated at the 30-second-level. This resulted in two time series: one with the number of tweets about Clinton every 30-seconds, and one with the number of tweets about Trump every 30-seconds. Because Twitter activity was high during this time, there were no gaps in the time seriesall equally-spaced time points had at least one tweet.

To perform the NLP analysis, we took all the tweets posted two minutes before each temporal outlier and constructed a corpus. We then took all the tweets posted two minutes after each temporal outlier to construct a second corpus. Each potential viral moment identified by the time series analysis, therefore, would have a corpora-pair (one corpus representing pre-viral tweets, and one representing post-viral tweets).

The second dataset is a C-SPAN video recording of the debate itself (this is analyzed in tandem with a transcript that has been manually time-stamped for every 10-second increment). C-SPAN is a public affairs programming network which televises and records U.S. political events, including U.S. Presidential debates. C-SPAN footage is made publicly available on their website. We analyzed the video in the "split-screen" format, wherein one camera is pointed to each candidate. The videos of both candidates are then shown side-by-side.

3.1 Time Series Analysis

This viral-moment identification process takes place in three steps. We begin with an analysis of temporal outliers in the two time series: one for

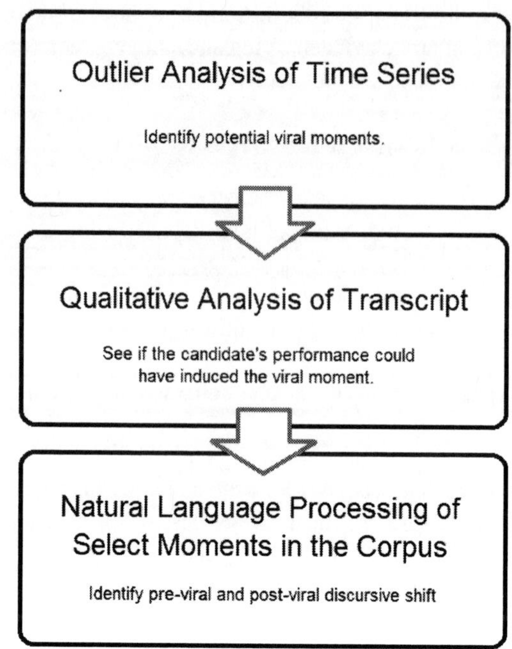

Figure 1: Three-step Method for identifying viral moments

mentions of Clinton and one for Trump. This is an inductive process. To identify outliers we estimate temporal outliers using an ARIMAX model. This is an extension of the popular univariate ARIMA model, which stands for a AutoRegressive, Integrated, Moving Average model (Brockwell et al., 2002). An ARIMA model attempts to identify and model the temporal data-generating process of a time series. In other words, to what degree (and how) is data at time "T" explained by its own prior values at time $t - 1$ or earlier $(t - n)$? It does so by looking at three possible dynamics, an autoregressive (AR) component, an integrated (I) component, and a moving average (MA) component. The ARIMAX model is an extension of the ARIMA that allows for control variables. Each of our models included one control: a dichotomous variable indicating the speaker. For the Clinton time series, the speaker was coded as "1" if Clinton was speaking, and "0" if she was not. For the Trump time series, the speaker was coded as "1" if Trump was speaking.

The R package $<$ tsoutliers $>$ estimates an ARIMAX model to identify three types of temporal outliers: a "pulse function", resulting in a quickly appearing or disappearing spike; a "transient change", where the series spikes quickly, but the effect dissipates slowly; and an "intervention outlier", representing "a shock in the innovations of the model" (López-de Lacalle, 2016). More colloquially, a pulse results in a short-term change, a transient change reflects an immediate change that slowly disappears over time, and an intervention indicates a fundamental shift or change in the time series.

Positive outliers indicate a fast increase in attention towards a candidate. Negative outliers indicate a fast decrease in attention towards a candidate. Because this study posits that viral moments result in more attention (not less), we focus only on the positive outliers.

3.2 Analyzing Debate Discourse

The positive outliers moments identified through the time series analysis are then studied further. As the time series analysis relies entirely on count data, an outlier analysis cannot tell us why there would be a spike in attention. To analyze these moments further, we study the debate content around the time of the social media time series outlier, using the C-SPAN video and debate transcript, focusing on the speaker's rhetoric, both in terms of content and performance, as well as the opponent's non-verbal presentation). This is a necessary process to weed out temporal outliers triggered by things unrelated to the event (e.g., a celebrity's tweet going viral, unrelated to the debate in real-time).

In addition to this, we also explore the debate content around the time of the social media time series outlier.This is an important feature, as this study focuses on viral moments induced by candidate discourse during the debate. We use this qualitative analysis to identify key terms in the debate for which there is likely to be a discourse shift.

3.3 Natural Language Processing of Discursive Shift

To confirm that the debate-induced temporal outliers also induces a discursive shift, we apply a NLP strategy that identifies key words that have changed in their discursive use between two corpora. There exist several embedding algorithms that produce highly optimized and efficient embeddings for words in an n-dimensional vector space. Typically, such algorithms are trained on large-sized generic bodies of text (e.g., Wikipedia), as larger datasets are beneficial for capturing a wide range of the semantics of a word in its vector representation.

Recent work by (Sarma et al., 2018) demonstrates how one can perform 'Domain Adaptation' in word embeddings for small-sized data sets, by shifting the space of generic word embeddings. In their work (Sarma et al., 2018), two sets of word embeddings are obtained for a single vocabulary of words. One set of embeddings, called 'generic' embeddings are obtained from off-the-shelf solvers like word2vec (Mikolov et al., 2013), GloVe (Pennington et al., 2014) etc that are trained on a generic corpus such a Wikipedia. A second set of 'domain specific' (DS) word embeddings are obtained by either i)re-training algorithms like word2vec/GloVe on a target data domain or ii) use LSA (Deerwester et al., 1990) based embedding approach if the target domain is small in size. In the LSA approach, a documents by words ($d \times N$) matrix of word counts is constructed. Then, a SVD step is performed followed by projecting the left singular vectors on to the k largest singular values to obtain word embeddings for the N words. Once, the generic and DS embeddings are a obtained, a new adapted subspace is learned for the two sets of embeddings using Kernel Canonical Correlation Analysis (KCCA). The objective of KCCA (Hotelling, 1936) is to obtain a non-linear subspace such that the statistical correlations between two sets of variables is maximized. Domain Adapted (DA) embeddings are obtained by learning a non-linear subspace between the generic and DS embeddings. In their work (Sarma et al., 2018), the authors demonstrate that DA embeddings perform particularly well on sentiment analysis tasks applied to small sized target domains.

In our work, we obtain DA embeddings for words in tweets posted two minutes before and two minutes after an time series-identified viral moment. First, we tokenize texts from tweets before and after the viral moment and construct two sets of vocabularies corresponding to tweets before and after the viral moment. We obtain DA embeddings for the two vocabularies using KCCA. Then, we look for words that are common in both vocabularies and extract their corresponding DA embeddings. Once we have these DA embeddings, we measure the semantic shift in words that occur both before and after the viral moment by measuring the L2 distance between the pre- and post- vector representations of a given word.

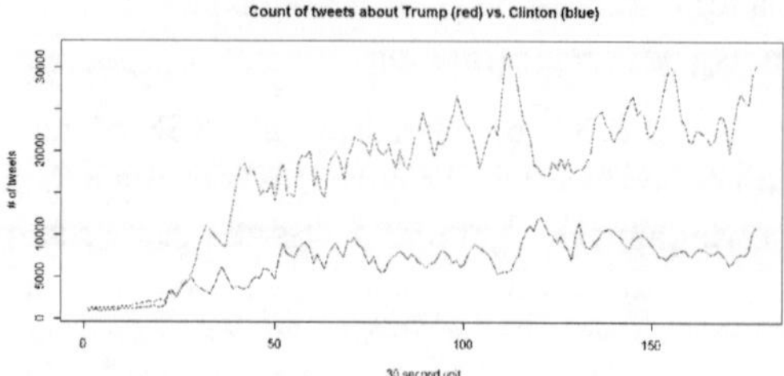

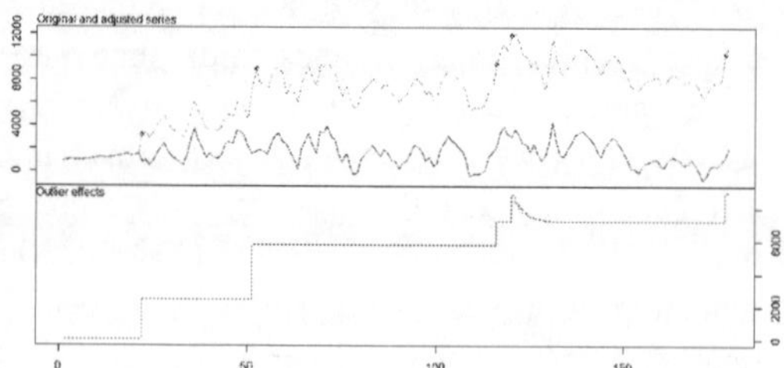

Figure 2: Time series of attention to Clinton (blue) and Trump (red)

Figure 3: Outliers identified in the Clinton Time Series

4 Results

4.1 Time Series Analysis

The debate was 1 hours and 29 minutes long. When using a 30-second interval as the time-unit, this results in 178 points. Figure 2 displays two time seriesone showing the mentions of Clinton and one representing the mentions of Trump.

We begin our time series analysis with a test for unit roots. Unit roots are an indicator that a time series is non-stationary (i.e., that the time series' mean, variance and covariance vary over time). This is a problem for time series models that rely on stationary time series. For ARIMA models, a unit root also indicates that the series has at least one integrated component (the 'I' in 'ARIMA' will be 1 or greater). It is also possible that a time series could be fractionally integrated, which means its 'I' would be between 0 and 1.

Two tests are common for finding unit roots: a KPSS test and an ADF test (Culver and Papell, 1997). Both are available in the R package $<$ tseries $>$. These test confirm one another and show that both the Clinton and the Trump time series have one unit root. To ensure that these unit roots are indicative of full integration, and not of fractional integration, we calculated an estimation of the integrated component of each time series (Haslett and Raftery, 1989). In both instances, the time series were well over 0.7, suggesting that both series have full or near-full integration components.

To diagnose the data-generating properties of each candidates Twitter count, we build two univariate auto-regressive integrated moving-average (ARIMA) models. We use the R package $<$ forecast $>$ to test the fit of various ARIMA models on each time series, relying on the Bayesian Information Criterion to select the optimal model.

This process yielded an optimal ARIMA model of (0,1,0) for Twitter attention to Trump (BIC = 3109.361) and an optimal ARIMA model of (0,1,1) for Twitter attention to Clinton (BIC = 2948.52).

Results of the outliers analysis identify several time series outliers. Because this study is only interested in positive spikes of attention, negative outliers are excluded from the subsequent analysis. For Clinton, there are four positive outliers (as a reminder: the time series is measured in 30-second intervals). The first occurs around 25:18 to 25:48 and is an intervention (coefficient = 2432.50, t = 5.37 , p < 0.01). The second occurs around 39:18 to 29:48 and is an intervention (coefficient = 3378.01, t = 9.09, p < 0.01). The third is between 1:12:18 to 1:12:48 and is another intervention (coefficient = 1048.00, t = 4.20, p<0.01). And finally, the fourth is between 1:14:48 to 1:15:18 and it is an intervention (coefficient = 1789.88, t = 3.11, p < 0.01).

For Trump, four outliers are also found. The first occurs between 42:18 and 42:48 and is a transient change outlier. The second happens between 46:18 and 46:48 and is a level shift. The third is between 1:09:18 to 1:09:48, and begins as a level-shift, but ends as a transient change. The fourth is a level shift that occurs between 1:22:48 to 1:23:18. Figure 2 displays Trumps positive outliers identified using this strategy. Figure 3 displays Clintons positive outliers identified using this strategy and Figure 4 displays Trump's positive outliers.

4.2 Analysis of Debate Discourse

To understand these outliers in more detail, we examine the candidates performative discourse at the seven aforementioned times. The first Clinton outlier occurs when she says, "Donald thinks that

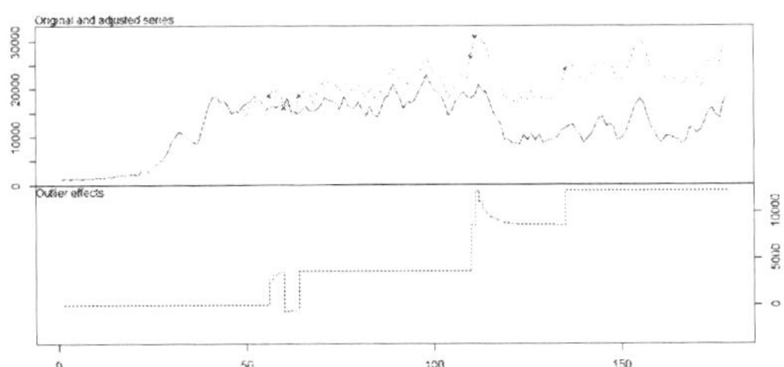

Figure 4: Outliers identified in the Trump Time Series

climate change is a hoax perpetrated by the Chinese" (0:25:37-0:25:49) in a response about climate change. The third outlier is a result of Clinton quoting First Lady Michelle Obama ("When they go low, we go high") during a question about Trump's Birther scandal (when Trump claimed that President Obama was not born in the United States). The fourth outlier happens in Clintons response to a question about cybersecurity. Curiously, the second outlier does not occur when Clinton is talking. Rather, mentions of Clinton increased when the moderator asked a question about Trumps tax returns:

> "Mr. Trump, we're talking about the burden that Americans have to pay, yet you have not released your tax returns. And the reason nominees have released their returns for decades is so that voters will know if their potential president owes money towho he owes it to and any business conflicts. Don't Americans have a right to know if there are any conflicts of interest?"

Because this event seemed to be induced by the moderators question, and not from either of the candidates, it was removed for subsequent analysis (this leaves us with 7 candidate-induced, temporally-identified viral moments). However, we posit that it remains a significant moment in the event worth noting.

The first outlier identified in the Trump attention time series occurred during the end of Trumps remarks regarding his taxes, and as Clinton begins her response. Following a back and forth that includes remarks about Clintons email scandal, the second outlier occurs when Trump uses the word "braggadocious" regarding his income: "I have a tremendous income. And the reason I say that

is not in a braggadocios way" (0:46:28-0:46:33). He continues with a lengthy critique of Clinton, her foreign policy decisions, and the perceived economic consequences (this includes describing the United States as a third-world country). The third outlier occurs when Trump answers a question about the Birther scandal: "I figured you'd ask the question tonight, of course. But nobody was caring much about it. But I was the one that got him to produce the birth certificate. And I think I did a good job" (1:09:28-1:09:36). The fourth outlier occurs when Trump attributes the formation of Iraq to Clinton: "Well, President Obama and Secretary Clinton created a vacuum the way they got out of Iraq [. . .] once they got in, the way they got out was a disaster. And ISIS was formed" (1:22:08-1:22:22).

4.3 Natural Language Processing

Owing to space constraints, we only discuss three of the six potential viral moments. These are: Trump's use of the word "braggadocious" regarding his income and competency (Trump Viral Moment 2), Clinton's statement that Trump "thinks that climate change is a hoax" (Clinton Viral Moment 1), and Clinton quoting Michelle Obama. However, we present the NLP results of all seven viral moments identified through the time series analysis in our Appendix.

To look at the discursive shift prior to and after the temporally-identified viral moments, we subset our full corpus of tweets about Trump or Clinton during the first debate into three corpora-pairs. For viral each moment, there were two corpora: one from tweets in the pre-viral moment, and one for tweets in the post-viral moment; this produced fourteen corpora. Tweets from these were tokenized, and unique vocabularies were constructed using the two minute data from before (the pre-) and after (the post-) the viral moment. Final vocabularies were constructed by retaining words that appear at least two times across all the tweets from the pre- and post- viral moment. We then took the intersection of the two vocabularies and to identify words that occurred often among the tweets from before and after the viral moment. Previous studies have shown that the social media effects of a candidate's rhetoric tend to last no longer than two minutes (Bucy et al., 2019).

Words are ranked as 'most different' in use by measuring the l2 distance between the vector embedding for a given word from the pre vocabulary and the corresponding embedding for the same word in the post vocabulary. Word embeddings for words in the pre and post vocabularies are obtained via the Kernel CCA projection method described in (Sarma et al., 2018). First domain specific word embeddings for both 'pre' and 'post' event vocabularies are constructed using LSA. Then, for words in common to both vocabularies a max-correlation subspace is constructed using KCCA. Projections of both sets of embeddings in this subspace are then compared to measure 'word-shift', i.e the l2 distance between the two projections of the same word in the KCCA derived vector subspace.

Among the three viral moments analyzed, many of the words that had the largest l2 distance in the pre-viral moment and the post-viral moment were words employed directly by a candidate during that time, or were relevant to the viral moment being discussed. This was especially true for Clinton's viral moments (regarding climate change and the Birther scandal). For example, in the first Clinton viral moment, words about climate change were among those with comparatively larger l2 distances, like green, climate, energy, and change.

Other discourse-specific words also had strong discursive shifts, such as hoax and China (words that originated directly from Clinton's statement). Similarly, the words with the largest l2-differences in Clinton's second viral moment were related to the Birther scandal, like Obama and Barack, or came directly from Clinton's statement, like response, high, go, and low. Clinton's statement also included a remark that Trump's accusation was "very hurtful" (the word "hurtful" also appeared to have a significant l2-difference in the pre-viral and post-viral corpora).

For Trump, the words with the largest l2-distance difference in the pre- and post-viral moment were related to the topic Trump was discussing. However neither the word braggadocious, nor the presumed root word brag, appeared on our list ("brag" appeared in this viral moment's pre-viral corpus, but "braggadocious" did not). Instead, the discourse shift on social media seemed to center around the foreign policy implications of his statement, which Trump pivoted to immediately following his statement about being a good businessman (this is what he was being 'braggadocious' about). Although Trump did not explic-

n	Word	Δ L2 distance
1	**wrong**	102.62
2	**Iraq**	101.83
3	**should**	73.67
4	take	62.94
5	**China**	57.53
6	there	53.07
7	security	51.86
8	really	51.56
9	talking	45.79
10	**money**	45.33
11	wants	45.02
12	racial	44.28
13	only	41.38
14	plan	41.30
15	even	41.00
16	better	40.14
17	maybe	39.66
18	endorse	38.90
19	lost	36.91
20	**International**	36.15

Table 1: Words with the greatest l2 distance difference between the pre-viral and post-viral moment for Trump's Viral Moment 2

itly mention any countries in his statement, social media discourse focused on countries like China and Iraq (two countries that Trump mentions frequently elsewhere). However, the prevalence of more unrelated words suggests that this potential viral moment did not result in as strong of a discourse shift as Clinton's viral moments. More succinctly put: Trump's statement likely resulted in a spike of attention; however, this shock did not focus attention specifically on Trump's words the way shocks in attention to Clinton did.

Figure 5, 6 and 7 provides words that changed the most between pre and post vocabularies and their corresponding differences in l2 distance for each viral moment studied.

5 Conclusion

Using a combination of time series techniques and natural language processing, this study finds several viral moments, or highlights, that have been induced by candidates during the first debate of the 2016 U.S. Presidential election. Though we find other spikes in attention towards either Trump or Clinton, they may be unrelated to the content of the debate itself (e.g., a celebrity watching the

n	Word	Δ L2 distance
1	blah	47.95
2	made	41.93
3	fuck	39.47
4	said	38.71
5	**green**	38.06
6	**climate**	37.57
7	**energy**	36.32
8	looks	36.28
9	again	35.19
10	**real**	33.80
11	because	33.71
12	sexist	33.68
13	**change**	33.54
14	**hoax**	33.38
15	important	32.93
16	please	32.21
17	bush	32.07
18	**china**	30.65
19	those	30.48
20	does	29.69

Table 2: Words with the greatest l2 distance difference between the pre-viral and post-viral moment for Clinton's Viral Moment 1

n	Word	Δ L2 distance
1	nothing	57.57
2	**response**	56.66
3	**high**	47.37
4	line	44.96
5	**go**	38.61
6	history	37.44
7	**they**	37.33
8	record	35.89
9	really	34.23
10	**hurtful**	33.45
11	vote	33.07
12	lester	31.75
13	**low**	31.67
14	went	31.64
15	**Obama**	31.26
16	**Barack**	31.12
17	**better**	30.77
18	there	30.75
19	watching	30.30
20	prepare	29.41

Table 3: Words with the greatest l2 distance difference between the pre-viral and post-viral moment for for Clinton's Viral Moment 2

debate that makes an unrelated comment that becomes popular). While those moments are important, we focus specifically on the stakeholders of the media storm, as they have the most to gain from viral moments.

Results of this analysis suggest that Trump and Clinton were both able to induce viral moments in the debate. Clinton's viral moments tended to produce a strong discursive shift that was directly related to her debate statement. This is indicated by the number of words that Clinton said which were also words that had the largest l2-difference in the pre-viral and post-viral corpus. By contrast, Trump's viral moment did not seem to have as prominent of a discursive shift. Nevertheless, Trump was seemingly able to focus attention on the topic of his interest. In the debate, Trump used his statement to pivot away from talk about his taxes to the present economic state of the country (in relation to other countries). On social media, attention also seemed to shift to his international critiques, reflecting Trump's ability to change public conversation at the time of the debate.

A more qualitative examination of the viral moments suggests that planned attacks or retorts, or those delivered in a more neutral tone, were not able to induce a viral event compared to unscripted words (e.g., braggadocious) and strong statements of condemnation (e.g., "Trump thinks climate change is a hoax perpetuated by the Chinese") were able to. We can note several instances where Trump or Clinton attempt to induce a viral moment, such as Clinton's use of Trumped-up, trickle-down economics and when Trump states: "Secretary Clinton doesn't want to use a few words like law and order." However, these statements did not induce temporally-evident viral moments, and likely did not result in a discursive shift.

Furthermore, even in instances where we may suspect the Twitter audience to focus on non-verbals or unique words (e.g., "braggadocious"), we find that the discourse shift occurs around words about policy issues, not words about the way a candidate behaves. This suggests that viral moments occur when the candidate makes a strong statement, often with critical audio or non-verbal cues but primarily if it relates to an already-salient political issue, such as a scandal (e.g., Birther scandal) or political decision (e.g., support for Iraq).

Combined, these results highlight the ability for debates to create politically salient viral moments, which carry symbolic meaning that lasts over the course of the debate, and beyond. As post-debate spin is important for audiences to understand how to interpret the debate ((Fridkin et al., 2007), (Shah et al., 2016)), we suspect that it is these viral moments that are subsequently identified as important highlights of the event. This is confirmed by news medias post-debate coverage of the top moment, which includes many of the viral moments identified here, though more of Trumps viral moments were listed at top moments by outlets like NBC, Fox News, and The New York Times. For example, both NBC and The New York Times highlighted Trumps remarks about Iraq, particularly when he attributed the creation of ISIS to Clinton and President Obama.

This debate may also be unique in its ability to induce viral moments. In particular, we found that the majority of the potential viral moments identified through the time series occurred during discussions of scandals, including the Birther Conspiracy, Trumps tax returns, and Clintons email and server scandal. Importantly, these scandals were not simple horserace stories. Rather, each candidate highlighted the other's scandals to emphasize their opponent's untrustworthiness or incompetence. The presence of so many scandals prior to, during, and after the election, likely fed into the ability for this debate to produce viral moments compared to other debates. Future work can explore this further by comparing insults that "go viral" in a debate to insults that do not.

5.1   Limitation

As with any study, there are several ways in which this work can be improved upon. In particular, the time series ends just as the debate ends. It is therefore difficult to interpret viral moments that occur early or late in the debate. Future studies on debates should therefore expand their time series into post-debate discourse so as to more accurately observe viral moments late in the debate.

While we highlight the importance of virality in spreading content, our study also does not empirically test the number of viral tweets that are produced as a result of viral moments. Though such analysis is beyond the scope of what this data can provide, future studies with more network information (i.e., retweets of a tweet over time) can also explore this phenomenon.

The addition of other control variables, such as interruptions, topic shifts and non-verbal features, would provide additional context that could help further explain why some insults or scandals induce viral events compared to others. For example, it is possible that insults induce virality when they are accompanied by aggressive gestures. Future studies can build upon this research by incorporating such data.

Nevertheless, we feel this study provides a substantive contribution to our understanding of debates as planned media storms that generate viral moments with potentially long-lasting implications in a political election. Rather than treating outliers as data to discard (for the purposes of better modeling), our research highlights the need to study why outliers appear the way they do, and to align these findings with our fields understanding of the media ecosystem.

Acknowledgments

This work was supported by the Ministry of Education of the Republic of Korea and the National Research Foundation of Korea (NRF-2016S1A3A2925033).

References

Nick Anstead and Ben OLoughlin. 2011. The emerging viewertariat and bbc question time: Television debate and real-time commenting online. *The international journal of press/politics* 16(4):440–462.

Marco Toledo Bastos, Rafael Luis Galdini Raimundo, and Rodrigo Travitzki. 2013. Gatekeeping twitter: message diffusion in political hashtags. *Media, Culture & Society* 35(2):260–270.

Amber E Boydstun, Anne Hardy, and Stefaan Walgrave. 2014. Two faces of media attention: Media storm versus non-storm coverage. *Political Communication* 31(4):509–531.

Peter J Brockwell, Richard A Davis, and Matthew V Calder. 2002. *Introduction to time series and forecasting*, volume 2. Springer.

Eric P Bucy, Jordan Foley, Josephine Lukito, Larisa Doroshenko, Dhavan V Shah, Jon CW Pevehouse, and Chris Wells. 2019. Performing populism: Trump's transgressive style and the dynamics of twitter response. In *2019 International Communication Association conference*. ICA, pages 1–28.

Andrew Chadwick, Ben OLoughlin, and Cristian Vaccari. 2017. Why people dual screen political debates and why it matters for democratic engagement. *Journal of broadcasting & electronic media* 61(2):220–239.

Sarah E Culver and David H Papell. 1997. Is there a unit root in the inflation rate? evidence from sequential break and panel data models. *Journal of Applied Econometrics* 12(4):435–444.

Daniel Dayan and Elihu Katz. 1994. *Media events.* harvard University Press.

Scott Deerwester, Susan T Dumais, George W Furnas, Thomas K Landauer, and Richard Harshman. 1990. Indexing by latent semantic analysis. *Journal of the American society for information science* 41(6):391–407.

Nicholas A Diakopoulos and David A Shamma. 2010. Characterizing debate performance via aggregated twitter sentiment. In *Proceedings of the SIGCHI Conference on Human Factors in Computing Systems.* ACM, pages 1195–1198.

Deen Freelon and David Karpf. 2015. Of big birds and bayonets: Hybrid twitter interactivity in the 2012 presidential debates. *Information, Communication & Society* 18(4):390–406.

Kim L Fridkin, Patrick J Kenney, Sarah Allen Gershon, and Gina Serignese Woodall. 2008. Spinning debates: The impact of the news media's coverage of the final 2004 presidential debate. *The International Journal of Press/Politics* 13(1):29–51.

Kim L Fridkin, Patrick J Kenney, Sarah Allen Gershon, Karen Shafer, and Gina Serignese Woodall. 2007. Capturing the power of a campaign event: The 2004 presidential debate in tempe. *The Journal of Politics* 69(3):770–785.

John Haslett and Adrian E Raftery. 1989. Space-time modelling with long-memory dependence: Assessing ireland's wind power resource. *Journal of the Royal Statistical Society: Series C (Applied Statistics)* 38(1):1–21.

Liangjie Hong, Ovidiu Dan, and Brian D Davison. 2011. Predicting popular messages in twitter. In *Proceedings of the 20th international conference companion on World wide web.* ACM, pages 57–58.

Harold Hotelling. 1936. Relations between two sets of variates. *Biometrika* 28(3/4):321–377.

Javier López-de Lacalle. 2016. tsoutliers r package for detection of outliers in time series. *CRAN, R Package* .

Shannon C McGregor and Logan Molyneux. 2016. Twitters influence on news judgment: An experiment among journalists. *Journalism* page 1464884918802975.

Tomas Mikolov, Ilya Sutskever, Kai Chen, Greg S Corrado, and Jeff Dean. 2013. Distributed representations of words and phrases and their compositionality. In *Advances in neural information processing systems.* pages 3111–3119.

Ethan Pancer and Maxwell Poole. 2016. The popularity and virality of political social media: hashtags, mentions, and links predict likes and retweets of 2016 us presidential nominees tweets. *Social Influence* 11(4):259–270.

Jeffrey Pennington, Richard Socher, and Christopher Manning. 2014. Glove: Global vectors for word representation. In *Proceedings of the 2014 Conference on Empirical Methods in Natural Language Processing (EMNLP).* Association for Computational Linguistics, Doha, Qatar, pages 1532–1543. http://www.aclweb.org/anthology/D14-1162.

Philip Pond. 2016. Twitter time: A temporal analysis of tweet streams during televised political debate. *Television & New Media* 17(2):142–158.

Vinodkumar Prabhakaran, Ashima Arora, and Owen Rambow. 2014. Staying on topic: An indicator of power in political debates. In *Proceedings of the 2014 Conference on Empirical Methods in Natural Language Processing (EMNLP).* pages 1481–1486.

Prathusha K Sarma, Yingyu Liang, and William A Sethares. 2018. Domain adapted word embeddings for improved sentiment classification. *arXiv preprint arXiv:1805.04576* .

Steven Schirra, Huan Sun, and Frank Bentley. 2014. Together alone: motivations for live-tweeting a television series. In *Proceedings of the 32nd annual ACM conference on Human factors in computing systems.* ACM, pages 2441–2450.

Dhavan V Shah, Alex Hanna, Erik P Bucy, David S Lassen, Jack Van Thomme, Kristen Bialik, JungHwan Yang, and Jon CW Pevehouse. 2016. Dual screening during presidential debates: Political nonverbals and the volume and valence of online expression. *American Behavioral Scientist* 60(14):1816–1843.

Chenhao Tan, Hao Peng, and Noah A Smith. 2018. You are no jack kennedy: On media selection of highlights from presidential debates. In *Proceedings of the 2018 World Wide Web Conference on World Wide Web.* International World Wide Web Conferences Steering Committee, pages 945–954.

Stefaan Walgrave, Amber E Boydstun, Rens Vliegenthart, and Anne Hardy. 2017. The nonlinear effect of information on political attention: media storms and us congressional hearings. *Political Communication* 34(4):548–570.

6 Supplemental Material

n	Word	Δ L2 distance
1	nothing	61.44
2	high	41.52
3	well	38.51
4	back	37.39
5	election	33.89
6	time	32.60
7	they	32.59
8	senator	31.87
9	also	31.73
10	prepare	30.50
11	drop	28.67
12	watching	28.04
13	movement	27.98
14	birth	27.84
15	business	27.40
16	literal	26.99
17	them	26.87
18	hurtful	25.41
19	issue	25.00
20	there	24.94

Table 4: Words with the greatest l2 distance difference between the pre-viral and post-viral moment for Clinton's Viral Moment 3

n	Word	Δ L2 distance
1	healing	43.71
2	wasn't	36.56
3	ever	30.48
4	take	29.96
5	much	29.13
6	born	28.77
7	lying	28.09
8	even	27.75
9	here	26.63
10	profil	26.37
11	years	26.25
12	first	26.03
13	produced	25.80
14	very	24.95
15	chicago	24.31
16	politicians	24.23
17	white	23.78
18	must	23.57
19	communities	23.41
20	vote	23.38

Table 6: Words with the greatest l2 distance difference between the pre-viral and post-viral moment for Trump's Viral Moment 3

n	Word	Δ L2 distance
1	paying	80.42
2	bubble	79.22
3	discurtir	75.57
4	smart	73.88
5	talk	71.58
6	Obama	69.45
7	federal	66.49
8	income	64.52
9	think	58.67
10	shit	57.66
11	rates	56.64
12	water	54.00
13	down	53.32
14	**ugly**	51.61
15	make	51.54
16	gold	51.42
17	need	51.41
18	interest	50.03
19	crook	48.75
20	tax	48.43

Table 5: Words with the greatest l2 distance difference between the pre-viral and post-viral moment for Trump's Viral Moment 1

n	Word	Δ L2 distance
1	iraq	103.84
2	wrong	100.95
3	internet	94.33
4	hacker	86.05
5	take	70.37
6	china	59.39
7	really	49.59
8	america	47.04
9	they	45.31
10	does	45.03
11	security	43.57
12	year	43.08
13	racial	42.96
14	talking	42.82
15	wants	41.49
16	very	38.46
17	better	37.95
18	even	37.48
19	russia	35.39
20	jacking	34.81

Table 7: Words with the greatest l2 distance difference between the pre-viral and post-viral moment for Trump's Viral Moment 4

Stance Classification, Outcome Prediction, and Impact Assessment: NLP Tasks for Studying Group Decision-Making

Elijah Mayfield and Alan W Black
Language Technologies Institute
Carnegie Mellon University
elijah@cmu.edu, awb@cs.cmu.edu

Abstract

In group decision-making, the nuanced process of conflict and resolution that leads to consensus formation is closely tied to the quality of decisions made. Behavioral scientists rarely have rich access to process variables, though, as unstructured discussion transcripts are difficult to analyze. Here, we define ways for NLP researchers to contribute to the study of groups and teams. We introduce three tasks alongside a large new corpus of over 400,000 group debates on Wikipedia. We describe the tasks and their importance, then provide baselines showing that BERT contextualized word embeddings consistently outperform other language representations.

1 Introduction

In the study of groups and teams, measuring discussion quality - plainly, what makes a group debate *good*? - is an open research area. Controlled behavioral studies have shown, for instance, that creativity, diversity, and conflict have major roles to play in the quality of teamwork (Caruso and Williams Woolley, 2008). But the value of diverse discussion and open conflict is complicated, with a long history of positive, negative, and null results, depending on the narrow construct being studied (Jehn et al., 1999). What is clear is that the particulars of how teams are composed and how teammates interact with each other matters a great deal for effective group work (Milliken et al., 2003; Kozlowski and Ilgen, 2006).

In behavioral science, questions are often explored through structured equation modeling and multivariate regressions, allowing behavior scientists sophisticated control over exogenous (fixed, external) variables, like demographics and task conditions, as well as *process* variables that describe observable behaviors in the groups being studied (Cheung and Lau, 2008). Reducing team dynamics from text transcripts to quantitative process variables is computationally complex; in practice, text data is often ignored in favor of proxies like count statistics or, more frequently, participant survey responses (Beal et al., 2003).

These proxies are reliable and effective as stand-ins, but put a limit on the types of questions that can be asked. Scientists studying teams may wish to evaluate which voices truly influenced a conversation, gauge the diversity of people or ideas represented in those influential roles, and measure observed conflicts and consensus-building. They may also want to assess whether any particular participant impacted the discussion and use these variables in aggregate to find which processes impact quality. This data is difficult to extract from discussion transcripts.

Of course, large-scale corpus analysis is common in natural language processing, with many efficient representations of the complex underlying meaning of texts. In this work, we use these methods in the domain of group decision-making research, with three tasks for studying groups:

- **Stance[1] classification**, a fine-grained, fully supervised classification task for individual contributions to a discussion.

- **Outcome prediction**, a distantly supervised task requiring far less annotated training data for new domains.

- **Individual impact assessment**, an unsupervised extension of outcome prediction to quantify how individual contributions or users influenced debate.

In the rest of this work, we demonstrate that these tasks are tractable for NLP researchers to-

---

[1] In other fields, the term "preference" is often used where NLP researchers would say "stance." Throughout this work, we use these terms mostly interchangeably.

Proceedings of the Third Workshop on Natural Language Processing and Computational Social Science, pages 65–77
Minneapolis, Minnesota, June 6, 2019. ©2019 Association for Computational Linguistics

day, especially with modern language representations like BERT (Devlin et al., 2018). This contextual representation is highly accurate in both supervised tasks and produces interpretable results for the unsupervised task, suggesting it is ready for immediate application in social science research. Alongside these results, we also introduce a real-world corpus of over 423,000 debates from Wikipedia, preprocessed and released under an open source license.

2 Background

2.1 Prior Work on Groups

Group discussion data is commonly used in NLP research. Datasets include the multiparty in-person group work of the AMI meeting corpus (McCowan et al., 2005) and the pair task-based dialogues in the MapTask corpora (Anderson et al., 1991; Bard et al., 1996). A range of core tasks have improved based on these corpora, including diarization (Anguera et al., 2012), laughter detection (Petridis and Pantic, 2008), and summarization (Riedhammer et al., 2010). In online contexts, group debates have been analyzed for tasks like argument mining (Mao et al., 2014) and stance classification (Sobhani et al., 2015), among others.

Outside of NLP venues, though, most studies of groups and organizations do not perform sophisticated text mining or analysis. Methods vary; some research focuses on fuzzy logic or economic agent modeling (see Pérez et al. (2018) for a recent systematic review), while others focus on social factors, network analysis, and the interactive aspects of teams (see Levine et al. (1993); Hackman (2011)). Here we do not address open-ended discussions, focusing on task-based debates where multiple people participate, a fixed set of options are available, and there is no gold standard "correct" answer (in social psychology, "Decision-Making Tasks," from McGrath (1984)).

In these tasks, dysfunction leads to poor outcomes. Low-quality group discussion can focus on already-shared knowledge, rather than new problem solving; high-performing groups by contrast have specific characteristics like shared values, mental models, and communication styles, and nuanced patterns of conflict and consensus-building (Stasser and Titus, 1985). But getting at these patterns quantitatively is complex - most social science research instead avoids the question of extracting structure directly from text, in-stead relying on direct observable variables and survey data (Jehn et al., 1999), or simulation with explicit preferences encoded in modeled agents (Chiclana et al., 2013). In most work on group decision-making (with the notable exception of some collaborative learning settings, see Rosé et al. (2008)), automated discourse analysis is rare.

2.2 Prior Work on Wikipedia

We situate our study in a corpus of Wikipedia data. Ours is far from the first work in this domain, with hundreds of papers published over the last two decades (Mesgari et al., 2015). Large corpora of user discussions on Wikipedia have previously been collected for NLP (Prabhakaran and Rambow, 2016; Hua et al., 2018), though most study discussion in the general case rather than in decision-making contexts. We specifically study *Articles for Deletion* debates (hereafter, *AfD*). In this setting, editors nominate pages for debate that they believe should be removed from the wiki, and other editors debate whether to keep or delete the page. Other reviews of deletion discussions were published during Wikipedia's peak almost a decade ago (Taraborelli and Ciampaglia, 2010; Lam et al., 2010; Geiger and Ford, 2011); since then, only a handful of studies have evaluated this domain, mostly in the context of argument structure mining (Schneider et al., 2013). Since the most recent comprehensive study of *AfD* (Lam et al., 2011), available data has nearly tripled.

The challenges of maintaining good discussion quality are directly applicable to Wikipedia. The health of production communities online requires good working conditions for users, who are volunteers (Halfaker et al., 2011); however, many attempts at improving experiences actually *decrease* productivity and retention (Schneider et al., 2014). The *AfD* process is not amenable to automation or algorithmic decision-making[2]; instead, it is the process itself and the quality of interactions that must be prioritized and improved over time. Better metrics for teamwork could therefore have an immediate effect on the site's policy and practice.

3 Context and Data

When a page is nominated to *AfD*, a group decision-making task begins. Any user (including unregistered users, provided they sign their

---

[2]Halfaker, personal communication.

Missed call [edit]

Missed call (edit | talk | history | links | watch | logs | views) -- (View log)

Seems to fail WP:NOT, is essentially social commentary and no references are given for the major assertions presented. Orderinchaos 09:13, 2 October 2007 (UTC)

- **Delete** Just a junk article, not notable. Jmlk17 09:52, 2 October 2007 (UTC)
- **Keep**. I don't know guys, this thing is very prevalent in our culture. See [1]. I don't know for other cultures though. --Lenticel (talk) 10:18, 2 October 2007 (UTC)
  - Could possibly be mentioned in an article on Telecommunications in India? Twenty Years 15:50, 6 October 2007 (UTC)
    - Philippines is not India.--Lenticel (talk) 00:35, 8 October 2007 (UTC)
- **Keep** as above. I don't see why we should not keep this. .. Elmao 10:23, 2 October 2007 (UTC)
- **Keep**, I added enough links to merit inclusion. it is not just a social commentary, it is a business, revenue and profit headache too. the apex body of indian telecom operators, coai has even instituted studies for tracking revenue loss. pls revisit the article to see the new links. Ankur Jain 12:23, 2 October 2007 (UTC)
  - **Comment:** hate to add this, but i believe there is a distinct anglo-american bias to article editing. just because you guys don't know about the widespread use of this thing, probably never having visited india or africa etc., that does not mean it does not exist. there is world beyond your countries.Ankur Jain 12:26, 2 October 2007 (UTC)
- **Delete** Generally, this sort of thing should be merged into another article. But, the lack of any sort of encyclopedic information seems to deter me from posting a merge. Some here have argued that its a business/profit making machine, if so, its lack of coverage certainly proves it, if some are to be found, this could easily be merged into telecommunications, as it wouldnt exactly merit an article on its own. If its prevalent in one culture, then woopdy-do, add it to the telecommunications article. Long story short: Its junk. Twenty Years 15:48, 6 October 2007 (UTC)
  - It is prevalent in more than one culture (not a good merge into India article alone) and just because it isn't notable in your country it is considered junk. --Lenticel (talk) 00:24, 8 October 2007 (UTC)

Figure 1: Excerpt from a single AfD discussion, with a nominating statement, five votes, and four comments displayed. Votes labeled in **"bold"** are explicit preferences (or stances), which are masked in our tasks.

post with an IP address) can participate, providing either votes or comments. Votes are public, signed, and timestamped; they contain a labeled stance followed by a rationale for why they believe an article should be kept or removed from the wiki. Non-voting *comments*, either in direct reply to the nomination, a vote, or other comments, contain only rationales and not labeled preferences. The structure of these votes and comments follows the standard "reply tree" model of online forums (Aragón et al., 2017).

After nomination, discussions are held open for at least seven days[3]. Discussions are then closed by an administrator, who determines the discussion outcome. While this is not a popular vote, administrators rarely deviate from group consensus. Administrators may also "re-list" debates to hold another seven days of discussion, or close discussions with a verdict of `No consensus`. When that happens, articles are kept by default.

Figure 1 gives an example of how these dynamics play out in practice for the article *"Missed Call."* The nominating statement cites the *"Wikipedia is not a dictionary"* policy and lack of sources to open the debate:

> **Orderinchaos** (nomination): *Seems to fail WP:NOT, is essentially social commentary and no references are given for the major assertions presented.*

This statement is followed by votes and comments, which also contain rationale texts. User preferences for `Delete` and `Keep` are given in **bold**, with some users voting to remove the page, some to keep, and discussion occurring through followup comments:

> **Jmlk** (voting for `Delete`): *"Just a junk article, not notable."*
>
> **Ankur Jain** (voting for `Keep`): *"I added enough links to merit inclusion"* .
>
> **Lenticel** (voting for `Keep`): *"this thing is very prevalent in our culture. See [1]."* .
>
> **Ankur Jain** (comment): *"just because you guys don't know about the widespread use of this thing, that does not mean it does not exist"*

After a long discussion and a total of eight votes and thirteen comments from ten total participants, the decision was made in favor of `Keep`.

3.1 Notation

For any discussion d, we say that it has length N corresponding to the number of contributions $[c_0, c_1, \ldots c_N]$, which are nominating statements, comments, or votes. Each contribution c_i has a corresponding tuple (u_i, t_i, r_i, l_i) representing extracted user, timestamp, rationale text, and stance label, respectively. In our corpus we provide two possible labeling schemes L, a 2-label case for binary classification (which we use), and a 5-label case for direct comparison with prior work like Lam et al. (2010):

$$L_2 = \{\texttt{Delete}, \texttt{Keep}\}$$

$$L_5 = \{\texttt{Delete}, \texttt{Keep}, \texttt{Merge}, \texttt{Redirect}, \texttt{Other}\}$$

In any discussion, the initial contribution c_0 is the nominating statement, which is assumed to have a preference $l_0 = \texttt{Delete}$. For comments, $l_i = \varnothing$. Table 1 gives distributions of these labels in our corpus; the two primary labels dominate. The largest difference between vote and outcome distributions is from `No consensus` results, which default to `Keep` in practice.

---

[3]Exceptions to this timeline exist and allow "speedy" resolution of discussions - for instance, libelous pages or plagiarism of copyrighted material.

Label	5-Label		2-Label	
	Vote	Final	Vote	Final
Delete	54.9	64.0	62.3	73.0
Keep	28.5	20.5	37.7	27.0
Merge	3.6	3.1		
Redirect	3.8	5.9		
Other	9.3	6.5		

Table 1: Distribution of preference labels in votes and final outcomes in our corpus.

3.2 Corpus and Experimental Details

We evaluate an offline database of all Articles for Deletion discussions[4]. The snapshot contains approximately 19 million pages. Over one third of the pages in the administrative `Wikipedia:` namespace are archives related to *AfD*. We include all data from January 1, 2005 to December 31, 2018. Prior to 2005, traffic was low and decision-making dynamics were erratic, while data from 2019 is (as yet) incomplete. This 14-year window includes over 423,000 discussions.

For all machine learning results, we train a logistic regression classifier implemented in Scikit-Learn (Pedregosa et al., 2011) with L2 regularization and the LIBLINEAR solver (Fan et al., 2008). Experiments represent average results of 10-fold cross-validation. All instances from a particular discussion appear in only one fold; there is never crossover from the same debate between train and test data. We report results on a randomized subset of 5% of the corpus, approximately 20,000 discussions. In preliminary evaluation, a 20x growth in training data increased computational resources beyond what is practical for social scientists, for model accuracy improvements of less than 1%; we exclude full analyses here but provide training splits (for potential future approaches that benefit from larger corpora) in the released data.

For further details on data release and corpus preprocessing, including how free-form preference labels were collapsed, see Appendix A.

3.3 Language Representations

We consider three representations of language. First, we extract standard binary unigram bag-of-words features $\phi_{BoW}(c)$. These were the standard representation of text data for decades and are still in widespread use (Jurafsky and Martin, 2014).

Bag-of-words models struggle in classification tasks for short texts, where sparsity is a significant problem. The most effective recent solution to this has been word *embeddings*, where words are represented not as a single feature but as dense vectors learned from large unsupervised corpora. This allows similar words to have approximately similar representations, and effectively manages sparsity. In our experiments we test a widely-used and effective word embedding model, GloVe (Pennington et al., 2014), set to the maximum of 300 dimensions and represented as $\phi_{GloVe}(c)$.

The newest word embedding models are *contextual*. Rather than encoding a word's semantics as a static high-dimensional vector, these models adjust the representation of words based on the words they appear near at classification time. This approach, combined with extensive pre-training, has led to improvements on numerous tasks. We use the most effective model to date, the $BERT_{BASE}$ model from Devlin et al. (2018) with 768-dimensional embeddings $\phi_{BERT}(c)$. This model was already trained on Wikipedia texts (and other sources), so we perform no fine-tuning[5].

4 Turn-Level Stance Classification

In most other collaborative team decision-making contexts, opinions are expressed but explicit stances are latent. Because of the unique format of Wikipedia discussions, those stances are easily extracted from '"**bolded**"' votes. We use this as a test case for building supervised classifiers which elicit participant stance based on their statements alone. All bolded text is masked from rationales and models must predict what vote is associated with a given rationale.

Similar tasks have been effective in labeling turns in prose text (see Wilson et al. (2005) and other work with their MPQA corpus), open-ended group dialogues (Stolcke et al., 2000; Mu et al., 2012), and in stance classification for more open-ended social media (Sobhani et al., 2015); here we apply the task to contributions in a structured group decision-making context.

Fundamentally this is a test of how closely the Wikipedia domain hews to other decision-making contexts. If rationales are *not* sufficient to predict

---

[4]From the January 1, 2019 snapshot
`dumps.wikimedia.org/enwiki/20180701`

[5]This may mean text from our corpus is included in $BERT_{BASE}$ training data, causing a minuscule exposure to test data in our experimental setup; we do not investigate this question here, but note it as a complicating factor.

Representation	Accuracy	
	%	κ
Majority Class	63.8	0.00
GloVe	76.0	0.45
Bag-of-Words	81.8	0.59
BERT	82.0	0.60

Table 2: Accuracy of stance classification models for individual contributions, based on rationale text alone.

stances accurately, it means one of two things. Either rationales do not carry information about user preferences, and so are not comparable to group decision-making in contexts where those preferences are not explicitly labeled with votes; or the rationales do carry this information, but they are not tractable with current NLP methods. To evaluate this, we define a task to label each vote in each *AfD* discussion:

- **Possible Labels:** $L = \{\texttt{Delete}, \texttt{Keep}\}$

- **Input:** Rationale text r_i from a single vote.

- **Features:** A representation vector $\phi(c_i)$.

- **Output:** A predicted stance $l \in L$.

We exclude the problem of classifying stance in non-voting comments from our analysis, as no gold labels are available for supervised training. Expansion to distant supervision, where user stances from votes are used as gold labels for that user's comments, is a possibility for future work.

4.1 Results

User stances are explicitly given by users in the original corpus and there is no ambiguity; the upper bound for this task is 100% accuracy and $\kappa = 1.0$. Individual votes or comments have short rationales, however, typically only a sentence or a few words. Despite this, n-gram models provide a robust baseline, and while the BERT model outperforms a unigram baseline, the difference is small. Comparing embeddings, the newer contextualized BERT model outperforms GloVe by more than 6% absolute and 10% relative. Overall, we find that this task is tractable, with good accuracy.

5 Discussion-Level Outcome Prediction

The prior task is a useful proof-of-concept that text rationales carry recognizable stance information and can be reliably recognized. With that being said, the task has limitations for practical use in other group decision-making research. Foremost, it requires training data with labeled votes; this is difficult to get in many cases. Moreover, the stances of individual votes in a discussion are too granular for process variables that aim to represent discussion dynamics overall.

A more relevant goal for social scientists is analysis of group discussions where the preferences of individuals are *unlabeled*, even in training data. Next, we aim to predict the consensus preference of a group, after discussion. This task measures whether language representations can model the many turns in a discussion and mimic the behavior of administrators. To do this, we give as input the rationale texts of nominations, votes, and comments throughout a discussion, and treat the label from administrative closure of a debate as the *only* supervised label of group consensus.

- **Possible Labels**: $L = \{\texttt{Delete}, \texttt{Keep}\}$

- **Input**: Discussion d, with nomination c_0, followed by votes and comments $c_1 \dots c_N$. Each contribution c_i consists of:
    - User ID u_i.
    - Timestamp t_i.
    - Rationale text r_i.
    - Stance label $l_i \in L$, or for comments, $l = \varnothing$. In experiments other than our gold-label comparison, l_i is masked.

- **Features:** A representation vector $\phi(d)$.

- **Output**: An outcome label $l \in L$.

For our embedding representations, we again extract features ϕ_{GloVe} and ϕ_{BERT}, but in this case there is a need to combine vectors from multiple contributions $[c_0, c_1, \dots c_N]$ into a single vector for discussion d. To do so, we encode each contribution's rationale r_i separately (again removing all occurrences of **"bolded"** text to mask votes). We then average each contribution's vector, normalized for length:

$$\phi(d) = \frac{\sum_{i=0}^{N} \frac{\phi(c_i)}{\ln(len(r_i))}}{N}$$

Unlike in the first task, outcome prediction is distantly supervised and the task is sometimes undecidable; as discussed previously, administrators occasionally close conversations with results of

Representation	Final		Real-Time	
	%	κ	%	κ
Majority Class	74.0	0.00	62.1	0.00
GloVe	81.7	0.49	69.1	0.31
Bag-of-Words	84.2	0.58	72.4	0.39
BERT	85.8	0.62	73.4	0.41
Gold Inputs	93.5	0.83	79.7	0.55

Table 3: Accuracy of outcome prediction models, for full discussions and in real-time predictions.

No consensus. To evaluate an upper bound on model accuracy with masked preferences, we include a gold feature vector $\phi^*(d)$ where gold-standard user preference labels *are* made available for modeling. Specifically, for each possible $l \in L$, this vector includes the raw count and percent of votes that label received. While Wikipedia is not a direct democracy, administrators rarely deviate from consensus; this represents a good approximation of an upper bound on meaning representation from rationales alone.

As in the first task, we compare binary bag-of-words, GloVe, and BERT representations. We evaluate these models in two scenarios. First, we consider the case where we only predict outcomes after a full discussion has elapsed (**Final**). Second, we consider a just-in-time classifier that predicts the outcome separately after *each* contribution to the discussion (**Real-Time**). While training data includes only final discussions, N separate instances are generated for testing. As such, long discussions have more influence on reported accuracy. By extension, discussions resulting in Keep are also over-weighted, as they tend to have more contributions.

5.1 Results

Table 3 shows our comparison of models. As expected, the model given access to stances of group members is highly accurate. That model is able to predict outcomes with a Cohen's $\kappa = 0.84$ for full discussions. The BERT model also reaches good levels of agreement, outperforming other language representations by at least 1.6% absolute. In the real-time evaluation, GloVe and bag-of-words models are more competitive, but BERT maintains the highest accuracy. All models (including the gold-standard) see significant performance degradation, suggesting that discussions are *not* foregone conclusions after early contribu-

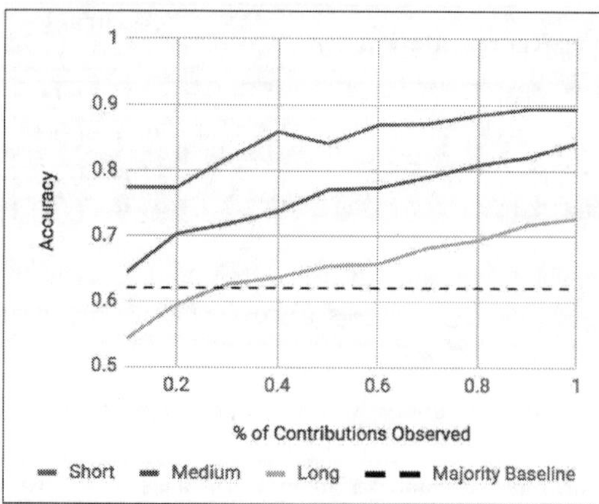

Figure 2: Real-Time BERT model accuracy mid-discussion, split by final debate length: short (5 or fewer), medium (6-10), and long (over 10).

tions. To demonstrate this more clearly, see Figure 2, where in conversations of any length, outcome prediction early in the debate is less reliable, then improves in accuracy steadily over time as more contributions are made visible to the classifier.

6 Assessing Individual Impact

The prior two tasks were important for understanding how participants use language, and whether preferences of an individual or group are revealed through rationale texts in a discussion. Next, we aim to provide more direct value to behavioral science research, by constructing a metric $Impact(u)$ to identify the primary sources of influence in these discussions.

Our definition of impact hinges on the idea that influential contributions immediately change the likely outcome of a debate. As the basis for this measurement we follow Chouldechova (2017). That work defined "disparate impact" as the difference in expected outcomes, given circumstances that differed by exactly one variable. We borrow this definition, and evaluate impact by varying only time; specifically, we measure the expected outcome of a discussion immediately before and after each contribution is posted[6]. To do so, we use the trained model from our outcome prediction task, in the real-time setting. For a discussion d at a timestamp t, this gives the expected outcome label l - represented as $\mathbb{E}(l|d, t)$, using

---

[6]For the special case of nominations ($i = 0$), for each possible $P(l)$, for $l \in L$, we instead subtract the baseline probability distribution of all outcomes $l \in L$ as measured from training data.

the model trained on BERT (ϕ_B). Thus:

$$\Delta(l, c_i) = \mathbb{E}(l|d, t_i) - \mathbb{E}(l|d, t_{i-1})$$

Probability movement in one label shifts that label upward, and another simultaneously downward, doubling the cumulative impact of changes; therefore, we sum the change in expected outcomes of all labels and introduce a normalizing factor of ½ to produce an impact value for each contribution ranging from [0,1].

$$Impact(c_i) = \frac{1}{2} \sum_{l \in L} |\Delta(l, c_i)|$$

Finally, we define impact for a user in a conversation as the sum of impacts of their contributions.

$$Impact(u) = \sum_{i=0}^{N} \begin{cases} Impact(c_i) & u_i = u \\ 0 & otherwise \end{cases}$$

This measurement of impact, based on probabilities learned from outcome prediction, again does *not* require any explicit labeling on the level of individuals or turns.

6.1 Evaluation

The prior two tasks were supervised, with labeled outcomes that could be measured for performance accuracy. Impact assessment has no specific ground truth to compare against. In this scenario, other NLP research has provided justifications for a mix of quantitative and qualitative evaluations, as well as validation with human annotators and evaluation based on performance improvement in downstream tasks (Louis and Nenkova, 2013; Yang, 2019). We present a mix of qualitative analysis and downstream tasks, while leaving room for future validation studies.

6.1.1 Application: Measuring Volatility

Wikipedia's cultural preference is for open debate and a willingness to voice contrasting views (discussions should be *"not a mere formality, but an integral part of writing the encyclopedia"*[7]). Using raw activity counts cannot measure this, partially because many contributors join late in discussions, mostly to voice agreement for foregone conclusion outcomes, a result of social rewards for editors who participate in more discussions and increase edit counts (Derthick et al., 2011).

To avoid reliance on counts, we define the volatility of a full discussion as the total amount of impact in that discussion, over all contributions:

$$Volatility(d) = \sum_{i=0}^{N} Impact(c_i)$$

We find that our this measure is effective in capturing highly contentious debates. As an illustration, the most volatile debate in our corpus was on the article[8], *"Justin Bieber on Twitter"*. This debate which resulted in nearly 100 votes and many more comments, an article rewrite, a followup deletion review (an appeals process meant to serve an oversight function for *AfD*), an extended external debate on Wikipedia's general purpose discussion board, and the establishment of prevailing policy thereafter for *"[X] on Twitter"* articles.

Other long debates with similarly large numbers of participants were given low volatility scores based on our outcome prediction metric. Upon inspection, these debates end with a string of repetitive votes, like *"**Delete. As per nom.**"* or *"**Delete. As above.**"* While these debates have high counting statistics, each late vote alters the expected outcome probabilities by well under 0.1%, and sometimes by less than $1 \times 10^{-5}\%$. This is an intuitive result, accurately reproducing the qualitative findings on behaviors from Derthick et al. (2011). Additionally, this means that more "talkative" users with many contributions do not necessarily make a greater impact, even though $Impact$ is a running sum rather than normalized by contribution count.

6.1.2 Application: Long-term Roles

We can also use outcome prediction to measure the role specific users play over time. By summing influence across all discussions, we find users who have had a disproportionate impact on the *AfD* process over Wikipedia's lifespan. Ranked highly, we find users like **TenPoundHammer** - a user influential enough to spawn an eponymous and well-cited policy essay[9], *"TenPoundHammer's Law."* The most impactful posts typically occur early in debates and are closely tied to policy (linked in double square brackets) and the broader context of Wikipedia's social norms.

---

[7]en.wikipedia.org/wiki/Wikipedia:
Dispute_resolution

[8]bit.ly/2FcSNY7
[9]en.wikipedia.org/wiki/Wikipedia:
TenPoundHammer%27s_Law

(voting for `Delete`) *"Unlikely redirect term, hasn't charted yet, the sources above only confirm that the single "will be" released and tell absolutely nothing else about it."*

(voting for `Keep`) *"I would think anyone who played the NFL for ten seasons is notable... [[WP:Notability (people)]] seems to suggest so."*

We can also evaluate *average* impact rather than cumulative. Here, we find users who are highly active and attentive to new debates, participating early in discussions. Our definition does not encode time explicitly, but in practice early contributions have a larger impact. This is particularly true for `Keep` votes to open debate, which are uniquely influential. Posting in favor of `Keep` immediately after a nomination influences probabilities by nearly three times as much as early `Delete` votes, and more than five times as much as votes that are the tenth or later contribution to a debate.

We can also find prolific users whose roles nevertheless do *not* had an impact on decision-making. User **Captain Raju**, for instance, is a highly active user primarily participating in administrative tasks like vandalism prevention and sorting, rather than voting. Despite frequent activity, their posts have an *Impact* measure of less than 2% on average. This matches the past finding of "mopping up" roles, which have high importance for the site and highly active users despite relatively low prestige (Burke and Kraut, 2008; Yang et al., 2017). The BERT-powered metric may therefore be useful for role identification.

Overall, our findings show that our $Impact(u)$ rating matches intuitions when given concrete examples, and is able to give interesting insights into group decision-making dynamics longitudinally and in specific circumstances.

7 Discussion

7.1 Opportunities for NLP

Our error analysis shows that on top of support for social sciences, the remaining errors in classification will only be resolved with improved NLP methods. For instance, in stance classification, there are some cases where individual contributions simply lack the content that is necessary to classify them accurately (e.g. *"Per all the above."*). These cases would benefit from a more detailed awareness of threads of conversation (Zhang et al., 2018). Even more often, classification errors occur when users *themselves* express uncertainty:

Final	ϕ	Short	Medium	Long
Delete	BERT	92.9	85.6	74.7
	Gold	97.3	92.9	85.4
		(-4.4)	(-7.3)	(-10.7)
Keep	BERT	71.9	80.6	75.0
	Gold	91.8	92.2	85.3
		(-19.9)	(-11.6)	(-10.3)

Table 4: Accuracy of outcome prediction, split by final outcome and total debate length (as in Figure 2).

(voting for `Delete`) *"[...] as I said, I am not really qualified to assess these sources in a deeper way, other than to indicate their existence, and "apparent" reliability under our usual sourcing guidelines."*

Instances like these require not just classification for stance but also for uncertainty (Forbes-Riley and Litman, 2011). Multi-task learning is a particularly fruitful domain for neural methods and the public release of our full corpus should be a resource for development of that field.

In outcome prediction, we find that text models underperform the gold-labels model when predicting an outcome of `Keep`, particularly for short debates. As seen in Table 4, when predicting `Delete` in short discussions, the BERT model is almost always accurate; as conversations grow, `Delete` predictions become less reliable, at just over 75% for debates longer than 10 contributions.

By contrast, when BERT predicts `Keep` it becomes *more* accurate as conversations grow. In short discussions where the final outcome was `Keep`, performance is at its worst, with a gap in accuracy over 22% compared to the gold model. In conjunction with our $Impact$ metric evaluation, this suggests that there is significant opportunity to better identify *persuasive* early `Keep` votes, which are elusive in existing representations.

Further technological advances may also focus on recognizing short discussions that *ought* to be enhanced with additional evidence, either through intelligent routing to potential participants or direct intervention with relevant content. When the outcome prediction expects a `Keep` decision and few users have participated, there is an opportunity for the gap in debate to be filled with decision support aids showcasing the potential of NLP.

7.2 Further Validation of Impact Measures

Our work evaluating impact as a metric, using downstream interpretation tasks as a measure of success, is preliminary. Prior work in the NLP community has developed evaluation metrics hand-in-hand with human input, aiming for high correlation with their judgments (cf. Papineni et al. (2002); Banerjee and Lavie (2005) in machine translation, and Lin (2004) in summarization). This is a natural next step for this work.

Once validated, impact assessment has immediate applications. Distinguishing the impact of individuals will enable deeper process analysis of the impact of diversity on teams (Bear and Williams Woolley, 2011), the interplay between individual participants and the process of resolving conflicts or disputes (Jehn et al., 1999), and the granular habits that lead to effective outcomes. These habits are often process-oriented, small-scale, and not adequately captured by survey or demographic variables (Riedl and Williams Woolley, 2017), opening exciting new dimensions for behavioral science research.

References

Anne H Anderson, Miles Bader, Ellen Gurman Bard, Elizabeth Boyle, Gwyneth Doherty, Simon Garrod, Stephen Isard, Jacqueline Kowtko, Jan McAllister, Jim Miller, et al. 1991. The hcrc map task corpus. *Language and speech*, 34(4):351–366.

Xavier Anguera, Simon Bozonnet, Nicholas Evans, Corinne Fredouille, Gerald Friedland, and Oriol Vinyals. 2012. Speaker diarization: A review of recent research. *IEEE Transactions on Audio, Speech, and Language Processing*, 20(2):356–370.

Pablo Aragón, Vicenç Gómez, David García, and Andreas Kaltenbrunner. 2017. Generative models of online discussion threads: state of the art and research challenges. *Journal of Internet Services and Applications*, 8(1):15.

Satanjeev Banerjee and Alon Lavie. 2005. Meteor: An automatic metric for mt evaluation with improved correlation with human judgments. In *Proceedings of the acl workshop on intrinsic and extrinsic evaluation measures for machine translation and/or summarization*, pages 65–72.

Ellen Gurman Bard, Catherine Sotillo, Anne H Anderson, Henry S Thompson, and Martin M Taylor. 1996. The dciem map task corpus: Spontaneous dialogue under sleep deprivation and drug treatment. *Speech Communication*, 20(1-2):71–84.

Daniel J Beal, Robin R Cohen, Michael J Burke, and Christy L McLendon. 2003. Cohesion and performance in groups: A meta-analytic clarification of construct relations. *Journal of applied psychology*, 88(6):989.

Julia B Bear and Anita Williams Woolley. 2011. The role of gender in team collaboration and performance. *Interdisciplinary science reviews*, 36(2):146–153.

Moira Burke and Robert Kraut. 2008. Mopping up: modeling wikipedia promotion decisions. In *Proceedings of the ACM conference on Computer supported cooperative work*, pages 27–36. ACM.

Heather M Caruso and Anita Williams Woolley. 2008. Harnessing the power of emergent interdependence to promote diverse team collaboration. In *Diversity and groups*, pages 245–266. Emerald Group Publishing Limited.

Gordon W Cheung and Rebecca S Lau. 2008. Testing mediation and suppression effects of latent variables: Bootstrapping with structural equation models. *Organizational research methods*, 11(2):296–325.

Francisco Chiclana, JM Tapia GarcíA, Maria Jose del Moral, and Enrique Herrera-Viedma. 2013. A statistical comparative study of different similarity measures of consensus in group decision making. *Information Sciences*, 221:110–123.

Alexandra Chouldechova. 2017. Fair prediction with disparate impact: A study of bias in recidivism prediction instruments. *Big data*, 5(2):153–163.

Katie Derthick, Patrick Tsao, Travis Kriplean, Alan Borning, Mark Zachry, and David W McDonald. 2011. Collaborative sensemaking during admin permission granting in wikipedia. In *International Conference on Online Communities and Social Computing*, pages 100–109. Springer.

Jacob Devlin, Ming-Wei Chang, Kenton Lee, and Kristina Toutanova. 2018. Bert: Pre-training of deep bidirectional transformers for language understanding. *arXiv preprint arXiv:1810.04805*.

Rong-En Fan, Kai-Wei Chang, Cho-Jui Hsieh, Xiang-Rui Wang, and Chih-Jen Lin. 2008. Liblinear: A library for large linear classification. *Journal of machine learning research*, 9(Aug):1871–1874.

Kate Forbes-Riley and Diane Litman. 2011. Benefits and challenges of real-time uncertainty detection and adaptation in a spoken dialogue computer tutor. *Speech Communication*, 53(9-10):1115–1136.

R Stuart Geiger and Heather Ford. 2011. Participation in wikipedia's article deletion processes. In *Proceedings of the 7th International Symposium on Wikis and Open Collaboration*, pages 201–202. ACM.

J Richard Hackman. 2011. *Collaborative intelligence: Using teams to solve hard problems*. Berrett-Koehler Publishers.

Aaron Halfaker, Aniket Kittur, and John Riedl. 2011. Don't bite the newbies: how reverts affect the quantity and quality of wikipedia work. In *Proceedings of the 7th international symposium on wikis and open collaboration*, pages 163–172. ACM.

Yiqing Hua, Cristian Danescu-Niculescu-Mizil, Dario Taraborelli, Nithum Thain, Jeffery Sorensen, and Lucas Dixon. 2018. Wikiconv: A corpus of the complete conversational history of a large online collaborative community. In *Proceedings of the 2018 Conference on Empirical Methods in Natural Language Processing*, pages 2818–2823. Association for Computational Linguistics.

Karen A Jehn, Gregory B Northcraft, and Margaret A Neale. 1999. Why differences make a difference: A field study of diversity, conflict and performance in workgroups. *Administrative science quarterly*, 44(4):741–763.

Dan Jurafsky and James H Martin. 2014. *Speech and language processing*, volume 3. Pearson London.

Steve WJ Kozlowski and Daniel R Ilgen. 2006. Enhancing the effectiveness of work groups and teams. *Psychological science in the public interest*, 7(3):77–124.

Shyong K Lam, Jawed Karim, and John Riedl. 2010. The effects of group composition on decision quality in a social production community. In *Proceedings of the 16th ACM international conference on Supporting group work*, pages 55–64. ACM.

Shyong K Lam, Anuradha Uduwage, Zhenhua Dong, Shilad Sen, David R Musicant, Loren Terveen, and John Riedl. 2011. Wp: clubhouse?: an exploration of wikipedia's gender imbalance. In *Proceedings of the 7th international symposium on Wikis and open collaboration*, pages 1–10. ACM.

John M Levine, Lauren B Resnick, and E Tory Higgins. 1993. Social foundations of cognition. *Annual review of psychology*, 44(1):585–612.

Chin-Yew Lin. 2004. Rouge: A package for automatic evaluation of summaries. In *Proc. of Workshop on Text Summarization Branches Out, Workshop at ACL 2004*.

Annie Louis and Ani Nenkova. 2013. Automatically assessing machine summary content without a gold standard. *Computational Linguistics*, 39(2):267–300.

Fiona Mao, Robert Mercer, and Lu Xiao. 2014. Extracting imperatives from wikipedia article for deletion discussions. In *Proceedings of the First Workshop on Argumentation Mining*, pages 106–107.

Iain McCowan, Jean Carletta, Wessel Kraaij, Simone Ashby, S Bourban, M Flynn, M Guillemot, Thomas Hain, J Kadlec, Vasilis Karaiskos, et al. 2005. The ami meeting corpus. In *Proceedings of the 5th International Conference on Methods and Techniques in Behavioral Research*, volume 88, page 100.

Joseph Edward McGrath. 1984. *Groups: Interaction and performance*, volume 14. Prentice-Hall Englewood Cliffs, NJ.

Mostafa Mesgari, Chitu Okoli, Mohamad Mehdi, Finn Årup Nielsen, and Arto Lanamäki. 2015. the sum of all human knowledge: A systematic review of scholarly research on the content of wikipedia. *Journal of the Association for Information Science and Technology*, 66(2):219–245.

Frances J Milliken, Caroline A Bartel, and Terri R Kurtzberg. 2003. Diversity and creativity in work groups. *Group creativity: Innovation through collaboration*, pages 32–62.

Jin Mu, Karsten Stegmann, Elijah Mayfield, Carolyn Rosé, and Frank Fischer. 2012. The acodea framework: Developing segmentation and classification schemes for fully automatic analysis of online discussions. *International journal of computer-supported collaborative learning*, 7(2):285–305.

Kishore Papineni, Salim Roukos, Todd Ward, and Wei-Jing Zhu. 2002. Bleu: a method for automatic evaluation of machine translation. In *Proceedings of the 40th annual meeting on association for computational linguistics*, pages 311–318. Association for Computational Linguistics.

Fabian Pedregosa, Gaël Varoquaux, Alexandre Gramfort, Vincent Michel, Bertrand Thirion, Olivier Grisel, Mathieu Blondel, Peter Prettenhofer, Ron Weiss, Vincent Dubourg, et al. 2011. Scikit-learn: Machine learning in python. *Journal of machine learning research*, 12(Oct):2825–2830.

Jeffrey Pennington, Richard Socher, and Christopher Manning. 2014. Glove: Global vectors for word representation. In *Proceedings of the 2014 conference on empirical methods in natural language processing (EMNLP)*, pages 1532–1543.

Ignacio J Pérez, Francisco Javier Cabrerizo, Sergio Alonso, YC Dong, Francisco Chiclana, and Enrique Herrera-Viedma. 2018. On dynamic consensus processes in group decision making problems. *Information Sciences*, 459:20–35.

Stavros Petridis and Maja Pantic. 2008. Audiovisual discrimination between laughter and speech. In *2008 IEEE International Conference on Acoustics, Speech and Signal Processing*, pages 5117–5120. IEEE.

Vinodkumar Prabhakaran and Owen Rambow. 2016. A corpus of wikipedia discussions: Over the years, with topic, power and gender labels. In *LREC*.

Korbinian Riedhammer, Benoit Favre, and Dilek Hakkani-Tür. 2010. Long story short–global unsupervised models for keyphrase based meeting summarization. *Speech Communication*, 52(10):801–815.

Christoph Riedl and Anita Williams Woolley. 2017. Teams vs. crowds: A field test of the relative contribution of incentives, member ability, and emergent collaboration to crowd-based problem solving performance. *Academy of Management Discoveries*, 3(4):382–403.

Carolyn Rosé, Yi-Chia Wang, Yue Cui, Jaime Arguello, Karsten Stegmann, Armin Weinberger, and Frank Fischer. 2008. Analyzing collaborative learning processes automatically: Exploiting the advances of computational linguistics in computer-supported collaborative learning. *International journal of computer-supported collaborative learning*, 3(3):237–271.

Jodi Schneider, Bluma S Gelley, and Aaron Halfaker. 2014. Accept, decline, postpone: How newcomer productivity is reduced in english wikipedia by prepublication review. In *Proceedings of the international symposium on open collaboration*, page 26. ACM.

Jodi Schneider, Krystian Samp, Alexandre Passant, and Stefan Decker. 2013. Arguments about deletion: How experience improves the acceptability of arguments in ad-hoc online task groups. In *Proceedings of the 2013 conference on Computer supported cooperative work*, pages 1069–1080. ACM.

Parinaz Sobhani, Diana Inkpen, and Stan Matwin. 2015. From argumentation mining to stance classification. In *Proceedings of the 2nd Workshop on Argumentation Mining*, pages 67–77.

Garold Stasser and William Titus. 1985. Pooling of unshared information in group decision making: Biased information sampling during discussion. *Journal of personality and social psychology*, 48(6):1467.

Andreas Stolcke, Klaus Ries, Noah Coccaro, Elizabeth Shriberg, Rebecca Bates, Daniel Jurafsky, Paul Taylor, Rachel Martin, Carol Van Ess-Dykema, and Marie Meteer. 2000. Dialogue act modeling for automatic tagging and recognition of conversational speech. *Computational linguistics*, 26(3):339–373.

Dario Taraborelli and Giovanni Luca Ciampaglia. 2010. Beyond notability. collective deliberation on content inclusion in wikipedia. In *Self-Adaptive and Self-Organizing Systems Workshop (SASOW), 2010 Fourth IEEE International Conference on*, pages 122–125.

Theresa Wilson, Janyce Wiebe, and Paul Hoffmann. 2005. Recognizing contextual polarity in phrase-level sentiment analysis. In *Proceedings of Human Language Technology Conference and Conference on Empirical Methods in Natural Language Processing*.

Diyi Yang. 2019. *Computational Social Roles*. Ph.D. thesis, Carnegie Mellon University.

Diyi Yang, Aaron Halfaker, Robert Kraut, and Eduard Hovy. 2017. Identifying semantic edit intentions from revisions in wikipedia. In *Proceedings of the 2017 Conference on Empirical Methods in Natural Language Processing*, pages 2000–2010.

Justine Zhang, Danescu-Niculescu-Mizil, Christy Sauper, and Sean Taylor. 2018. Characterizing online public discussions through patterns of participant interactions. In *Proceedings of CSCW*.

A Appendix

A.1 Corpus Preprocessing

Compared to the broader internet, Wikipedia is simpler to preprocess due to the rigid formality of the archival process, the MediaWiki markup language, and enforced community standards. For most tasks, we are able to extract names, timestamps, and labels with only regular expressions.

Extracting Timestamps

AfD discussion norms require that all contributions are signed using a standard format, which includes the contributor's username or IP address and a timestamp in UTC format[10]. All lines following the outcome are checked for timestamps in Wikipedia standard format[11]:

```
\d\d:\d\d, \w+ \d+, 20\d\d (UTC)
```

Extracting outcomes

AfD discussions are archived in a specific format with only minor variation, and can be easily extracted for structured representation. We define a discussion as having an *outcome* if its archival page includes a header line with one of three fixed phrases (ignoring whitespace):

```
The result of the debate was [x]
The result was [x]

The result of this discussion was [x]
```

We save the captured string `[x]` as the debate outcome. When these lines are timestamped, we also log the user and timestamp of the outcome.

Extracting nominations, votes, and comments.

If a timestamped contribution appears at the top of the discussion, prior to any votes, it is treated as a *nomination*. These statements have become more common over time: while they occur in only 67% of nominations in 2005, they were rapidly adopted and are present in 98% of nominations since 2008[12].

Following the nominating statement, any timestamped line is captured as either a vote or a comment. We define votes as any timestamped line beginning with a bolded phrase, following Wikipedia convention for contributions:

```
* ```[y]'''
```

Posts beginning with one or more leading asterisks creates a bulleted, threaded discussion. Words or phrases surrounded with three apostrophes creates *'''**bolded**'''* text. The value of this bolded text `[y]` is captured and stored. If no bolded phrase is present, but the line is still signed and timestamped, that line is treated as a *comment*[13]. Lines with no timestamped signature are discarded.

Several alternative solutions to deletion exist; each maintains the content of the page while deleting the page itself. In the five-label case, `Merge` and `Redirect`, the two most common alternate outcomes, are represented separately in line with prior work; in the two-label case they are merged in with Delete. All other values are grouped together as `Other` in the five-label case[14]; in the two-label case they are merged in with `Keep`. Votes and outcomes of "Close", "Withdraw", and "Cancel" are treated as "Keep" outcomes as the page as well as its content is fully maintained. Copyright violations are treated as a "Delete" outcome, as the content is deleted as a result of the outcome. Any given vote or outcome is represented as a set that can contain zero or more normalized labels. Therefore, the probability of a vote for a particular label is not drawn from a distribution; probabilities of each label in L are disjoint.

Extracting users

For each nomination, outcome, vote, or comment, we log the user whose signature immediately appears before the timestamp, either with a MediaWiki link to their User page or their User Talk page:

```
[[User Talk:[z]
[[User:[z]
```

We extract `[z]` as a username and associate it with the nomination, outcome, vote, or comment where it was captured. When user signatures link to both User and User Talk pages and those usernames differ, the Talk page's username is prioritized.

---

[10]These signatures are highly formulaic and easy to extract, because they can be automatically generated by MediaWiki's ~~~~ shorthand. When users do not sign contributions, bots add them, along with a citation to the SIGNATURES policy.

[11]In regular expressions, \w matches any letter and \d can match any numeric character. A + suffix captures one or more consecutive characters of that type.

[12]Under present policy, omitting a nominating statement is an acceptable reason for "speedy" dismissal and default "Keep" outcome for an AfD nomination.

[13]Lines beginning with the bolded phrase **"Comment"** are also treated as comments. Lines beginning with **"Note"** are automatically generated, typically for categorizing discussions by topic, and are discarded. Lines with "Relist" bolded are administrative notes to keep the discussion open for longer than the typical seven days, and are also discarded.

[14]"Userfy", "Transwiki", "Move", and "Incubate"

A.2 Reproducibility

The public release of this corpus will include
designated fold assignments for reproducible results and future comparisons against baselines
on the 5% subset used in this work. We will
also include two formats for experimenting with
the full corpus: a 10-fold cross-validation split,
as well as a single train/validation/test split for
use with more resource-intensive classifiers, especially neural methods.

The library that we developed for producing
these variables is written in Python and compat-
ible with standard implementation of BERT and a
standard JSON format for representing group discussions.

A Sociolinguistic Study of Online Echo Chambers on Twitter

Nikita Duseja *
Computer Science and Engineering
Texas A&M University
nduseja@tamu.edu

Harsh Jhamtani *
School of Computer Science
Carnegie Mellon University
jharsh@cmu.edu

Abstract

Online social media platforms such as Facebook and Twitter are increasingly facing criticism for polarization of users. One particular aspect which has caught the attention of various critics is presence of users in echo chambers - a situation wherein users are exposed mostly to the opinions which are in sync with their own views. In this paper, we perform a socio-linguistic study by comparing the tweets of users in echo chambers with the tweets of users not in echo chambers with similar levels of polarity on a broad topic. Specifically, we carry out a comparative analysis of tweet structure, lexical choices, and focus issues, and provide possible explanations for the results.

1 Introduction

An echo chamber refers to a social phenomenon in which most of the content one receives in one's social media feed is heavily skewed toward one's own opinion, often defined in context of controversial political topics (Garimella et al., 2018). In social media environments, users are exposed to several polarized views on political topics. According to the selective exposure theory (Frey, 1986), individuals have a tendency to consume information from like minded individuals content and avoid contrasting perspectives. This leads to the existence of polarized segregated communities in social media, with resounding similar views. This can be concerning as such users are not exposed to alternate or opposing perspectives, which may adversely impact deliberative democratic processes.

In this work we carry out a comparative analysis of tweets from users in echo chambers versus tweets from users not in echo chambers. Specifically, we compare some properties pertaining to tweet structure, lexical choices, and top-

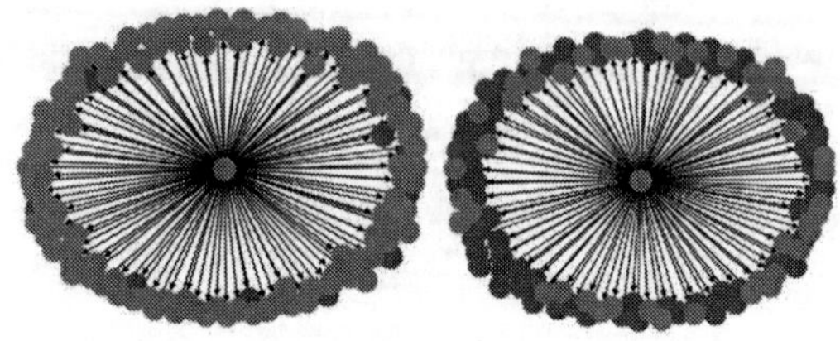

Figure 1: Visualizing user-followee network for a user in echo chamber (center of left sub-figure) and another user not in echo chamber (center of right sub-figure) on Twitter. A red circle represents a user with positive polarity scores for the topic *Obamacare*, while a blue circle represents a user with negative polarity scores. An arrow from x to y means that user x follows user y. A user in an echo chamber is exposed only to views very similar to his/her own opinions while a user not in an echo chamber witnesses opposing views as well. We focus on analyzing differences in tweets from the two types of users.

ics/attributes discussed in tweets. Table 1 summarizes some hypotheses of interest we framed to compare the tweets. To perform the analysis, we identify two sets of users with similar polarity levels on a topic, with one set of users being in echo chambers, while the other control set of users are not in echo chambers. We build on prior works (Garimella et al., 2018) to identify such sets of twitter users on topics such as Affordable Care Act (*Obamacare*), a comprehensive health care reform law that was enacted under the Obama administration. Figure 1 provides a pictorial overview of the network of a user in an echo chamber and another user not in an echo chamber.

There have been many recent works focusing on echo chambers in online social media (Garimella et al., 2018; Grömping, 2014; Barberá et al., 2015; Kwon et al., 2012). Many prior works point out presence of a large number of social media users in echo chambers (An et al., 2014; Bakshy et al., 2015; Lawrence et al., 2010). Our primary contribution is a comparative analysis of tweets from users in echo chambers versus users not in echo

---

* ND and HJ contributed equally for this paper

Proceedings of the Third Workshop on Natural Language Processing and Computational Social Science, pages 78–83
Minneapolis, Minnesota, June 6, 2019. ©2019 Association for Computational Linguistics

chambers. We build on work of Garimella et al. (2018), who focus on identifying users in echo chambers and characterizing various social network properties of such users. We believe our study can help in further characterizing and understanding online echo chambers, which may help in mitigating negative impacts associated with echo chambers.

2 Dataset

We use data from Garimella et al. (2018) who calculated polarity of twitter users towards topics such as *Obamacare* on twitter. The dataset contains polarities of users, as well as the user-follower graph for the same set of users.

We choose to work with *Obamacare* topic for the analysis in this paper. All the polarity scores of users are in the range $(-2.5, 2.5)$. A higher positive score represents more *conservative* viewpoint, while a more negative score represents a more *liberal* viewpoint (Garimella et al., 2018) (Not to be confused with sentiment towards the topic). In general, positive score users can be considered as *conservative* users, while negative score users can be considered as *liberal* users.

The dataset also consists of user-follower network in Twitter for the relevant set of users. We are mainly interested in finding the followees of users since a user is typically exposed to tweets and re-tweets of his/her followees in the social media feed.

2.1 Echo chambers

We consider following notation for a twitter user $u \in U$, where U is the set of all users under consideration.

- $S(u)$: Set of followees of u having same polarity as the user u

- $D(u)$ Set of followees of u having different polarity as the user u

To characterize an echo chamber, we define *Homophily score* $H(u)$ for a user u as follows:

$$H(u) = \frac{|S(u)| - |D(u)|}{|S(u)| + |D(u)|} \quad (1)$$

Thus, $H(u) \in (-1, 1)$ range (both inclusive). A score of $H(u) = 1$ means that all the followees of the user u have same polarity about the given topic as u himself/herself. This characterizes an

extreme case of being in an echo chamber. On the other hand, score close to 0 would suggest that the user has followees of both polarity, i.e they belong to classes on both sides of the spectrum in equal number. We define a threshold of θ_1 such that users with $H(u)$ above θ_1 are said to be in echo chamber **EC**. Users having $H(u) < \theta_2$ ($\theta_2 < \theta_1$) are said to not be in an echo chamber **NE**. We first report results for $\theta_1 = 0.9$, $\theta_2 = 0.7$, and later discuss the robustness to these choices.

$$EC = \{u : u \in U, H(u) \geq \theta_1\} \quad (2)$$
$$NE = \{u : u \in U, H(u) < \theta_2\} \quad (3)$$

3 Methodology

Our aim is to compare tweets from users in echo chambers against tweets of users not in echo chambers. Towards this end, we control for the polarity of the users, so that we could study any differences in nature of tweets which correlates with being in an echo chamber. Specifically, we restrict users to polarity range 0.5 to 1.5. We term users in this polarity region as *moderate conservatives* (MC).

We work with moderate conservatives and compare the tweets of users in echo chambers versus users not in echo chambers. Next, we filter to retain only those tweets which talk about *Obamacare* (the original data contains all tweets of users over a long time duration). This leaves us with 47,533 tweets for moderate conservatives in echo chambers **MC-EC**, and 35,820 tweets of moderate conservatives not in echo chamber **MC-NE**, talking about Obamacare.

Table 1 lists our main hypotheses which we test on the dataset. We use chi-squared tests for testing statistical significance while comparing counts of features. The chi-squared test (Greenwood and Nikulin, 1996) is used to determine whether a perceived association between two categorical variables is by chance or reflects a real association between these two variables in the data. It compares the observed frequency with expected frequency (expected assuming no correlation).

We perform some pre-processing on the tweet texts before conducting the experiments. We use Twitter tokenizer from NLTK (Bird et al., 2009) to tokenize the tweets. We retain the hashtags and URLs as they are needed in the experiments and analysis.

Type	Hypothesis	Holds in data?
Tweet-structure	MC-NE tweets are more likely than MC-EC to cite external resource	Yes
Tweet-structure	MC-EC tweets are more likely than MC-NE to contain hashtags	Yes
Vocabulary	MC-NE tweets are more likely than MC-EC to express uncertainty	Yes
Vocabulary	MC-NE tweets are more likely than MC-EC to use swear words	Yes
Topical	Certain topics are talked about more in MC-EC tweets and vice versa	Yes

Table 1: Summary of the hypotheses and the results. We carry out tweet structure analysis, vocabulary choice analysis, and a topic-level analysis, and observe significant difference in the tweets from the two types of users.

4 Experiments

In this section, we describe more details about the experiments and corresponding observations. We define three types of hypotheses: 1) Tweet Structure Analysis 2) Vocabulary Analysis 3) Topic Analysis.

4.1 Tweet structure analysis

Tweet structure analysis aims to uncover differences in tweets from the two types of users with regard to aspects like use of hash-tags, use of accompanying URLs, etc. Our first hypothesis is based on intuition that MC-EC users feel less compelled to cite an external resource while tweeting, as all the tweets in their feed already resonate with their own view-points. Our second hypothesis is that MC-EC tweets are more likely to contain hash-tags, as MC-EC users may more strongly believe in correctness of their own viewpoint, and may use more hash-tags with the intention to spread their strongly believed view-points.

4.1.1 Evidence / Link citing

Hypothesis: We hypothesize that users not in echo chamber may be more likely to tweet or re-tweet with citing external news link or other sources. This follows the general idea that users in an 'echo chamber' might feel less of a need to justify their claims or opinions as people (followees) around them *echo* with similar opinions.

Analysis: We perform the test using a chi-squared test. We first identify URLs using simple regular expressions. We notice that most of the urls were shortened URLs. We leverage python library BeautifulSoup (Richardson, 2007) to identify the expanded URLs, and then filter out any twitter URLs (since these often correspond to other user's status'). We observe that tweets from MC-NE users are much more likely to contain external URLs, which are often news or opinion pieces,

compared to users in echo chambers($p < 0.01$ as per chi-squared test). Specifically, about 35% tweets from MC-NE users had an external link while only about 19% of the tweets from MC-EC contained an external link.

4.1.2 Use of hashtag

Hypothesis: Hashtags are widely used in tweets, often to explicitly tag the tweet about being a specific topic or point, and are often used with the intention to spread messages or viewpoints. We hypothesize that MC-EC users' tweets are more likely to use hashtags.

Analysis: We explore the degree to which hashtags are used in tweets between the two types of users. We observe that our hypothesis holds in the dataset - tweets and re-tweets from MC-EC users are much more likely to contain hashtags($p < 0.01$ as per chi-squared test). Specifically, 45909 MC-EC tweets out of 47533 had at least one hashtag, while only 17097 MC-NE tweets out of 35820 had hashtags.

4.2 Vocabulary analysis

We inspect if being in an echo chamber is correlated with more/less usage of specific types of words. For example, MC-NE users are exposed to varying viewpoints, and therefore their vocabulary choice might reflect some uncertainty in views.

4.2.1 Words expressing uncertainty

Hypothesis: Since users in echo chambers are exposed only to opinions similar to theirs in the online media, they might show more certainty in their tweets. Similarly, users not in echo chambers are exposed to alternative views also in online social media, and as such may use uncertainty expressing words more frequently. We hypothesize that tweets from MC-NE users are more likely to contain uncertainty depicting words.

We use following list of uncertainty depicting words: 'may','might','perhaps', 'maybe/may-be', 'possibly', 'likely' .

Analysis: We test the hypothesis using chi-squared test and observe that the usage is more frequent in users outside of echo chambers ($p <$ 0.01). For example, word 'might' appears 238 times in MC-NE tweets, while occurs only 159 times in MC-EC tweets. Word 'may' appears 720 times in MC-NE, while occurs only 581 times in MC-EC.

4.2.2 Use of swear words

Hypothesis: We hypothesize that users not in echo chambers are more likely to express frustration through swear words on witnessing opposing viewpoints. We use the list of common English swear words [1]. We do expand the list to include commonly occurring variants. For example, *f**cking* is a commonly used word which would not have shown up on doing exact token match to *f**ck*. This expansion was done manually, as automatic lemmatization tools did not work satisfactorily. Improving swear word detection would be part of future work.

Analysis: We inspect the total count of swear words used in the two set of tweets. We observe that the proposed hypothesis holds in the data ($p <$ 0.01 using a chi-squared test). For example, word 'f**k' appears 41 times in MC-NE tweets, while occurs only 1 time in our set of MC-EC tweets. This analysis suggests that being in echo chamber is correlated with lesser use of swear words.

4.3 Topic analysis

We had filtered the tweets to be about the broad topic of Obamacare. In this analysis, we are interested in comparing the main (sub-)topics about Obamacare that are discussed in the two user groups. Towards this goal, we run a topic model on the set of tweets from each user group.

Hypothesis: We hypothesize that certain topics would be correlated with presence in echo chamber i.e. some topics would be talked about more in MC-EC tweets while certain other topics would be covered more in MC-NE tweets. We believe that presence in echo chambers might have an effect on the aspects of *Obamacare* that users are tweeting about.

Analysis: We run LDA (Latent Dirichlet Allocation) topic model to extract the topics for the combined set of tweets from both user types. LDA is a generative model, where each 'document' is supposed to have been generated using a multinomial distribution over the set of topics, and each word in the document can be thought of being generated from a topic picked up based on the drawn topic distribution for that document. Each topic itself is a multinomial distribution over the vocabulary of words.

Towards this end, we run the topic model for K number of topics on all the tweets i.e. tweets from MC-NE and MC-EC combined. We limit the vocabulary to 1000 most frequently occurring words in the dataset excluding the English stop words. The model approximates the multinomial distribution over vocabulary for each topic, and also computes the relative proportion of each topic for every *document* (tweet). For each of the two types of tweets (from MC-NE and MC-EC users), we compute an aggregated topic distribution for that type by summing the topic distribution vectors of corresponding tweets. This can be thought of summing up fractional counts of occurrence of topics, and this provides us with two topic occurrence pseudo-counts, one for each set of tweets.

For each topic, we test if it's pseudo count is significantly different between the two types of tweets. We experiment with $K = 10, 15, 20$, and observe that 11 (for $K = 20$), 6 (for $K = 10$) and 3 (for $K = 5$) topics had statistically significant different occurrence in the two sets of tweets ($p < 0.01$). For example, for $K = 20$, topic *future* ('time','year','watch','future') occurs much more in MC-EC tweets while topic *repeal* ('repeal','vote','repeal','senate') is present much more in MC-NE.

4.4 Sensitivity to homophily threshold parameters θ_1 and θ_2

Above experiments were reported for homophily thresholds $\theta_1 = 0.9, \theta_2 = 0.7$. These values were selected such that users with very high homophily scores are marked as being in echo chambers. We repeat the all the experiments with more sets of parameter values ($\theta_1 = 0.8, \theta_2 = 0.8$) and ($\theta_1 = 0.9, \theta_2 = 0.9$), and observe very sim-

---

[1] Available at `https://en.wiktionary.org/wiki/Category:English_swear_words`

ilar results, with all the tested hypotheses leading to same conclusions. This demonstrates that the analysis is robust to changes in these parameter values.

5 Discussions

Since we were interested in comparing the linguistic properties of the tweets from two types of users, we control for polarity levels, and select MC-EC and MC-NE sets of users. It is possible to extend the work on other such pairs of categories, such as ML-EC and ML-NE (ML: moderate liberals), and test the generality of the proposed hypotheses to other such groups. Moreover, we experiment with tweets on only one topic: Obamacare - it would be interesting to test the generalizability of the hypotheses to other data sets as well. Such extensions to the current work are part of future directions.

There are certain limitations of the current analysis. We did not take into account many network and content popularity effects. Moreover, we do not comment on any causality aspect: for example, does one's presence in an echo chamber makes one's tweet less likely to contain uncertainty depicting words, or if less polarized users are less likely to get trapped in an echo chamber. This remains an important possible future extension.

Related Work Garimella et al. (2018) propose methods to identify partisan and bipartisan users, and characterize such users based on network effect, profile information, and interaction actions such as retweets. We leverage their work and dataset to define echo chambers. However, our main focus is to do a linguistic comparison of tweets based on whether the tweet is from a user in an echo chamber or not.

Many prior works (Garimella et al., 2018) aim to study echo chambers in context of various network effects. Some prior works correlate retweet network with political ideology of the users (Barberá et al., 2015). Bakshy et al. (2015) study the consumption of online content generated by users of opposing views. Gilbert et al. (2009) conduct a comment based study on political blogs and find that, to a great extent, comments are in agreement with the views of the author of the blog. We on the other hand correlate some linguistic properties of tweets with presence in an online echo chamber.

6 Conclusion

We have carried out a comparison of tweets between moderate conservatives in echo chambers with moderate conservatives not in echo chambers, on the topic *Obamacare*. We carry out analysis at three different levels: tweet-structure level, topic level, and word-group level. We observe statistically significant difference in frequency of usage of uncertainty depicting words, hashtags, swear words, and external URL links, as well as a difference in the aspects of *Obamacare* talked about frequently between the two types of tweets. We also highlight possible future extensions to our work.

Acknowledgements

We are thankful to David R. Mortensen for insightful comments and discussions. We also acknowledge Lori Levin, Vidhisha Balachandran, Sanket V. Mehta, Kundan Krishna, and anonymous workshop reviewers for providing valuable feedback. We are thankful to Kiran Garimella for sharing dataset with us.

References

Jisun An, Daniele Quercia, Meeyoung Cha, Krishna Gummadi, and Jon Crowcroft. 2014. Sharing political news: the balancing act of intimacy and socialization in selective exposure. *EPJ Data Science*, 3(1):12.

Eytan Bakshy, Solomon Messing, and Lada A Adamic. 2015. Exposure to ideologically diverse news and opinion on facebook. *Science*, 348(6239):1130–1132.

Pablo Barberá, John T Jost, Jonathan Nagler, Joshua A Tucker, and Richard Bonneau. 2015. Tweeting from left to right: Is online political communication more than an echo chamber? *Psychological science*, 26(10):1531–1542.

Steven Bird, Ewan Klein, and Edward Loper. 2009. *Natural language processing with Python: analyzing text with the natural language toolkit.* " O'Reilly Media, Inc.".

Dieter Frey. 1986. Recent research on selective exposure to information. In *Advances in experimental social psychology*, volume 19, pages 41–80. Elsevier.

Kiran Garimella, Gianmarco De Francisci Morales, Aristides Gionis, and Michael Mathioudakis. 2018. Political discourse on social media: Echo chambers, gatekeepers, and the price of bipartisanship. In *Proceedings of the 2018 World Wide Web Conference on World Wide Web*, pages 913–922. International World Wide Web Conferences Steering Committee.

Eric Gilbert, Tony Bergstrom, and Karrie Karahalios. 2009. Blogs are echo chambers: Blogs are echo chambers. In *2009 42nd Hawaii International Conference on System Sciences*, pages 1–10. IEEE.

Priscilla E Greenwood and Michael S Nikulin. 1996. *A guide to chi-squared testing*, volume 280. John Wiley & Sons.

Max Grömping. 2014. echo chambers partisan facebook groups during the 2014 thai election. *Asia Pacific Media Educator*, 24(1):39–59.

K Hazel Kwon, Onook Oh, Manish Agrawal, and H Raghav Rao. 2012. Audience gatekeeping in the twitter service: An investigation of tweets about the 2009 gaza conflict. *AIS Transactions on Human-Computer Interaction*, 4(4):212–229.

Eric Lawrence, John Sides, and Henry Farrell. 2010. Self-segregation or deliberation? blog readership, participation, and polarization in american politics. *Perspectives on Politics*, 8(1):141–157.

Leonard Richardson. 2007. Beautiful soup documentation. *April*.

Uphill from here: Sentiment patterns in videos from left- and right-wing YouTube news channels

Felix Soldner[1], Justin Chun-ting Ho[2], Mykola Makhortykh[3],
Isabelle van der Vegt[1], Maximilian Mozes[1,4] and Bennett Kleinberg[1,3]

[1]University College London
[2]University of Edinburgh
[3]University of Amsterdam
[4]Technical University of Munich

[1]{felix.soldner, isabelle.vandervegt, bennett.kleinberg}@ucl.ac.uk

[2]justin.ho@ed.ac.uk, [3]m.makhortykh@uva.nl, [4]mozes@cs.tum.edu

Abstract

News consumption exhibits an increasing shift towards online sources, which bring platforms such as YouTube more into focus. Thus, the distribution of politically loaded news is easier, receives more attention, but also raises the concern of forming isolated ideological communities. Understanding how such news is communicated and received is becoming increasingly important. To expand our understanding in this domain, we apply a linguistic temporal trajectory analysis to analyze sentiment patterns in English-language videos from news channels on YouTube. We examine transcripts from videos distributed through eight channels with pro-left and pro-right political leanings. Using unsupervised clustering, we identify seven different sentiment patterns in the transcripts. We found that the use of two sentiment patterns differed significantly depending on political leaning. Furthermore, we used predictive models to examine how different sentiment patterns relate to video popularity and if they differ depending on the channel's political leaning. No clear relations between sentiment patterns and popularity were found. However, results indicate, that videos from pro-right news channels are more popular and that a negative sentiment further increases that popularity, when sentiments are averaged for each video.

Keywords: linguistic temporal trajectory analysis, online news, left-wing, right-wing, sentiment analysis, YouTube

1 Introduction

Today, news is increasingly consumed through online platforms. Approximately nine out of ten adults (93%) in the US acknowledge reading news online (Center, 2018); similar, if slightly lower rates, are observed for many European countries (e.g. 65% of Germany and 79% in the Netherlands) (Newman et al., 2018). The reasons for the growing online consumption of news are many: digital outlets provide higher interactivity and greater freedom of choice for news readers (Van Aelst et al., 2017), and the possibility to access them through mobile devices enables more flexibility and convenience in consuming news content (Schrøder, 2015).

Despite the multiple benefits associated with "the digital turn" in news consumption, it also raises concerns regarding possible changes in the societal role of news media (Coddington, 2015). It has been established that there is a relationship between news consumption and the formation of public agendas, including political attitudes of the general population (McCombs, 2014). However, the possible impact of digitalization on these relationships remains a subject of academic debate (Helberger, 2015; Eskens et al., 2017; Van Aelst et al., 2017). An increasing number of studies examine the possible connection between online news consumption and the formation of isolated ideological communities, which can nurture biases and limit citizens' societal participation (Gentzkow and Shapiro, 2011; Flaxman et al., 2016; Sunstein, 2017). Such formations can lead to increased political or personal radicalization, which is a concern for societal cohesion.

Polarization concerns related to audience segmentation are amplified by the use of affective language for producing online news stories (Soroka et al., 2015). Despite the widespread belief that news stories tend to use balanced and unbiased language, recent studies suggest that this is not necessarily true, in particular in the case of news stories crafted for online environments such as news websites (Young and Soroka, 2012). A number of studies suggest that the use of affective language can increase audience engagement with

Proceedings of the Third Workshop on Natural Language Processing and Computational Social Science, pages 84–93
Minneapolis, Minnesota, June 6, 2019. ©2019 Association for Computational Linguistics

news content (e.g. stories with a negative tone seem to be more popular (Trussler and Soroka, 2014; Soroka et al., 2015)). At the same time, the relationship between a narrative's popularity and the specific patterns of sentiment remains under-investigated, as well as the ways this relationship varies among audiences with different political leanings.

In this paper, we contribute to the debate on the use of emotionally loaded language in online news stories as well as its variations between outlets with different political leanings. Specifically, we examine the sentiment trajectories of YouTube news channels related to major English-language media outlets. Our interest in YouTube is attributed to the platform's significant impact on information consumption as users increasingly consume news in the video format (al Nashmi et al., 2017). Together with Facebook, YouTube is the main platform used by consumers to watch news outside of news organizations' own websites (Newman et al., 2018). News content produced by news organizations for YouTube usually follows traditional broadcast standards (Peer and Ksiazek, 2011) and formats (al Nashmi et al., 2017) and often serves as an extension of their distribution model. At the same, YouTube also enables experimenting with new formats and engaging audiences in more interactive or provocative ways (al Nashmi et al., 2017).

Using YouTube as a case platform, we test for differences in the dynamic use of sentiment in news coverage between channels leaning to the political left (e.g. CNN) and right (e.g. Fox News). Additionally, we examine if sentiment patterns have predictive value for news videos' popularity on YouTube.

2   Related Work

Since the mid 2000s, sentiment analysis remains one of the fastest growing fields of machine learning and computational linguistics (Mäntylä et al., 2018). Defined by Liu (2010) as a collection of methods for detecting and extracting subjective information (e.g. opinions, attitudes and emotions) from language, sentiment analysis is increasingly adopted for multiple academic areas, varying from from media studies (Sivek, 2018) to literature (Gao et al., 2016) to political science (Cambria, 2016) and conflict studies (Welch, 2018).

The growing adoption of sentiment analysis as a research tool is accompanied by methodological improvements. Originally employed for classifying user reviews coming from the commercial domain (Pang and Lee, 2008), early approaches to sentiment analysis were focused on producing a single sentiment score for the specific document or a text section using binary assessments of polarity. Such approaches, however, resulted in rather simplified evaluations, which reduced sentiment complexity to binary constructs under which the whole document could be either positive or negative or (in some cases) neutral. This can lead to incorrect conflations of sentiment variations within a text.

The response to these limitations included the advancement towards more fine-grained assessments of sentiment, including the identification of a more complex spectrum of emotions (Cambria et al., 2015), but also the transition towards the dynamic assessment of sentiment shifts throughout texts (Jockers, 2015; Tanveer et al., 2018; Kleinberg et al., 2018).

Until now, the sentiment of news stories remains a rather under-investigated subject. Kaya et al. (2012) note that unlike user reviews of products (e.g. movies), news stories are considered to be written in a neutral way. A different study found that news stories about the economy and the environment were overall more positive than about crime or international topics, which were overall more negative (Young and Soroka, 2012). Despite the growing number of studies on news sentiment, only a few of them so far approach it by considering the dynamic shifts of sentiment. A study, examining sentiments of different topics (e.g. earthquakes) included time stamps over a three months period, to model the sentimental change of news stories (Fukuhara et al., 2007). In that way, they were able to show a sudden increase of negative emotions in news corpora, when an earthquake occurred. These negative emotions slowly decreases over time. While this approach models sentiment change over time, it cannot account for shifts within single stories.

Among multiple areas of research on news story sentiment, the issue of variation in the use of affective language by news outlets with different political leanings (e.g. left- or right-wing) is both under-investigated and urgent. The language of politics-related texts does not only reflect, but can also influence the sentiments of the audience (Brader,

2005). A number of studies point to the distinct features of online political communication depending on the actors' political leaning (e.g. (Engesser et al., 2017; Bracciale and Martella, 2017; Hameleers et al., 2017; Schoonvelde et al., 2019a)). Engesser et al. (2017) identify that social media usage of right-wing political actors is characterized by the use of a few key features, such as emphasizing the sovereignty of the people, advocating for the people, attacking the elite, ostracizing others, and invoking the concept of a "heartland". Similarly, Bracciale and Martella (2017) show that communication styles of populist actors tend to involve highly emotional language and that they are particularly keen on referring to negative emotions (e.g. fear) to mobilize their supporters.

The studies mentioned above, however, focus on political statements produced and distributed through different media; yet, little is known how different political sentiments materialize in online news stories, in particular in the YouTube video format, which is the major focus of our study. A number of studies discuss the impact of news outlet ideological leanings on the way specific subjects are covered (de Vreese, 2005). Most of these works, however, tend to focus on traditional formats of news stories (i.e. text) and use qualitative approaches to examine coverage of a specific subject, such as climate change (Dotson et al., 2012; Feldman et al., 2012) or protest campaigns (Ha and Shin, 2016; Shahin et al., 2016). In our paper, we propose to look at the intra-textual dynamics of the overall sentiment of content produced by the outlet in question and employ a quantitative approach to trace if there are differences between right- and left-wing news outlets.

3 Method

The data used in this study are publicly available[1] and the current work is the joint product of a workshop on linguistic temporal trajectory analysis at the European Symposium Series on Societal Challenges in Computational Social Science in 2018. This includes the pre-processing and feature extraction[2] of the data, which is needed for the analyses we performed in the current study. The data has not been used in other research and was specifically collected to devise the current work.

3.1 News channels selection

The data consist of all English-language channels from the top 250 news channels on YouTube, which were ranked by SOCIAL-BLADE[3] (www.socialblade.com, retrieved November 2018). From that pool, 18 news channels were selected, which were identified as the ones holding political bias (i.e. either left- or right-wing) by Media Bias/Fact Check[4]. The website uses a rating method to identify biases among information sources and has been used by previous studies dealing with media bias (Bentley et al., 2019; Bovet and Makse, 2019; Mehta and Guzmán, 2018).

3.2 Obtaining video transcripts

Video transcripts were scraped with the help of "www.downsub.com", which retrieves the transcripts of specific YouTube video URLs, and the "beautifulsoup" python package (Richardson, 2019) (for more details see Kleinberg et al. (2018)). Downloaded transcripts were manually or automatically generated. Videos without transcripts were not included in further analyses. Retrieved transcripts were cleaned by removing XML tags and merged into one string, without punctuation for each video. Selected transcripts for further processing adhered to the following criteria: at least 100 words; at least 50% of words are matched English words; at least 90% of words are ASCII-encoded; and from channels with more than 2000 valid transcripts. Subsequently, for 4 left and 4 right channels (randomly selected) 2000 transcripts were selected, 7 non-English transcripts from Business Insider and Russian today were then excluded, resulting in a balanced dataset of 15993 transcripts (table 1).

3.3 Popularity rating

Since we are interested in the popularity rating of each video and its association to sentiment style, we created an adjusted popularity rating. We calculated a popularity index defined as the number of upvotes divided by the total views for each video, which would be a score between 0 (no upvotes) and 1 (upvotes is equal to views). The adjustment allows us to compare the popularity be-

---

tween videos, which have different upload dates, because videos available over a prolonged period of time have the advantage of accumulating more upvotes.

3.4 Feature extraction

The organizers of the workshop provided us with the necessary features for further analyses, who were inspired by Jockers (2015) and Gao et al. (2016); (for more details see Kleinberg et al. (2018)). Features were generated from the transcripts, which capture the sentiment change throughout the transcript. The applied method is based on the approach of the R package "sentimentr" (Rinker, 2019a), which generates sentiments on a sentence level, but the current approach extends it to continuous text without punctuation as is the case with video transcripts. The "naive context" sentiment extractor (Kleinberg et al., 2018) accounts for valence shifters, which influence the meaning of the sentiment. Negators (e.g., not, doesn't), [de-]amplifiers (e.g., really, hardly), and adversative conjunctions (e.g., but, however) were included. This is important when generating the sentiments for sentences like "I had a really good day" (amplifying "good" through "really") or "My day was not bad" (changing "bad" from a negative to a positive sentiment through "not"). In order to extract sentiment values, each word is assigned a sentiment value based on the "Jockers and Rinker Polarity Lookup Table" from the lexicon R package (Rinker, 2019b). For the extractions of the features a window approach is taken, by which the sentiment of the core word and its surrounding words of $+/-3$ are considered. This cluster of seven words is assigned an adjusted sentiment value by calculating the product of all the sentiment values in the cluster. The features are represented in vectors, containing zeros and weighted sentiment values. Theses values are standardized to a narrative time from 0 to 100, with a discrete cosine transformation from the "syuzhet" R package (Jockers, 2015) and scaled from -1 to $+1$ (i.e. lowest sentiment (negative) per transcript to highest sentiment (positive) per transcript).

4 Results

4.1 Data

The total data set consists of 15993 video transcripts, which are distributed between eight news channels, and are equally divided into political

Channel	Pol	N. of videos	Avg. wc
Al Jazeera English	Left	2000	1000.49
Business Insider	Left	1997	501.56
Fox news channel	Right	2000	777.85
MSNBC clean forward	Left	2000	1499.25
Russia today[5]	Right	1996	1422.71
The young turks	Left	2000	1504.59
The daily wire	Right	2000	4845.80
Rebel Media	Right	2000	1250.73

Table 1: YouTube news channels distribution; Pol = Political leaning; N. = number; wc = word count

leanings (table 1).

4.2 Clustering

In order to examine sentiment patterns within the YouTube videos and their predictive value on popularity, we examined whether overarching sentiment patterns are present. We used an unsupervised k-means clustering method and determined the number of k through the within cluster sum of squares inflexion method (Thorndike, 1953) for 1 to 30 clusters (figure 1). Following this, we used a k-means method with $k = 7$, which resulted in seven clusters, each representing a sentiment behavior pattern found in the transcripts. All the patterns are displayed in figure 1, showing the average sentiment trajectory for the adjusted timescale from 0 to 100, and sentiments from -1 (most negative) to $+1$ (most positive). The patterns correspond well with the patterns found in related work (Kleinberg et al., 2018). Thus, we assigned the corresponding taxonomy names to our patterns. The dotted blue line indicates the average behavior pattern for the cluster and the red lines indicate standard deviation of $+/-1$. Table 2 shows the taxonomies and descriptive statistics of the sentiment clusters.

4.3 Sentiment styles and political stance

We also examined whether there is a relationship between political stance and sentiment clusters. A significant association was found with a 2 (political stance) by seven (cluster) Chi-square test ($\chi^2(14) = 25.31, p < 0.001$). Table 3 shows that the cluster "Downhill from here" was significantly $p < 0.01$ more used by politically right leaning news channels. The reversed effect was observed for the cluster "Uphill from here", which

---

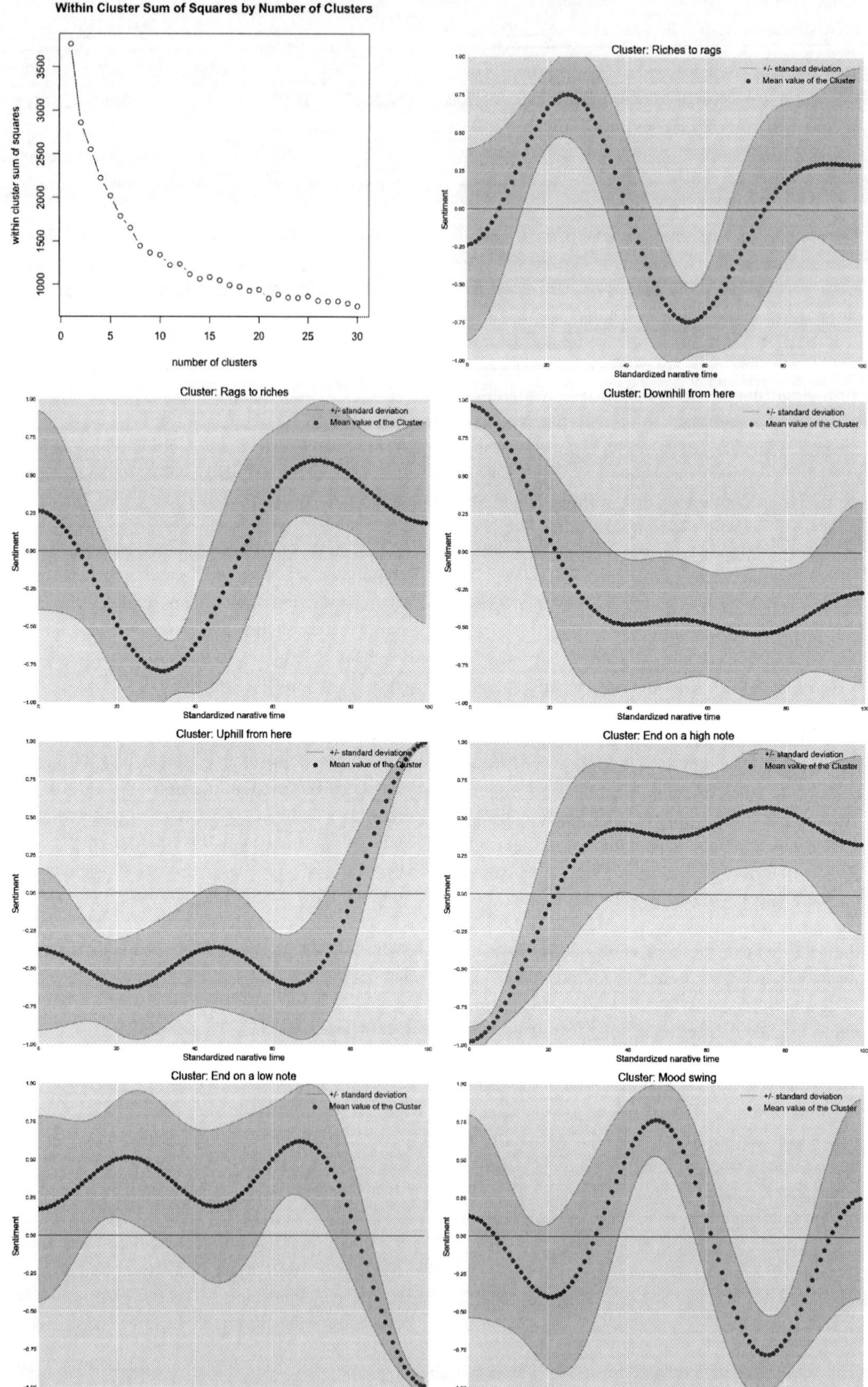

Figure 1: Cluster plot and sentiment behavior patterns for each cluster.

Cluster	Description	N. of videos	% of videos	Avg. vc	Avg. up v.
Rags to riches	Negative curve turns into positive curve	2675	16.73	827.00	15.53
Riches to rags	Positive curve turns into negative curve	2587	16.18	1002.47	17.11
Downhill from here	Short positive turns into consistent negative	2177	13.61	919.94	16.82
End on a high note	Short negative turns into consistent positive	2194	13.72	928.78	17.03
Uphill from here	Consistent negative turns into short positive	2085	13.04	823.17	14.37
End on a low note	Consistent positive turns into short negative	1547	9.67	846.80	16.81
Mood swing	Small positive start into negative-positive-negative curves with small positive ending	2728	17.06	910.83	16.57
Total	All	15993	100	897.71	16.32

Table 2: Sentiment styles taxonomy (adopted from Kleinberg et al. (2018)) and descriptive statistics; Average (Avg.) scores are adjusted by the number of days the videos were uploaded; N = Number; vc = view count; v = votes.

	Political leaning	
Cluster	Left	Right
Rags to riches	-0.96	0.96
Riches to rags	1.09	-1.09
Downhill from here	-3.25*	3.25*
End on a high note	1.28	-1.28
Uphill from here	2.74*	-2.74*
End on a low note	-2.44	2.44
Mood swing	1.13	-1.13

Table 3: Chi-Square residuals; * = statistically significant ($\alpha = 0.01$).

were used more often by politically left leaning news channels.

4.4 Sentiment clusters and popularity

To assess the relationship between the sentiment clusters and political orientations on popularity rating, we conducted three least square regression models in R with the "caret" package (Kuhn, 2008). The different sentiment clusters were the predictors for the adjusted popularity rating. We used the cluster "mood swing" as the reference category as it was closest to the overall average of the adjusted upvotes, all other clusters were treated as a separate dichotomous variable. Our first regression model included sentiment clusters, which consisted of all news channels. The second regression model included the channel as a fixed effect along with sentiment clusters. The analysis indicated that there was no significant difference in the adjusted popularity rating between the clusters in the second model; "Rags to riches" ($\beta = -1.28, se = 1.60, p = .42$), "Riches to rags" ($\beta = .47, se = 1.61, p = .77$), "Down hill from here" ($\beta = -1.25, se = 1.69, p = .46$), "End on a high note" ($\beta = .4, se = 1.69, p = .81$), "Up hill from her" ($\beta = -1.71, se = 1.71, p = .32$), "End on

a low note" ($\beta = .02, se = 1.87, p = .99$). Neither model explains a sufficient proportion of the variance to be considered informative, $R^2 = 0.00$ and $R^2 = 0.03$, for the first and second model, respectively.

We also split the transcripts in three equal sized components (beginning, middle, and end) and calculated the average sentiment rating for each part and used a OLS regression model to test for an effect of the components on the adjusted popularity ($F(10, 15982) = 52.46, p < .001, r^2 = 0.03$). No significant effects were found, after controlling for channel: "Beginning" ($\beta = -1.28, se = 1.02, p = .68$), "Middle" ($\beta = -1.65, se = -1.65, p = .11$), "End" ($\beta = -1.79, se = 1.09, p = .1$).

In addition we used an OLS regression model to test if the average sentiment score of each transcript and political leaning had an effect on the adjusted popularity ($F(3, 15989) = 1759, p < .001, r^2 = 0.248$). It seems that the model can account for 24% of the variance in adjusted popularity. The model exhibits a significant constant ($\beta = 0.013, se < 0.001, p < 0.001$), a significant main effect of political leaning (right) ($\beta = 0.021, se < 0.001, p < 0.001$), an insignificant main effect for average sentiment ($\beta = -0.0004, se = 0.001, p = 0.66$), and a significant interaction between average sentiment and political leaning (right) ($\beta = -0.003, se < 0.001, p = 0.034$). The model predicted adjusted popularity for left wing channel when average sentiment equals to zero is 0.013 and 0.013 + 0.02 = 0.033 for right wing channels. The slope of the regression line for the left wing channel is -0.0004 and -0.0004 - 0.003 = -0.0034 for right wing channels, suggesting that the effect of average sentiment is greater in magnitude for right wing than for left wing channels.

5 Discussion

In this study we examined sentiment patterns in news videos published on YouTube channels with different political leanings. Using sentiment trajectory analysis, we identified recurring patterns of sentiment changes, which were then grouped through k-means clustering into seven major categories of videos based on their sentiment patterns (e.g. "rags to riches" or "mood swings"). These patterns correspond to the ones identified in previous research on sentiment patterns of vloggers on YouTube (Kleinberg et al., 2018). While YouTube videos of vloggers and news channels differ in their domain, the persistence of similar sentiment clusters might indicate the presence of a few consistent sentiment styles that are shared between specific content domains and themes across YouTube. Future research could further examine whether similar patterns persist across various domains of YouTube content.

5.1 Sentiment pattern by political stance

Our results show, that political leanings seem to influence the usage of sentiment patterns: "Downhill from here" was used more often by pro-right news channels than by pro-left news channels, and conversely "Uphill from here" was used more often by pro-left news channels. It is interesting that both sentiment patterns exhibit the same proportion of negative and positive sentiment (80/20 respectively), but are different in sentiment order (see figure 1).

It is important to note that previous studies show that the sentiment of politics-related content, such as political ads, can affect the emotional state of the viewer (Brader, 2005). For the "Downhill from here" and "Uphill from here" patterns, viewers of pro-right news channels are left with a more negative sentiment and viewers of pro-left news channels are left with a more positive sentiment after watching the whole video.

At the same time, while some sentiment patterns seem to be more commonly used by channels with specific political leaning, it is difficult to propose a strong theoretical background which can explain this link. The complexity of this task is related to the large number of factors (both ideological, but also contextual) which can influence the use of language for political purposes (for a more detailed discussion see recent work on linguistic complexity of political speeches (Schoonvelde

et al., 2019b)).

Further research could examine the distribution of sentiment patterns between specific YouTube channels and investigate how factors, such as viewership or content influence them. This could include how pro-right/left channels differ in the amount of content creation for specific topics and how sentiment is used within this content. In addition, future work could examine if political leaning has predictive value on sentiment clusters for specific topics. This could be useful to ascertain whether news channels with a right or left political leaning discuss specific topics more often and differently than others and with what type of sentiment style.

5.2 Predicting video popularity through sentiment patterns

Our study indicated that sentiment patterns are weak predictors of news video popularity. A number of studies suggest that content-based features, in particular sentiment, have a strong impact on news content popularity (Trussler and Soroka, 2014; Soroka et al., 2015). However, our findings align with results of other studies that emphasize the importance of looking at a broader set of features, in particular contextual ones (e.g., the time of publication), for predicting the popularity of news content (Tatar et al., 2012; Keneshloo et al., 2016). Additionally, in the case of YouTube, the importance of other content-agnostic factors (e.g., the total views a channel received previously) for predicting the popularity of videos has been noted (Borghol et al., 2012; Figueiredo et al., 2014).

It is important to note that the current prediction task, with sentiment clusters, does not account for the temporal properties of the sentiment trajectories. Future research could utilize the sequential alignment of the raw sentiment scores by integrating this aspect into a prediction task of video popularity. That way, the features could be used without condensing information (e.g., into clusters) and acknowledge the sequential nature of sentiment trajectories.

5.3 Predicting popularity through average sentiment and political stance

We also tested for effects of average sentiment scores and political leaning on popularity with. The regression model was able to account for 24% of the variance of video popularity. Examining the model's coefficients more closely show, that popularity seem to be higher when the video originated from a pro-right news channel. Furthermore, the interaction of political leaning and sentiment scores shows, that a negative sentiment will increase popularity, while a positive sentiment will decrease popularity more for videos from pro-right news channels. Our findings support earlier work, which show that a negative tone seem to be more popular overall (Trussler and Soroka, 2014; Soroka et al., 2015).

5.4 Limitations

The current dataset consists of transcripts of YouTube videos and it is important to recognize that aspects such as video and audio of the clips are not integrated in the analyses. News channels might utilize audio and visual effects differently, which could affect text sentiment and video popularity.

In addition, the obtained transcripts in our analyses could have been generated manually or automatically, hence might differ in quality. Since there is no direct indicator of this, we do not know in what proportion they are represented in our corpus.

Generating appropriate and accurate bias ratings for news channels is not easy. Therefore, it is not guaranteed that the bias rating of Media Bias/Fact Check is accurate in all regards. However, it has a comprehensive list of news channels, which are not always covered by other bias rating resources (Budak et al., 2016; Center, 2018).

Finally, in our study we specifically focused on YouTube videos. While earlier studies (Peer and Ksiazek, 2011; al Nashmi et al., 2017) demonstrate that content produced by legacy media for YouTube often follows the same standards and formats as stories produced for other platforms, there also exceptions from this rule. Some news organizations (for instance, RT) tend to push more provocative stories to YouTube, whereas others (such as CNN) preferred to publish more lighter content on the platform (al Nashmi et al., 2017). These distinct features of content distributed through YouTube news channels can impact our observations.

6 Conclusion

In this study we showed that news channels on YouTube exhibit different sentiment patterns, which can be clustered into overarching groups. We found seven sentiment shapes similar to those found in previous research. The cluster "Mood swings" was most prominent whereas "End on a low note" was least prominent. Two additional sentiment clusters seemed to be used differently depending on political leaning of the channels: the cluster "Downhill from here" was used more often by pro-right news channels than by pro-left news channels. The reversed effect was observed for the cluster "Uphill from here". In addition, sentiment clusters seem to have no predictive value on popularity ratings. However, we found that pro-right videos were more popular and that negative sentiments increased popularity, for averaged sentiment scores of each video. Future research on dynamic approaches to sentiment analysis might help overcome some of the current limitations and offer more nuanced insights into language use in online media.

References

Frank Bentley, Katie Quehl, Jordan Wirfs-Brock, and Melissa Bica. 2019. Understanding Online News Behaviors. page 11.

Youmna Borghol, Sebastien Ardon, Niklas Carlsson, Derek Eager, and Anirban Mahanti. 2012. The untold story of the clones: Content-agnostic factors that impact YouTube video popularity. In *Proceedings of the 18th ACM SIGKDD International Conference on Knowledge Discovery and Data Mining - KDD '12*, page 1186, Beijing, China. ACM Press.

Alexandre Bovet and Hernán A. Makse. 2019. Influence of fake news in Twitter during the 2016 US presidential election. *Nature Communications*, 10(1).

Roberta Bracciale and Antonio Martella. 2017. Define the populist political communication style: The case of Italian political leaders on Twitter. *Information, Communication & Society*, 20(9):1310–1329.

Ted Brader. 2005. Striking a Responsive Chord: How Political Ads Motivate and Persuade Voters by Appealing to Emotions. *American Journal of Political Science*, 49(2):388.

Ceren Budak, Sharad Goel, and Justin M. Rao. 2016. Fair and Balanced? Quantifying Media Bias through Crowdsourced Content Analysis. *Public Opinion Quarterly*, 80(S1):250–271.

E. Cambria. 2016. Affective Computing and Sentiment Analysis. *IEEE Intelligent Systems*, 31(2):102–107.

Erik Cambria, Jie Fu, and Federica Bisio. 2015. AffectiveSpace 2: Enabling Affective Intuition for Concept-Level Sentiment Analysis. page 7.

Pew Research Center. 2018. Trends and Facts on Online News | State of the News Media.

Mark Coddington. 2015. Clarifying Journalism's Quantitative Turn: A typology for evaluating data journalism, computational journalism, and computer-assisted reporting. *Digital Journalism*, 3(3):331–348.

Claes H de Vreese. 2005. News framing: Theory and typology. page 12.

Devin M. Dotson, Susan K. Jacobson, Lynda Lee Kaid, and J. Stuart Carlton. 2012. Media Coverage of Climate Change in Chile: A Content Analysis of Conservative and Liberal Newspapers. *Environmental Communication*, 6(1):64–81.

Sven Engesser, Nicole Ernst, Frank Esser, and Florin Büchel. 2017. Populism and social media: How politicians spread a fragmented ideology. *Information, Communication & Society*, 20(8):1109–1126.

Sarah Eskens, Natali Helberger, and Judith Moeller. 2017. Challenged by news personalisation: Five perspectives on the right to receive information. *Journal of Media Law*, 9(2):259–284.

Lauren Feldman, Edward W. Maibach, Connie Roser-Renouf, and Anthony Leiserowitz. 2012. Climate on Cable: The Nature and Impact of Global Warming Coverage on Fox News, CNN, and MSNBC. *The International Journal of Press/Politics*, 17(1):3–31.

Flavio Figueiredo, Jussara M Almeida, Marcos Andre Gonc Alves, and Fabricio Benevenuto. 2014. On the Dynamics of Social Media Popularity: A YouTube Case Study. *ACM Transactions on Internet Technology*, 1(1):22.

Seth Flaxman, Sharad Goel, and Justin M. Rao. 2016. Filter Bubbles, Echo Chambers, and Online News Consumption. *Public Opinion Quarterly*, 80(S1):298–320.

Tomohiro Fukuhara, Hiroshi Nakagawa, and Toyoaki Nishida. 2007. Understanding Sentiment of People from News Articles: Temporal Sentiment Analysis of Social Events. page 2.

J. Gao, M. L. Jockers, J. Laudun, and T. Tangherlini. 2016. A multiscale theory for the dynamical evolution of sentiment in novels. In *2016 International Conference on Behavioral, Economic and Socio-Cultural Computing (BESC)*, pages 1–4.

Matthew Gentzkow and Jesse M. Shapiro. 2011. Ideological Segregation Online and Offline *. *The Quarterly Journal of Economics*, 126(4):1799–1839.

Jae Sik Ha and Donghee Shin. 2016. Framing the Arab Spring: Partisanship in the news stories of Korean Newspapers. *International Communication Gazette*, 78(6):536–556.

Michael Hameleers, Linda Bos, and Claes H. de Vreese. 2017. " *They* Did It": The Effects of Emotionalized Blame Attribution in Populist Communication. *Communication Research*, 44(6):870–900.

Natali Helberger. 2015. Merely Facilitating or Actively Stimulating Diverse Media Choices? Public Service Media at the Crossroad. page 17.

Matthew Jockers. 2015. » Revealing Sentiment and Plot Arcs with the Syuzhet Package Matthew L. Jockers.

Mesut Kaya, Guven Fidan, and Ismail H. Toroslu. 2012. Sentiment Analysis of Turkish Political News. In *2012 IEEE/WIC/ACM International Conferences on Web Intelligence and Intelligent Agent Technology*, pages 174–180, Macau, China. IEEE.

Yaser Keneshloo, Shuguang Wang, Eui-Hong (Sam) Han, and Naren Ramakrishnan. 2016. Predicting the Popularity of News Articles. In *Proceedings of the 2016 SIAM International Conference on Data Mining*, pages 441–449. Society for Industrial and Applied Mathematics.

Bennett Kleinberg, Maximilian Mozes, and Isabelle van der Vegt. 2018. Identifying the sentiment styles of YouTube's vloggers. *In Proceedings of the 2018 Conference on Empirical Methods in Natural Language Processing*, page 10.

Max Kuhn. 2008. Building Predictive Models in *R* Using the **caret** Package. *Journal of Statistical Software*, 28(5).

Bing Liu. 2010. Sentiment Analysis and Subjectivity. page 38.

Mika V. Mäntylä, Daniel Graziotin, and Miikka Kuutila. 2018. The evolution of sentiment analysis—A review of research topics, venues, and top cited papers. *Computer Science Review*, 27:16–32.

Maxwell E. McCombs. 2014. *Setting the Agenda: The Mass Media and Public Opinion*, 2. ed edition. Polity Press, Cambridge. OCLC: 935284613.

Rohit Mehta and Lynette DeAun Guzmán. 2018. Fake or Visual Trickery? Understanding the Quantitative Visual Rhetoric in the News. *Journal of Media Literacy Education*, page 19.

Eisa al Nashmi, Michael North, Terry Bloom, and Johanna Cleary. 2017. Promoting a global brand: a study of international news organisationsâĂŹ youtube channels. *The Journal of International Communication*, 23(2):165–185.

N. Newman, R. Fletcher, A. Kalogeropoulos, D. Levy, and R. K. Nielsen. 2018. Reuters Institute Digital News Report. http://www.digitalnewsreport.org/.

Bo Pang and Lillian Lee. 2008. Opinion mining and sentiment analysis. page 94.

Limor Peer and Thomas B Ksiazek. 2011. Youtube and the challenge to journalism: new standards for news videos online. *Journalism Studies*, 12(1):45–63.

Leonard Richardson. 2019. Beautiful Soup.

Tyler Rinker. 2019a. A data package containing lexicons and dictionaries for text analysis: Trinker/lexicon.

Tyler Rinker. 2019b. Dictionary based sentiment analysis that considers valence shifters: Trinker/sentimentr.

Martijn Schoonvelde, Anna Brosius, Gijs Schumacher, and Bert N. Bakker. 2019a. Liberals lecture, conservatives communicate: Analyzing complexity and ideology in 381,609 political speeches. *PLOS ONE*, 14(2):e0208450.

Martijn Schoonvelde, Anna Brosius, Gijs Schumacher, and Bert N Bakker. 2019b. Liberals lecture, conservatives communicate: Analyzing complexity and ideology in 381,609 political speeches. *PloS one*, 14(2):e0208450.

Kim Christian Schrøder. 2015. News Media Old and New: Fluctuating audiences, news repertoires and locations of consumption. *Journalism Studies*, 16(1):60–78.

Saif Shahin, Pei Zheng, Heloisa Aruth Sturm, and Deepa Fadnis. 2016. Protesting the Paradigm: A Comparative Study of News Coverage of Protests in Brazil, China, and India. *The International Journal of Press/Politics*, 21(2):143–164.

Susan Currie Sivek. 2018. Both Facts and Feelings: Emotion and News Literacy. *Journal of Media Literacy Education*, page 16.

Stuart Soroka, Lori Young, and Meital Balmas. 2015. Bad News or Mad News? Sentiment Scoring of Negativity, Fear, and Anger in News Content. *The ANNALS of the American Academy of Political and Social Science*, 659(1):108–121.

Cass R. Sunstein. 2017. *#Republic: Divided Democracy in the Age of Social Media*. Princeton University Press, Princeton ; Oxford.

M. Iftekhar Tanveer, Samiha Samrose, Raiyan Abdul Baten, and M. Ehsan Hoque. 2018. Awe the Audience: How the Narrative Trajectories Affect Audience Perception in Public Speaking. In *Proceedings of the 2018 CHI Conference on Human Factors in Computing Systems - CHI '18*, pages 1–12, Montreal QC, Canada. ACM Press.

A. Tatar, P. Antoniadis, M. D. de Amorim, and S. Fdida. 2012. Ranking News Articles Based on Popularity Prediction. In *2012 IEEE/ACM International Conference on Advances in Social Networks Analysis and Mining*, pages 106–110, Istanbul. IEEE.

Robert L. Thorndike. 1953. Who belongs in the family? *Psychometrika*, 18(4):267–276.

Marc Trussler and Stuart Soroka. 2014. Consumer Demand for Cynical and Negative News Frames. *The International Journal of Press/Politics*, 19(3):360–379.

Peter Van Aelst, Jesper Strömbäck, Toril Aalberg, Frank Esser, Claes de Vreese, Jörg Matthes, David Hopmann, Susana Salgado, Nicolas Hubé, Agnieszka Stępińska, Stylianos Papathanassopoulos, Rosa Berganza, Guido Legnante, Carsten Reinemann, Tamir Sheafer, and James Stanyer. 2017. Political communication in a high-choice media environment: A challenge for democracy? *Annals of the International Communication Association*, 41(1):3–27.

Tyler Welch. 2018. Theology, heroism, justice, and fear: An analysis of ISIS propaganda magazines *Dabiq* and *Rumiyah*. *Dynamics of Asymmetric Conflict*, 11(3):186–198.

Lori Young and Stuart Soroka. 2012. Affective News: The Automated Coding of Sentiment in Political Texts. *Political Communication*, 29(2):205–231.

Simple dynamic word embeddings for mapping perceptions in the public sphere

Nabeel Gillani
MIT
ngillani@mit.edu

Roger Levy
MIT
rplevy@mit.edu

Abstract

Word embeddings trained on large-scale historical corpora can illuminate human biases and stereotypes that perpetuate social inequalities. These embeddings are often trained in separate vector space models defined according to different attributes of interest. In this paper, we develop a single, unified dynamic embedding model that learns attribute-specific word embeddings and apply it to a novel dataset—talk radio shows from around the US—to analyze perceptions about refugees. We validate our model on a benchmark dataset and apply it to two corpora of talk radio shows averaging 117 million words produced over one month across 83 stations and 64 cities. Our findings suggest that dynamic word embeddings are capable of identifying nuanced differences in public discourse about contentious topics, suggesting their usefulness as a tool for better understanding how the public perceives and engages with different issues across time, geography, and other dimensions.

1 Introduction

Language has long been described as both a cause and reflection of our psycho-social contexts (Lewis and Lupyan, 2018). Recent work using word embeddings—low-dimensional vector representations of words trained on large datasets to capture key semantic information—has demonstrated that language encodes several gender, racial, and other common contemporary biases that correlate with both implicit biases (Caliskan et al., 2017) and macro-scale historical trends (Garg et al., 2018).

These studies have validated the use of word embeddings to measure a range of psychological and social contexts, yet in most cases, they have failed to leverage the full power of available datasets. For example, the historical biases presented in (Garg et al., 2018) are computed using decade-specific word embeddings produced by training different Word2Vec (Mikolov et al., 2013) models on a large corpus of historical text from that decade. The authors then use a Procrustes alignment to project embeddings from different models into the same vector space so they can be compared across decades (Hamilton et al., 2016). While this approach is reasonable when there are large-scale datasets available for a given attribute of interest (e.g. decade), it requires an additional optimization step and also disregards valuable training data that could be pooled and leveraged across attribute values to help with both training and regularization. This latter property is particularly appealing—and necessary—in the context of limited data.

In this paper, we use a simple, unified dynamic word embedding model that jointly trains linguistic information alongside any categorical variable of interest—e.g. year, geography, income bracket, etc.—that describes the context in which a particular word was used. We apply this model to a novel data corpus—talk radio transcripts from stations located in over 64 US cities—to explore the evolution of perceptions about refugees during a one-month period in late 2018. The results from our model suggest the potential to use dynamic word embeddings to obtain a granular, near real-time pulse on how people feel about different issues in the public sphere.

2 Model

2.1 Overview

Our dynamic embedding for word w is defined as

$$E(w, A) = \gamma_w + \Sigma_{a \in A} \, \beta_w^a \tag{1}$$

where γ_w is an attribute-invariant embedding of w computed across the entire corpus, β_w^a is the off-

Proceedings of the Third Workshop on Natural Language Processing and Computational Social Science, pages 94–99
Minneapolis, Minnesota, June 6, 2019. ©2019 Association for Computational Linguistics

set for w with respect to attribute a across the set of attributes A we are interested in computing the word embedding with respect to. For example, if we wish to compute the embedding for the word "refugee" as it was used on the 25th day of a particular 30-day corpus of talk radio transcripts, we would set $w = refugee$ and $A = \{25\}$. This approach, as formalized in Equation 1 above, is identical to one introduced by (Bamman et al., 2014), though finer details of our model and training differ slightly, as described below.

To learn γ_w and β_w^a, we train a neural network. Our model is a simple extension to the distributed memory (DM) model for learning paragraph vectors originally introduced in (Le and Mikolov, 2014). The DM model uses a continuous bag-of-words architecture to jointly train a paragraph ID with a sequence of words sampled from that paragraph to predict a particular word given the words that surround it. The output of this model includes a semantic vector representation of a) each paragraph, and b) each word in the vocabulary.

Our model extends the DM model by adding an additional dimension to the paragraph vector to learn specific *paragraph-by-word*—or, in our context, *attribute-by-word*—embeddings (i.e., β_w^a). The penultimate layer (before word prediction) is computed as an average of the dynamic embeddings for each context word, i.e., $X = \frac{1}{N}\Sigma_{i=1}^{N} E(w_i, S, A)$, where N is the size of our context window. This average embedding is then multiplied by the output layer parameters and fed through the final layer for word prediction. Figure 1 depicts our model architecture.

2.2 Implementation

We build on an existing PyTorch implementation of paragraph vectors[1] to implement our model, setting the dimensionality of γ_w and β_w^a to be 100. We use the Adam optimization algorithm with a batch size of 128, word context window size of 8 (sampling four words to the left and right of a target prediction word), learning rate of 0.001, and L2 penalty to regularize all model parameters. We only train embeddings for words that occur at least 10 times in the corpus. For training, we use the negative sampling loss function, described in (Mikolov et al., 2013) to be much more efficient than the hierarchical softmax and yield competi-

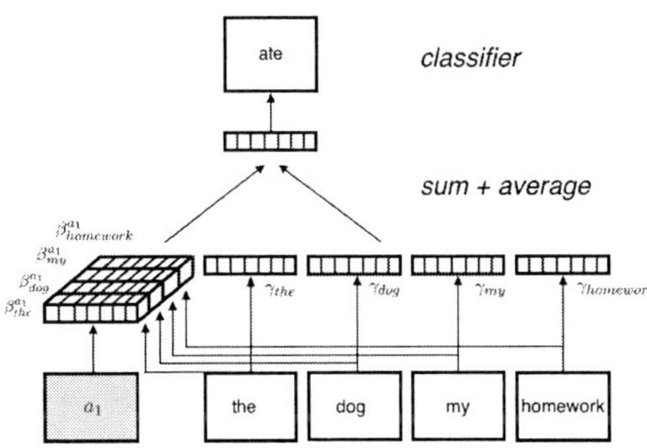

Figure 1: Our dynamic embedding model learns an attribute invariant embedding for each training word w (i.e., γ_w), along with an attribute-specific offset for attribute $A = \{a_1\}$ (i.e., $\beta_w^{a_1}$). The γ_w and $\beta_w^{a_1}$ terms are summed to compute $E(w, A)$ for each context word and averaged across words before classification. Figure inspired by (Le and Mikolov, 2014).

tive results[2]. We train for 1 to 3 epochs and select the model with the lowest loss.

2.3 Validation

To validate our model, we compare our results to those produced via the decade-by-decade models trained in (Garg et al., 2018) using the Corpus of Historical American English (Davies, 2010). We use the same metric and word lists as the authors to compute bias scores. In particular, we compute linguistic bias scores for two analyses presented in (Garg et al., 2018): the extent to which female versus male words are semantically similar to occupation-related words, and the extent to which Asian vs. White last names are semantically similar to the same, from 1910 through 1990. We then compute correlations between changes in these scores and the actual changes in female and Asian workforce participation rates (relative to men and Whites, respectively) over the same time period.

Figure 2 depicts these results. The correlation between our scores and changes in workforce participation rates are similar to the correlation between the scores from (Garg et al., 2018) and the same ($r = 0.8, p = 0.01$ and $r = 0.81, p < 0.01$, respectively, for gender occupation bias; $r = 0.84, p < 0.01$ and $r = 0.79, p = 0.01$, respectively, for Asian/White occupation bias). Qualitative inspection of Figure 2 suggests that our model also produces smoother decade-by-decade scores, suggesting that it not only identifies attribute-

---

[1]Available at: `https://github.com/inejc/paragraph-vectors`.

[2]We include three noise words when computing the loss.

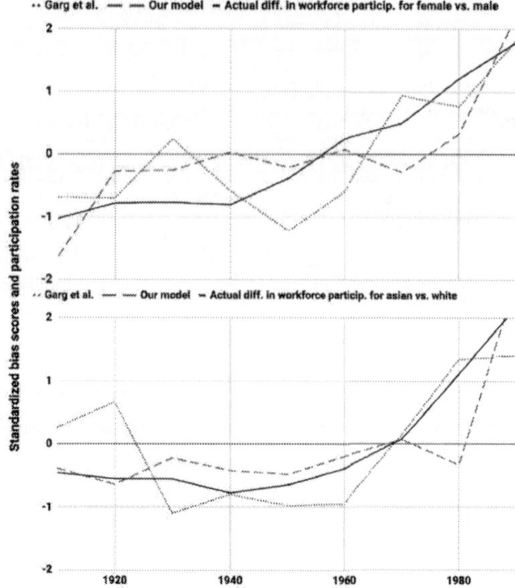

Figure 2: Scores produced by (Garg et al., 2018) and our model (blue dotted and green dashed lines, respectively) compared to actual workforce participation rates (solid lines) for gender (top) and Asian/White (bottom) linguistic biases. To compare all values on a single y-axis, we standardize both sets of bias scores and workforce participation rates by subtracting the mean and dividing by the standard deviation across decades.

specific fluctuations in word semantics, but also, may provide a more general, regularized model for learning attribute-conditioned word embeddings. Future research should include a comparison of our model's outputs to the outputs of other dynamic word embedding models that treat time as a continuously-valued attribute, e.g. (Bamler and Mandt, 2017; Rudolph and Blei, 2018; Yao et al., 2018).

3   Case study: refugee bias on talk radio

We are interested in applying our dynamic embedding model to better-understand talk radio-show biases towards refugees. Talk radio is a significant source of news for a large fraction of Americans: In 2017, over 90% of Americans over the age of 12 listened to some type of broadcast radio during the course of a given week, with news/talk radio serving as one of the most popular types (Pew, 2018). With listener call-ins and live dialog, talk radio provides an interesting source of information, commentary, and discussion that distinguishes it from discourse found in both print and social media. Given the proliferation of refugees and dis-

placed peoples in recent years (totalling nearly 66 million individuals in 2016 (UNHCR, 2017))—coupled with the rise of talk radio as a particularly popular media channel for conservative political discourse (Mort, 2012)—analyzing bias towards refugees across talk radio stations may provide a unique window into a large portion of the American population's views on the issue.

3.1   Dataset and analyses

Our data is sourced from talk radio audio data collected by the media analytics nonprofit Cortico[3]. Audio data is ingested from nearly 170 different radio stations and automatically transcribed to text. The data is further processed to identify different speaker turns into "snippets"; infer the gender of the speaker; and compute other useful metrics (more details on the radio data pipeline can be found in (Beeferman and Roy, 2018)).

We train our dynamic embedding model on two talk radio datasets sourced from 83 stations located in 64 cities across the US. Dataset 1 includes 4.4 million snippets comprised of 114 million words produced by 390 shows between September 1 and 30, 2018. Dataset 2 includes over 4.8 million snippets comprised of 119 million total words produced by 433 shows between August 15, and September 15, 2018[4]. These datasets are used for analyses 1 and 2, respectively, described below.

Finally, we define bias towards refugees similar to how the authors of (Garg et al., 2018) define bias against Asians during the 20th century, measuring to what extent radio shows associate "outsider" adjectives like "aggressive", "frightening", "illegal", etc. with refugee and immigrant-related terms in comparison to all other adjectives. To compute refugee bias scores with respect to the attribute set A, we use the relative norm distance metric from (Garg et al., 2018):

$$bias_A = \Sigma_{r \in R} ||E(r, A) - \overline{all}||_2 - ||E(r, A) - \overline{out}||_2$$

Where $E(r, A)$ is the dynamic embedding for a given word refugee word r in the set of all refugee-related words R (e.g. "refugee", "immigrant", "asylum", etc); $\overline{all}$ is the average dynamic embedding computed for each w in the set of all adjectives with respect to A; $\overline{out}$ is analogously defined for outsider adjectives; and $|| \cdot ||_2$ is the L2 norm.

---

[3] http://cortico.ai.

[4] As a rough proxy for removing syndicated content, we include only those snippets produced by a talk radio shows that air on one station.

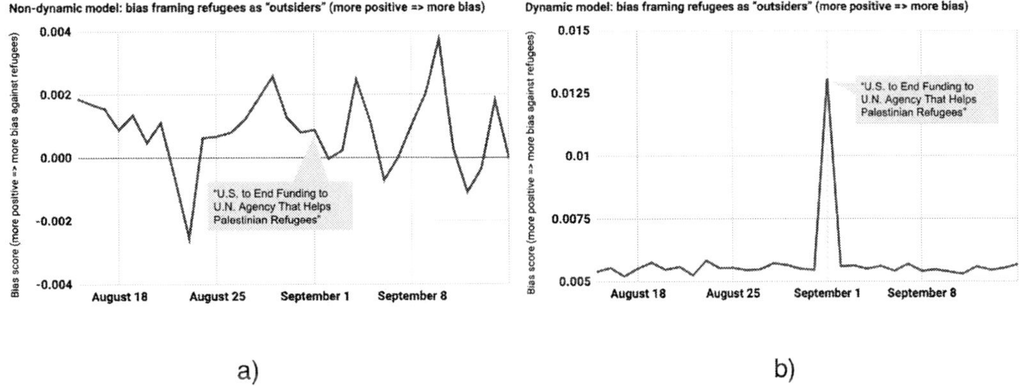

Figure 3: Bias towards refugees as outsiders across talk radio shows from mid-August to mid-September 2018: (a) depicts bias scores computed using a "non-dynamic model", i.e., training multiple Word2Vec models (one per day of data) and then projecting these models into the same vector space using orthogonal Procrustes alignment, and (b) depicts bias scores computed using our dynamic model. From qualitative inspection, the dynamic model appears to regularize scores across days during which refugee-related news is likely less-salient in public discourse.

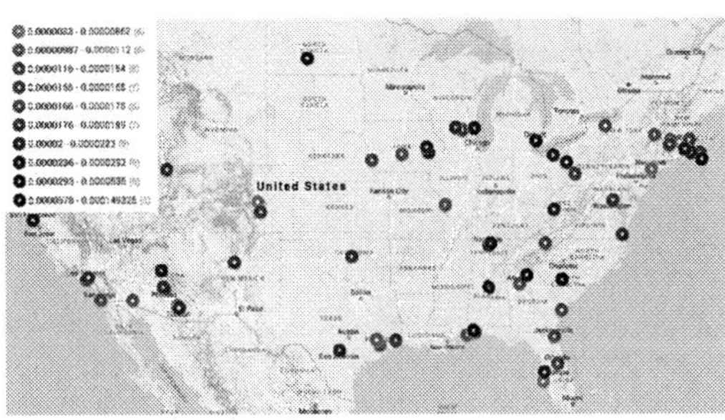

Figure 4: Bias towards refugees as outsiders computed across cities for radio shows aired between September 1 and 30, 2018 (darker means more biased).

3.2 Analysis 1: refugee bias over time

We analyze how refugee biases on talk radio vary by day between August 15 and September 15, 2018. We choose this interval to center on the August 31, 2018 news story regarding the Trump administration's contentious decision to pull funding from a UN agency that supports Palestinian refugees[5]. Our attribute of interest is the day in which a particular snippet occurred. Figure 3(b) illustrates the temporal variation in bias scores, highlighting a notable shift towards *greater bias* against refugees in response to the news story. Interestingly, bias towards refugees returns to pre-event levels very quickly after the spike. Computing the correlation between daily bias scores and the number of mentions of the keyword "refugee" across stations yields $r = 0.56, p < 0.001$, suggesting that additional discourse about refugees tends to be biased against them.

As a comparison, we also compute bias scores by training one Word2Vec model per day and projecting all day-by-day models into the same vector space using orthogonal Procrustes alignment[6] similar to (Hamilton et al., 2016). The resulting scores from this non-dynamic model are depicted in 3(a). From qualitative inspection, the day-by-day scores produced by the non-dynamic model appear much less smooth, and hence, fail to show the relative shift in discourse that likely occurred in response to a major refugee-related news event. One possible reason for this is that the median number of words for each day in the talk radio corpus is 4 million—over 5x fewer than a median of 22 million words per decade used to train each decade-specific model in (Garg et al., 2018). These results suggest that using our dynamic embedding approach is particularly valuable when data is sparse for any given attribute.

3.3 Analysis 2: refugee bias by city

Next, we analyze how bias towards refugees varies by city for talk radio produced between September 1 and 30, 2018. We first train our model to learn a city-specific embedding for each word

---

[5]For historical coverage of different refugee-related news events, please see https://www.nytimes.com/topic/subject/refugees-and-displaced-people.

[6]We use the Gensim implementations of Word2Vec and orthogonal Procrustes alignment, aligning hyperparameters as closely as possible to our dynamic model.

and then use these embeddings to compute corresponding bias scores, which are depicted in figure 4. Qualitatively, cities in the Southeastern US, those closer to the US-Mexico border, and some that have suffered from economic decline in recent years (e.g. Detroit, MI; Youngstown, OH) tend to have talk radio coverage that is more biased towards refugees, though the trends are quite varied. Interestingly, there is a weak negative, though marginally insignificant, correlation between the level of bias per city and the number of refugees the city admitted in 2017[7] ($r = -0.21, p = 0.1$). This relationship persists even after controlling for state fixed effects. A more thorough analysis with additional cities and other city-level covariates may reveal meaningful patterns and perhaps even help illuminate which geographies are particularly welcoming towards refugees.

4 Conclusion

In this paper, we present a unified dynamic word embedding model mirroring the earlier work of (Bamman et al., 2014) to learn attribute-specific embeddings. We validated our model by replicating gender and ethnic stereotypes produced in (Garg et al., 2018) by training multiple word embedding models and applied it to a novel corpus of talk radio data to analyze how perceptions of refugees as "outsiders" vary by geography and over time. Our results illustrate that dynamic word embeddings capture salient shifts in public discourse around specific topics, suggesting their potential usefulness as a tool for obtaining a granular understanding of how the media and members of the public perceive different issues, especially when data is sparse.

Opportunities for future work include a) comparing the results of our model to other existing dynamic embedding models, particularly when the attribute of interest is temporal in nature, b) exploring embeddings defined with respect to other attributes of interest, perhaps in combination with other contextual embedding models like (Peters et al., 2018), c) exploring alternative definitions of bias towards refugees and other groups, and d) learning a dynamic embedding model for continuous attributes in order to limit the need to impose (perhaps arbitrary) discretizations. We be-

lieve these approaches hold promise in helping us illuminate evolving attitudes and perceptions towards different issues and groups across a rapidly expanding digital public sphere.

Acknowledgments

We thank Doug Beeferman, Prashanth Vijayaraghavan and David McClure for their valuable input on this project. We also thank Nikhil Garg for sharing prior results to help us benchmark our model.

References

R. Bamler and S. Mandt. 2017. Dynamic Word Embeddings. In *Proceedings of the International Conference on Machine Learning (ICML)*.

D. Bamman, C. Dyer, and N. A. Smith. 2014. Distributed Representations of Geographically Situated Language. In *Proceedings of the 52nd Annual Meeting of the Association for Computational Linguistics (Volume 2: Short Papers)*.

D. Beeferman and B. Roy. 2018. Making radio searchable. `https://medium.com/cortico/making-radio-searchable-f337de9fa325`. Accessed: March 10, 2019.

A. Caliskan, J. J. Bryson, and A. Narayanan. 2017. Semantics derived automatically from language corpora contain human-like biases. *Science*, 356(6334):183–186.

M Davies. 2010. The 400 million word corpus of historical American English (1810 2009). In *Selected Papers from the Sixteenth International Conference on English Historical Linguistics (ICEHL 16)*.

N. Garg, L. Schiebinger, D. Jurafsky, and J. Zhou. 2018. Word embeddings quantify 100 years of gender and ethnic stereotypes. *Proceedings of the National Academy of Sciences*, 115(16):E3635–E3644.

W. Hamilton, J. Leskovec, and D. Jurafsky. 2016. Diachronic word embeddings reveal statistical laws of semantic change. In *Proceedings of the 54th Annual Meeting of the Association for Computational Linguistics (Volume 1: Long Papers)*, pages 1489–1501.

Q.V. Le and T. Mikolov. 2014. Distributed Representations of Sentences and Documents. *arXiv: 1405.4053*.

M. Lewis and G. Lupyan. 2018. Language use shapes cultural norms: Large scale evidence from gender. In *The Annual Meeting of the Cognitive Science Society*, pages 2041–2046.

T. Mikolov, I. Sutskever, K. Chen, G. S. Corrado, and J. Dean. 2013. Distributed representations of words and phrases and their compositionality. *NIPS*.

---

[7]We sourced per-city 2017 refugee arrival numbers from the Refugee Processing Center's interactive reporting webpage: `http://ireports.wrapsnet.org/`.

S. Mort. 2012. Tailoring Dissent on the Airwaves: The Role of Conservative Talk Radio in the Right-Wing Resurgence of 2010. *New Political Science*, 34(4):485–505.

M. E. Peters, M. Neumann, M. Iyyer, M. Gardner, C. Clark, K. Lee, and L. Zettlemoyer. 2018. Deep contextualized word representations. *arXiv: 1802.05365*.

Pew. 2018. Audio and podcasting fact sheet. `http://www.journalism.org/fact-sheet/audio-and-podcasting/`. Accessed: March 10, 2019.

M. Rudolph and D. Blei. 2018. Dynamic Embeddings for Language Evolution. In *WWW 2018: The 2018 Web Conference*, pages 1003–1011.

UNHCR. 2017. Forced displacement in 2016. Global Trends Report.

Z. Yao, Y. Sun, W. Ding, N. Rao, and H. Xiong. 2018. Dynamic Word Embeddings for Evolving Semantic Discovery. In *Proceedings of the The Eleventh ACM International Conference on Web Search and Data Mining (WSDM)*.

Modeling Behavioral Aspects of Social Media Discourse for Moral Classification

Kristen Johnson and Dan Goldwasser
Department of Computer Science
Purdue University, West Lafayette, IN 47907
{john1187, dgoldwas}@purdue.edu

Abstract

Political discourse on social media microblogs, specifically Twitter, has become an undeniable part of mainstream U.S. politics. Given the length constraint of tweets, politicians must carefully word their statements to ensure their message is understood by their intended audience. This constraint often eliminates the context of the tweet, making automatic analysis of social media political discourse a difficult task. To overcome this challenge, we propose simultaneous modeling of high-level abstractions of political language, such as political slogans and framing strategies, with abstractions of how politicians behave on Twitter. These behavioral abstractions can be further leveraged as forms of supervision in order to increase prediction accuracy, while reducing the burden of annotation. In this work, we use Probabilistic Soft Logic (PSL) to build relational models to capture the similarities in language and behavior that obfuscate political messages on Twitter. When combined, these descriptors reveal the moral foundations underlying the discourse of U.S. politicians online, *across* differing governing administrations, showing how party talking points remain cohesive or change over time.

1 Introduction

Over the last decade social media has taken a central role in facilitating and shaping political discourse. Such platforms are regularly used by politicians across the political spectrum to directly address the public and influence its opinion on a wide range of current issues. This phenomenon provides a tantalizing opportunity to study political discourse at a large-scale by using computational methods to shed light on the ways in which politicians express their views and frame the discussion to help promote these views. However, the short and often ambiguous nature of social media posts makes this analysis extremely challenging. For example, consider the discussion around gun regulation in the United States. Proponents of the two opposing views, supporting and objecting the imposing of gun regulations, tend to use similar vocabulary when mass shooting events occur, such as *"thoughts and prayers"*. This common phrase can express solidarity with the victims and their families or indicate that these actions are not sufficient and further regulations should be imposed. Given the wide range of real-world events and policy issues discussed online, and the purposeful ambiguity in the way in which they are discussed, there is a clear need for abstracting over the specific issues and word choices in order to find commonalities in the way issues are presented.

Previous works in social psychology and political science suggest moral framing as a way to explain the ideological differences that underlie the stances taken by liberals and conservatives on different issues (Graham et al., 2009). The Moral Foundations Theory (MFT) (Haidt and Joseph, 2004; Haidt and Graham, 2007) provides a theoretical framework for analyzing moral framing, suggesting that human morality is based on five key values, emerging from evolutionary, social, and cultural origins. These values are referred to as the moral foundations and consist of *Care/Harm, Fairness/Cheating, Loyalty/Betrayal, Authority/Subversion* and *Purity/Degradation*. These foundations are defined in more detail in Section 3.

Consider the following examples, in the context of the immigration debate, in which different moral foundations can be used to justify different stances. A conservative stance might view immigration as a potential safety threat, and then frame the discussion using the Care/Harm moral foundation by emphasizing the lives lost at the hands of *"illegal immigrants"*.

100

Proceedings of the Third Workshop on Natural Language Processing and Computational Social Science, pages 100–109
Minneapolis, Minnesota, June 6, 2019. ©2019 Association for Computational Linguistics

---

I know the faces of the parents of half the children pictured below. Every victim below would be alive today if we enforced our immigration laws.

Alternatively, a liberal point of view could highlight the origins of the United States as a nation founded by immigrants and argue that immigrants today should receive a similar treatment. This stance can be expressed using the Fairness moral foundation by emphasizing that current immigrants should have access to the same rights.

We are a country of immigrants & refugees, of people fleeing religious persecution & seeking freedom, a country made strong by diversity.

Our goal in this paper is to make headway towards large-scale analysis of political discourse using the Moral Foundations Theory. Traditionally, analyzing text using Moral Foundations Theory relied on lexical resources, such as the Moral Foundations Dictionary (Haidt and Graham, 2007; Graham et al., 2009), which provides relevant keywords for each foundation. This tool is not well suited for text analysis on social media, given the diversity of topics discussed and their ambiguity. Using machine learning methods to automatically predict the relevant moral foundations is a partial solution, as keeping the model up-to-date as the discussion shifts and new terms are introduced can be difficult and time consuming.

Instead, we follow the intuition that when analyzing political messaging on social media, the *context* in which a message appears provides valuable information which can help support the decision and provide an alternative source of supervision. Instead of viewing the problem as a text classification problem, defined over the text alone, we take into account the author of the tweet, as well as their activities and social interactions (such as retweeting and following other users). This information is incorporated into a probabilistic graphical model, which makes a global inference decision forcing consistency across the messages by similar party members on the same issues. We use Probabilistic Soft Logic (PSL) (Bach et al., 2013), which specifies high level rules over relational representations of the textual content and social interactions between politicians on social media.

In this paper, we make two main contributions: (1) We suggest global computational models for operationalizing the Moral Foundations Theory. Given the highly connected structure of the political sphere on social media, identifying the similarity between users' ideologies based on their behavior can significantly improve performance. Our experiments in Section 5 validate this hypothesis, showing that our modeling approach is able to perform better than human annotation for moral foundations classification in both supervised and unsupervised settings, and highlighting that models using behavioral information can outperform language-based baselines.

(2) We perform large-scale analyses, providing both intrinsic evaluations of moral foundations prediction using our models, as well as case study analyses of trends in U.S. political discourse on various policy issues across administrations. Our experiments show that there are distinct patterns in which moral foundations are used to discuss issues and that these patterns can shift over time in response to the occurrence of new events.

2 Related Works

To the best of our knowledge, this is the first work to leverage the interaction of social networks and behavioral features on Twitter, in addition to language, for the task of weakly-supervised modeling and unsupervised classification of moral foundations implied in social media political discourse. Similar studies have used models which only employ language features for this task in a supervised setting (Johnson and Goldwasser, 2018). These language-based models serve as the baselines in our experimental analyses.

Ideology measurement (Iyyer et al., 2014; Bamman and Smith, 2015; Sim et al., 2013; Djemili et al., 2014), political sentiment analysis (Pla and Hurtado, 2014; Bakliwal et al., 2013), and polls based on Twitter political sentiment (Bermingham and Smeaton, 2011; O'Connor et al., 2010; Tumasjan et al., 2010) are related to the study of abstract language, specifically political framing analysis which is a key feature in the language baseline of our approach. The association between Twitter and framing in molding public opinion of events and issues (Burch et al., 2015; Harlow and Johnson, 2011; Meraz and Papacharissi, 2013; Jang

Table 1: Brief Descriptions of Moral Foundations.

and Hart, 2015) has also been studied.

Connections between morality dimensions and political ideology have been analyzed in the fields of psychology and sociology (Graham et al., 2009, 2012). Moral foundations have also been used via the Moral Foundations Dictionary (MFD) to identify the foundations in partisan news sources (Fulgoni et al., 2016) and to construct features for other downstream tasks (Volkova et al., 2017). Several recent works have explored using data-driven methods that go beyond the MFD to study tweets related to specific events, rather than policy issues, such as natural disasters (Garten et al., 2016; Lin et al., 2017).

3 Moral Foundations Theory and Datasets

Moral Foundations Theory. The Moral Foundations Theory (Haidt and Graham, 2007) was proposed by psychologists and sociologists as a way to analyze how morality develops, including its similarities and differences, across cultures. The theory consists of the five moral foundations described in Table 1. Each foundation has a positive and negative aspect, e.g., the Care/Harm foundation has a positive aspect, Care, and a negative aspect, Harm. The goal of this work is to build a relational model capable of classifying the *implied* moral foundations which are used to express stances in the tweets of U.S. politicians. To do so, three datasets are used in our model design, evaluation, and application.

The Congressional Tweets Dataset. The Congressional Tweets Dataset (Johnson and Goldwasser, 2018) consists of the tweets of the 114th Congress covering varying years and is annotated to indicate which moral foundation is used in each tweet. This dataset was collected in June 2016 using Twitter API collection methods. Therefore, for each politician in this dataset, only the most recent 3200 tweets were recovered. In this work, we use this dataset to design and evaluate our model in a supervised and unsupervised setting.

Senate Tweets 2016. Using a combination of web scraping and the Twitter API, we collected the available tweets of all Senators during the year 2016. This approach allows us to overcome the recovery limit of the Twitter API by scraping for available tweet IDs, while still adhering to the terms of service, i.e., if a politician deletes a tweet, we are *unable* to recover it. This dataset will be made publicly available for use by the community.

CongressTweets. CongessTweets is a collection of the tweets of all congressional members in 2018 [1]. To facilitate comparison with the Senate Tweets 2016 dataset, we used only the tweets of senators from this collection. This dataset and the Senate Tweets 2016 dataset (described previously) are used in Section 6 for the qualitative application of our models to the analysis of real world political behavior.

4 Weakly-supervised Model Design

Global Modeling Using PSL. PSL is a declarative modeling language used to specify weighted, first-order logic formulas which are compiled into the rules of a graphical model, specifically a hinge-loss Markov Random Field. This model defines a probability distribution over possible continuous value assignments to the random variables of the model (Bach et al., 2015). The defined probability density function is represented as follows:

$$P(\mathbf{Y} \mid \mathbf{X}) = \frac{1}{Z} \exp\left(-\sum_{r=1}^{M} \lambda_r \phi_r(\mathbf{Y}, \mathbf{X}) \right)$$

where Z is the normalization constant, λ is the vector of weights, and

$$\phi_r(\mathbf{Y}, \mathbf{X}) = (\max\{l_r(\mathbf{Y}, \mathbf{X}), 0\})^{\rho_r}$$

---

[1]The dataset is available for download at: https://github.com/alexlitel/congresstweets/tree/master/data.

is the hinge-loss potential which represents a rule instantiation. This potential is specified by the linear function l_r and the optional exponent $\rho_r \in 1, 2$. PSL has been used in a variety of network modeling applications; for more details we refer the reader to Bach et al..

PSL rules have the following form:

$$\lambda_1 : P_1(x) \wedge P_2(x, y) \rightarrow P_3(y)$$
$$\lambda_2 : P_1(x) \wedge P_4(x, y) \rightarrow \neg P_3(y)$$

where P_1, P_2, P_3, P_4 are predicates describing language or behavioral features and x, y are variables. Each rule has a learned weight λ which reflects that rule's importance in the prediction. Contrary to other probabilistic logical models, concrete constants a, b (e.g., specific tweets or other features), which instantiate the variables x, y, are mapped to soft [0,1] assignments with preference given to rules with larger weights.

Predicate Design. For each feature of interest, represented as a *predicate* in PSL notation, scripts are written to identify and extract the relevant information from tweets. Because of this initial step, which operates on keywords to identify the appropriate information for extraction, we refer to our overall approach as *weakly-supervised*. Once isolated, this information is transcribed into PSL predicate notation and input to the rules of the PSL models. Table 2 presents one example rule for each PSL model used in this work.

The BASELINE model consists of language-based features only. For this work, we recreated the model and features of Johnson and Goldwasser (2018): unigrams based on the Moral Foundations Dictionary, *political slogans* represented by bigrams and trigrams associated with each party for each issue, ideological phrase indicators, and frames. For more details on each of these features, we refer the reader to their work.

The first row of Table 2 shows the use of unigram indicators from the Moral Foundations Dictionary ($\text{MFD}_M(T, U)$) and ideological phrases ($\text{PHRASE}(T1, S)$). For example, the predicate $\text{MFD}_M(T, U)$ indicates that this tweet T has unigram U from the Moral Foundations Dictionary (MFD) list of unigrams for an expected Moral Foundation M. The rule in this row would therefore read as: if tweet T has unigram U from the MFD list for moral M and has slogan S that belongs to a group of phrases, then we expect moral M is implied in tweet T.

The next model, RETWEETS, builds upon the language-based baseline by adding retweet information into the prediction. Retweets are useful because they are both textual indicators and miniature representations of the network structure inherent in the political sphere of Twitter. This feature is therefore able to simultaneously capture both the impact of language and social connections.

The FOLLOWING model takes this one step further and incorporates the actual social network into the PSL model. This predicate, FOLLOWS(T1, T2), indicates that the author of tweet T1 follows the author of tweet T2. Since politicians are likely to follow other politicians or Twitter accounts that share similar ideologies and ideology has been shown to be associated with moral foundations, this PSL model can exploit the social network relationships of politicians to detect similar moral foundations patterns.

Lastly, the TEMPORAL PSL model adds information about similar time activity between tweets. Rules in this model indicate if tweets occur within the same time frame as one another. For this work, a time window of one day was used. This feature is motivated by the observation that most politicians tweet about an event on the day it occurs, and discussion of the event declines over time. Therefore, if two politicians share similar moral viewpoints, we expect them to use the same moral foundations to discuss an event at the same time.

5 Quantitative Results

In this section, we present the quantitative results of our weakly-supervised modeling approach evaluated under both supervised and unsupervised settings. For both tasks, the weakly-supervised models are evaluated using the Congressional Tweets Dataset because the annotations of this dataset allow the predicted classifications to be verified. For the supervised experiments, tweets were classified using five-fold cross validation with randomly chosen splits. The results are shown in Table 3. For the unsupervised experiments, shown in Table 4, tweets were classified using the PSL-provided implementation of a hard expectation-maximization algorithm.

Evaluation Metrics. For evaluation, we use traditional multilabel classification metrics for precision and recall. These metrics are used in order to accurately reflect how each tweet can represent more than one moral foundation. The F_1 score is

PSL Model	Features	Example of PSL Rule
Baseline	Language	$\text{MFD}_M(\text{T, U}) \wedge \text{Phrase(T1, S)} \rightarrow \text{Moral(T, M)}$
+Retweets	Retweets	$\text{Retweets(T1, T2)} \wedge \text{Moral(T1, M)} \rightarrow \text{Moral(T2, M)}$
+Following	Social Network	$\text{Follows(T1, T2)} \wedge \text{Moral(T1, M)} \rightarrow \text{Moral(T2, M)}$
+Temporal	Time Patterns	$\text{Temporal(T1, T2)} \wedge \text{Follows(T1, T2)} \rightarrow \text{Moral(T1, M)}$

Table 2: Examples of PSL Model Rules. Each row shows an example of how the model combines rules from previous models to build an increasingly comprehensive model.

Moral Fdn.	Results of PSL Model Predictions			
	Baseline	+Retweets	+Following	+Temporal
Care	67.78	67.78	69.75	**75.59**
Harm	73.68	73.64	73.32	**77.65**
Fairness	75.48	75.48	80.14	**85.40**
Cheating	60.00	60.00	61.02	**65.81**
Loyalty	64.20	64.19	65.57	**75.10**
Betrayal	70.00	70.00	71.67	**72.11**
Authority	69.61	69.62	70.67	**71.43**
Subversion	79.61	81.19	85.82	**88.58**
Purity	80.41	80.43	81.29	**85.95**
Degradation	73.47	72.30	72.83	**74.42**
Non-moral	83.33	83.35	88.27	**92.31**
Average	72.49	74.16	76.02	**81.63**

Table 3: F_1 Scores of Supervised Experiments. Numbers in boldface indicate the highest prediction. The average is the macro-weighted average F_1 score over all moral foundations.

Moral Fdn.	Results of PSL Model Predictions			
	Baseline	+Retweets	+Following	+Temporal
Care	55.49	56.37	63.99	**67.23**
Harm	53.11	53.21	55.07	**64.40**
Fairness	56.22	56.22	64.78	**68.80**
Cheating	38.06	40.00	44.29	**47.92**
Cheating	49.91	50.34	54.82	**59.09**
Loyalty	50.00	50.00	51.79	**57.78**
Betrayal	52.32	52.73	56.43	**58.15**
Authority	55.80	57.61	62.04	**64.40**
Subversion	62.11	62.54	63.422	**67.50**
Purity	52.34	52.34	57.27	**60.95**
Degradation	57.51	57.88	71.01	**73.98**
Average	52.69	53.57	61.20	**64.75**

Table 4: F_1 Scores of Unsupervised Experiments. Numbers in boldface indicate the highest prediction. The average is the macro-weighted average F_1 score over all moral foundations.

the harmonic mean of these two measures. In this work, the precision is calculated as the ratio of the number of correctly predicted labels:

$$Precision = \frac{1}{T} \sum_{t=1}^{T} \frac{|Y_t \cap h(x_t)|}{|h(x_t)|} \qquad (1)$$

The recall then represents how many of the true labels were predicted:

$$Recall = \frac{1}{T} \sum_{t=1}^{T} \frac{|Y_t \cap h(x_t)|}{|Y_t|} \qquad (2)$$

In both formulas, T is the total number of tweets, Y_t is the gold label for a tweet t, x_t is a specific tweet, and $h(x_t)$ are all the model-predicted labels for tweet x_t.

Analysis of Supervised Experiments. Supervised experiments were conducted using five-fold cross validation with randomly chosen splits. The first column of Table 3 shows the results when using only language-based features in the PSL models (Johnson and Goldwasser, 2018). Since we are interested in showing the benefits of modeling social network and behavioral features in addition to language features, we use this as our baseline to show improvement against. The second column presents results when politician retweet information, i.e., when politicians retweet each other, is included into the language model. Similarly, the third column is when following information, i.e., when politicians are following another politician,

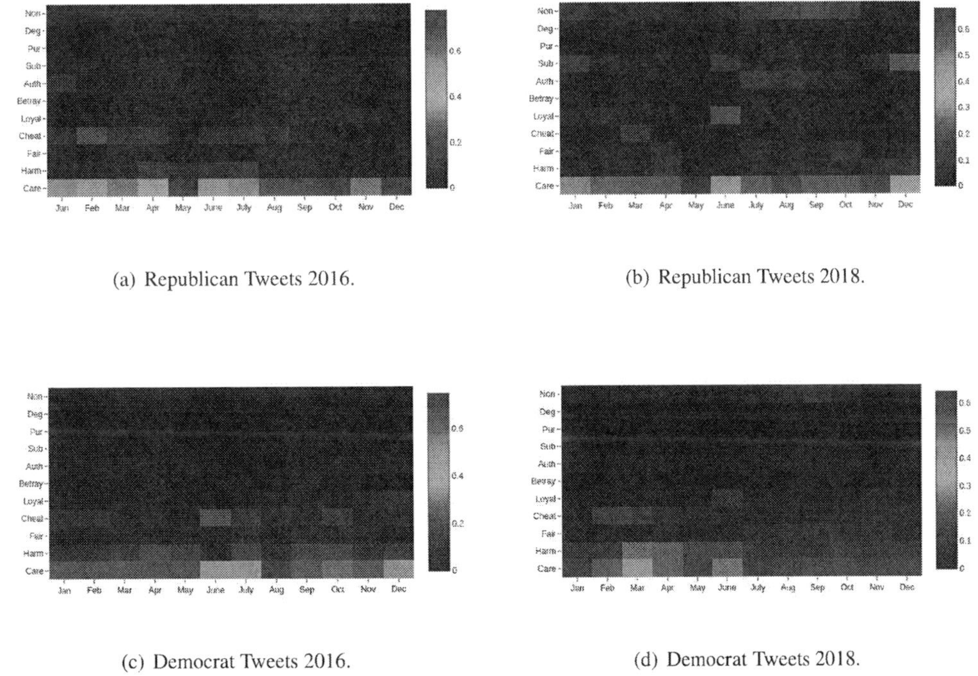

<table>
<tr><td align="center">(a) Republican Tweets 2016.</td><td align="center">(b) Republican Tweets 2018.</td></tr>
<tr><td align="center">(c) Democrat Tweets 2016.</td><td align="center">(d) Democrat Tweets 2018.</td></tr>
</table>

Figure 1: Monthly Coverage of Moral Foundations in Republican and Democrat Tweets.

is used in the prediction. Finally, the last column indicates the results when features related to the timing of tweets are incorporated into the model.

This table shows that for all moral foundations adding features of social or behavioral information extracted from politician's Twitter networks improves the overall prediction, with a 9.14 point increase in average F_1 score over all foundations.

For most foundations however, incorporation of retweet information did not increase the score, and in some cases lowered the score. This could be due to two likely reasons: first, there is a low quantity of retweet information in this dataset, resulting in too little social information to increase the score, or second, many retweets are a copy of the original tweet with little new information added. In such cases, the model would only have access to the language-based features used in the baseline. However, based on the results of Table 3, retweet information is a useful predictor of the Subversion moral foundation. This is reflected in the data in tweets where a politician from one political party retweets a politician from the opposite party in order to criticize their statement in the original tweet.

Analysis of Unsupervised Experiments. To the best of our knowledge, this is the first work to evaluate the classification of moral foundations in political tweets in an unsupervised fashion. Moreover, prior works did not provide unsupervised analyses for their findings. Therefore, we reconstructed the language-based features to create a language only PSL model, with results shown in column one of Table 4). The remaining columns of Table 4 correspond to the addition of each social-behavioral network feature, similar to the supervised testing approach.

From these results, we observe that the addition of social and behavioral information results in the best prediction in an unsupervised setting as well. The final combined model has an improved average F_1 score of 12.06 points over the language-only baseline. Furthermore, approximately half of the predictions exceed the reported inter-annotator agreement of 67.2% for this dataset, calculated using Cohen's Kappa coefficient (Johnson and Goldwasser, 2018), suggesting that weakly-supervised models incorporating social and behavioral information can help overcome the need for annotation, even in an unsupervised approach.

6 Qualitative Results

In this section, we present two case studies showing the usefulness of the weakly-supervised models in an unsupervised setting for the analysis of the relationships between moral foundations used in social media discourse and real world political behavior. Predicted moral foundations were obtained by running the tweets from the two Senate collections of 2016 and 2018, as described in Section 3, through the unsupervised PSL model.

Figure 1 shows the predicted moral foundations for each political party over the two years of 2016 and 2018. Figures 2 through 4 show the distributions of moral foundations used by each party in tweets discussing specific events.

Case Study 1: Trends by Year. Figure 1(a) and Figure 1(b) show the predicted moral foundations of Republicans' tweets in 2016 and 2018, respectively, concerning the six issues studied in this work: health care, women's rights, gun violence, immigration, terrorism, and LGBTQ rights. From these two figures, we can see that Republicans favor the Care foundation, but still use the other foundations as well throughout the year. However, there is a greater concentration of tweets expressing Care in 2016 compared to 2018, in which use of this foundation drops. Consequently, the use of other moral foundations increases in 2018 and is more evenly spread out throughout the year.

In Figure 1(a), there are two areas with peak use of the Care foundation during 2016. The first is around June and corresponds to increased Twitter activity during *Whole Woman's Health v. Hellerstedt*, a Supreme Court case concerning women's rights to health care, and the Orlando Pulse Nightclub shooting, an event related to both terrorism and gun violence. The second peak is during the months of September and October and corresponds to increased activity in the months proceeding November in which the midterm elections were held. Figure 1(b) also reflects this peak in the months proceeding the midterm elections for 2018. Furthermore, activity in this time frame spiked in July due to the Brett Kavanaugh nomination hearings. Figures 1(c) and 1(d) similarly show the predicted moral foundations of Democrats' tweets in 2016 and 2018, respectively. Figure 1(c) shows that Democrats favor the first four moral foundations (Care, Harm, Fairness, and Cheating) more evenly. This only changes during

a spike in activity in June, over the same issues which caused an increase in Republican activity. However, the lower frequency of foundations used in 2016 correlates with the more infrequent use of Twitter by Democratic Senators. This changes dramatically in Figure 1(d), which shows that Democratic activity discussing these issues on Twitter *triples*. Additionally, more moral foundations are used throughout 2018 by Democrats.

Similar to Republicans in 2018, Democrats also show a spike in activity and moral foundations during the months of July to October. Tweets from these months also correspond to the Kavanaugh hearings and pre-election activity. An interesting point between the two 2018 heatmaps is that both Republicans and Democrats use the Care foundation in their tweets in similar proportions during these months, but their use of other foundations is more varied.

Case Study 2: Event-specific Trends. We have observed that when events occur, such as a shooting, Twitter activity discussing the event peaks on the day of the event and gradually diminishes over the following weeks. Figures 2 through 4 highlight key events in 2016 and 2018 for three different policy issues: gun violence, women's rights, and LGBTQ rights. Each heat map shows the frequency of each moral foundation used by Republicans and Democrats to discuss these specific events, for one month after the event occurs.

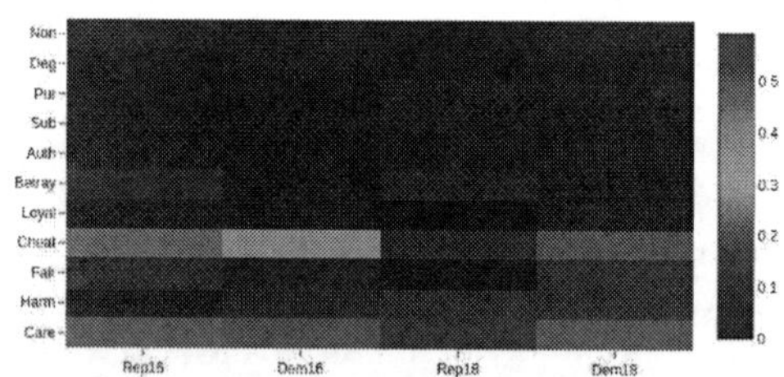

Figure 2: Moral Foundations of Tweets Discussing Shooting Events. The two columns on the left are predictions for tweets one month after the Orlando Pulse Nightclub shooting. The two columns on the right are predictions for tweets one month after the Marjory Stoneman Douglas High School shooting.

Gun Violence. Figure 2 shows the predicted moral foundations for tweets discussing two events related to gun violence. The first is the June 12, 2016 shooting at the Pulse Nightclub in Orlando, Florida. The first column of the heat map shows Republican moral foundations used to discuss this shooting. The second column shows the foundations used by Democrats. Columns three and four are the Republican and Democrat foundations used to discuss the Marjory Stoneman Douglas High School shooting on February 14, 2018. For both parties, over both years, the first four moral foundations (i.e., Care, Harm, Fairness, and Cheating) are used more frequently than all others. Similar to the yearly trends, Care is the most used foundation to discuss these events. This is to be expected because after shootings both parties express their concern for the victims and families and offer their "thoughts and prayers" to those affected. Two interesting trends are shown in this heat map: (1) an increase from 2016 to 2018 in the use of the Care foundation by Republicans and the Harm and Fairness foundations by Democrats, and (2) increased use of the Cheating moral foundation when compared to other events. This foundation appears in tweets related to a lack of justice for the victims of the shootings and their families, as well as tweets discussing the need for blood donations for the Orlando victims being hindered by unjust blood donor restrictions.

for the *Whole Woman's Health v. Hellerstedt* Supreme Court case which determined that laws enacted by Texas placed an undue burden on women seeking a legal abortion, and thus were unconstitutional. The second two columns correspond to predicted foundations for tweets discussing the testimony of Dr. Christine Blasey Ford in the Brett Kavanaugh Supreme Court nomination hearing. For both parties and years, the top moral foundations used are Care, Harm, Authority, and Non-moral. Interestingly, Democrats in 2016 discuss this issue in terms of Fairness, but the use of Fairness in 2018 declines and is replaced with Non-moral arguments. In 2016, both parties use the Authority foundation to discuss support or lack thereof for the Supreme Court and President Obama on this issue. However, in 2018, there is a significant decrease in the use of this foundation, while the use of the Non-moral foundation increases for both parties. For Republicans in 2018, the top foundations are Care and Authority, reflected in tweets which discuss a simultaneous care and support for the hearing proceedings and Kavanaugh's reputation. Democrats, however, use Care, Harm, and Fairness as their top foundations to express concern about the potentially harmful effect on legislation pertaining to women's rights that his nomination to the Supreme Court might cause.

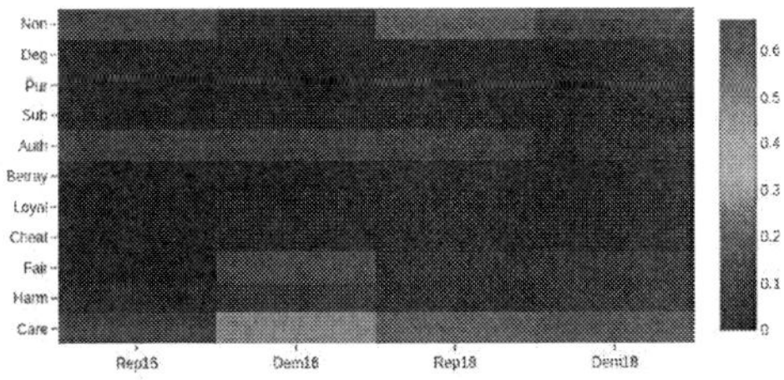

Figure 3: Moral Foundations of Tweets Discussing Events Related to Women's Rights and the Supreme Court. The two columns on the left are predictions for tweets one month after the *Whole Women's Health v. Hellerstedt* Supreme Court case. The two columns on the right are predictions for tweets during the month of testimonies during the Brett Kavanaugh hearing.

Women's Rights. Figure 3 presents a similar heat map for two events related to women's rights. The first two columns are the predicted moral foundations of Republican and Democrat tweets

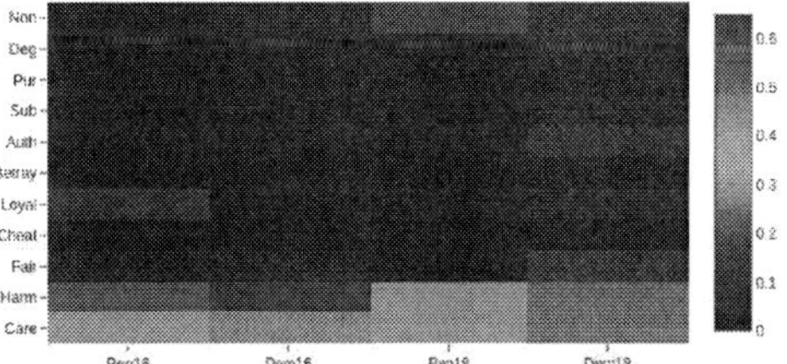

Figure 4: Moral Foundations of Tweets Discussing Events Related to Transgender Rights. The two columns on the left are predictions for tweets one month after the North Carolina "bathroom bill". The two columns on the right are predictions for tweets one month after the current administration announced transgender people would not be allowed to serve in the military.

LGBTQ Rights. Figure 4 presents a heat map of predicted moral foundations concerning two events related to transgender rights. The leftmost columns represent tweets discussing the passage of the *Public Facilities Privacy & Security Act* in North Carolina which constrains transgender people to only access bathrooms corresponding to their gender at birth. The rightmost columns represent tweets discussing the current administration's proposed ban prohibiting transgender people from serving in the military.

For this issue, both parties use a dual Care-Harm foundation to express concern over how the legislation will harm differing populations. Different from most issues, there is a greater emphasis on the harm such legislation could cause, as evidenced by the significantly higher representation of Harm foundation predictions for all groups, except the Republicans in 2016.

7 Future Work and Conclusion

In this work, we concentrated our qualitative analyses on a subset of issues and used only the tweets of senators. In the future, we will expand the issue coverage to include more in-depth analysis of currently trending issues. We are also collecting the tweets for the members of the House of Representatives for the last 5 years and will incorporate these tweets into our dataset.

We presented global, relational models for the classification of moral foundations in political discourse on social media microblogs. We have shown the usefulness of incorporating social and behavioral information into the predictive models, which perform well in both supervised and unsupervised settings. These models can be used to shed light on political discourse trends over time and their relation to real-world events and policy issues.

References

Stephen H Bach, Matthias Broecheler, Bert Huang, and Lise Getoor. 2015. Hinge-loss markov random fields and probabilistic soft logic. *arXiv preprint arXiv:1505.04406*.

Stephen H. Bach, Bert Huang, Ben London, and Lise Getoor. 2013. Hinge-loss Markov random fields: Convex inference for structured prediction. In *Proc. of UAI*.

Akshat Bakliwal, Jennifer Foster, Jennifer van der Puil, Ron O'Brien, Lamia Tounsi, and Mark Hughes. 2013. Sentiment analysis of political tweets: Towards an accurate classifier. In *Proc. of ACL*.

David Bamman and Noah A Smith. 2015. Open extraction of fine-grained political statements. In *Proc. of EMNLP*.

Adam Bermingham and Alan F Smeaton. 2011. On using twitter to monitor political sentiment and predict election results.

Lauren M. Burch, Evan L. Frederick, and Ann Pegoraro. 2015. Kissing in the carnage: An examination of framing on twitter during the vancouver riots. *Journal of Broadcasting & Electronic Media*, 59(3):399–415.

Sarah Djemili, Julien Longhi, Claudia Marinica, Dimitris Kotzinos, and Georges-Elia Sarfati. 2014. What does twitter have to say about ideology? In *NLP 4 CMC*.

Dean Fulgoni, Jordan Carpenter, Lyle Ungar, and Daniel Preotiuc-Pietro. 2016. An empirical exploration of moral foundations theory in partisan news sources. In *Proc. of LREC*.

Justin Garten, Reihane Boghrati, Joe Hoover, Kate M Johnson, and Morteza Dehghani. 2016. Morality between the lines: Detecting moral sentiment in text. In *IJCAI workshops*.

Jesse Graham, Jonathan Haidt, and Brian A Nosek. 2009. Liberals and conservatives rely on different sets of moral foundations. *Journal of personality and social psychology*, 96(5):1029.

Jesse Graham, Brian A Nosek, and Jonathan Haidt. 2012. The moral stereotypes of liberals and conservatives: Exaggeration of differences across the political spectrum. *PloS one*, 7(12):e50092.

Jonathan Haidt and Jesse Graham. 2007. When morality opposes justice: Conservatives have moral intuitions that liberals may not recognize. *Social Justice Research*, 20(1):98–116.

Jonathan Haidt and Craig Joseph. 2004. Intuitive ethics: How innately prepared intuitions generate culturally variable virtues. *Daedalus*, 133(4):55–66.

Summer Harlow and Thomas Johnson. 2011. The arab spring— overthrowing the protest paradigm? how the new york times, global voices and twitter covered the egyptian revolution. *International Journal of Communication*, 5(0).

Iyyer, Enns, Boyd-Graber, and Resnik. 2014. Political ideology detection using recursive neural networks. In *Proc. of ACL*.

S. Mo Jang and P. Sol Hart. 2015. Polarized frames on "climate change" and "global warming" across countries and states: Evidence from twitter big data. *Global Environmental Change*, 32:11–17.

Kristen Johnson and Dan Goldwasser. 2018. Classification of moral foundations in microblog political discourse. In *Proc. of ACL*.

Ying Lin, Joe Hoover, Morteza Dehghani, Marlon Mooijman, and Heng Ji. 2017. Acquiring background knowledge to improve moral value prediction. *arXiv preprint arXiv:1709.05467*.

Sharon Meraz and Zizi Papacharissi. 2013. Networked gatekeeping and networked framing on #egypt. *The International Journal of Press/Politics*, 18(2):138–166.

Brendan O'Connor, Ramnath Balasubramanyan, Bryan R Routledge, and Noah A Smith. 2010. From tweets to polls: Linking text sentiment to public opinion time series. In *Proc. of ICWSM*.

Ferran Pla and Lluís F Hurtado. 2014. Political tendency identification in twitter using sentiment analysis techniques. In *Proc. of COLING*.

Sim, Acree, Gross, and Smith. 2013. Measuring ideological proportions in political speeches. In *Proc. of EMNLP*.

Andranik Tumasjan, Timm Oliver Sprenger, Philipp G Sandner, and Isabell M Welpe. 2010. Predicting elections with twitter: What 140 characters reveal about political sentiment. In *ICWSM*.

Svitlana Volkova, Kyle Shaffer, Jin Yea Jang, and Nathan Hodas. 2017. Separating facts from fiction: Linguistic models to classify suspicious and trusted news posts on twitter. In *Proceedings of the 55th Annual Meeting of the Association for Computational Linguistics (Volume 2: Short Papers)*, volume 2, pages 647–653.

Author Index

Association for Computational Linguistics
209 N. Eighth Street
Stroudsburg, Pennsylvania 18360

ISBN 978-1-5108-8775-6